I0001730

Book About Real Estate

Accelerate Your Real Estate Education and Growth

By: Matt Jones

Copyright © 2020

All rights reserved.

Published by Hawkwing Capital, LLC.

Disclaimer

The information contained in the book and its related guides are deemed to serve as a part of the author's collection of books, which may increase their revenue and income passively. The tips, strategies, tricks, and the information in this book take no guarantee that someone else's research will also produce results synonymous to it.

The material can include content or information from the third parties, but the author takes full charge of quoting genuine resources that may be subjected to copyright issues. The author takes no charge of the opinion that any of the third-parties or unrelated individuals have. If the content inculcated in the publication becomes obsolete due to technical reasons or whatsoever, the author or the publication house are entitled to no blame. All of the events indicated in the book are the result of primary research, secondary research, and the personal experience of the person(s) involved in formulating the book and bringing it into the form it is in today. All the content used in this book belongs solely to the author. No part of this shall be reproduced, sold, or transmitted in any medium by the third party except after the author's approval.

Table of Contents

Introduction

Why real estate? If you are counting on Medicare and Social Security to take care of you when you retire, what will you do if/when they run out of money? I looked at the projections of my retirement accounts through work to see how much I would have in retirement, considering inflation. That is when, I realized that I had to do something different. For me, real estate makes a lot of sense. It is a risk, but it's the kind of gamble where you can stack the cards in your favor through knowledge and good planning. Plus, I love to share the knowledge that I have gained. That's why I wrote this book about real estate.

How would you like to read 20+ books about real estate in the time it takes to read just one book? If that sounds good, then this book is for you! There are a ton of different ways to invest in real estate. By reading this book, you will gain a layman's understanding of the spectrum of real estate investment options in no time at all. This will make you more effective at talking with other people about real estate, and deciding which path in real estate you want to take.

There are many similarities between the different ways of investing in real estate as you will see across the chapters. The lessons within ring true regardless of whether there is a recession, pandemic, or even a riot going on where you invest. Don't try to invest in every type of real estate. Instead of that, choose one type, and even one specific role in that type, so you can excel at it. Educate yourself about that investment type. Network with other people so that you can build a team to help you. Find ways to add value to both other people and to properties.

My insight into the various topics can be found in parentheses throughout the book. That is also found in each chapter's introduction and conclusion sections. Since each chapter can be read by itself, you may choose to skip chapters that don't interest you. Therefore, there is some repeated information between the chapters when it is relevant to the topic within those chapters.

Each chapter in this book is a condensed version of another great book about real estate. I have done all the research. I have selected what I found to be the top books in different aspects of real estate investing. I have reviewed and summarized each book to give you the most important and useful information from them. This way, you can get all the information in one place instead of reading all the other books.

The original books had some formatting and grammar errors. I wasn't focused on critiquing these as the quality information found within them is what's most important. Some of the authors provide contradicting information based upon their own experience, opinions, and what works in their choice of investment classes. It's up to you to decide which advice you are willing to accept.

You will see various concepts and terminology repeated across the chapters. That is because they are important enough across the various real estate investment types to be of worthwhile knowledge to you. The more familiar you are with these concepts and terms, the more competent you will be when you are investing and networking. Use those repeats to engrain that essential information into your mind.

There are a gazillion great books about ways to invest in real estate that I have not covered in this book. For example, I could not find suitable books about hotel, motel, resort, or casino investing.

If you're wondering how this book is even legal, it's because of the Fair Use Law. I am not word-for-word repeating the words of the original authors. Instead, I just get straight to the point with the information the authors were saying. I add my humor and thoughts about the books as well.

I don't know about you, but the older I get, the worse my memory becomes. Even though I've read all of the books described in this book, I find it handy to use this book as a reference to remind me of the lessons that I learned from each book. All of these books are indeed excellent, which is why they made the cut to be included in here. I highly recommend that you purchase and read these books. Since each chapter is just an abbreviation of each book, there is naturally a ton more good info that you can learn by reading the full versions. I will include links to where you can purchase each book if you choose to do so.

I am not a lawyer or an accountant. As such, my comments in this book should not be considered to be official, legal, or financial advice. There are so many ways to approach real estate investing, and they all come with risks attached. I hope that the information in this book will guide you to the path that you wish to take up in the real estate business.

You need to do three things to set you up for success with real estate investing: network, educate yourself, and take action. Network with other people in the business by adding value to them first. Then, you will naturally gain more knowledge and opportunities. Educate yourself with the mountain of real estate material out there to be equipped for real estate investing. And perhaps most importantly, take action so that you're not stuck in "analysis paralysis." Networking and education are nothing if you don't take action on what you have learned. The mantra here is to learn and act! Thanks, good luck, and enjoy the book!

Matt Jones

www.HawkwingCapital.com

Chapter 1: Investor Mindset

Rich Dad Poor Dad by Robert Kiyosaki and Sharon Lechter

Introduction

Of all the books I have highlighted, *Rich Dad Poor Dad* (RDPD) has been the most impactful on my journey in real estate. While it's not specifically about real estate itself, it describes the mindset that you will need to adapt to be successful in real estate. Many real estate investors point to this book as the one that started their real estate journey. While all of the books I have written about are awesome, this one is one of the best of the best. It was originally published in 1997, and I am giving you the information from the updated 20th anniversary edition.

If you've read this book at least once as many real estate investors have, then you likely know that it is worthwhile to read again. The lessons within it deem repeating. It is sometimes called the "Purple Bible" because of the purple cover and the life lessons included within it. The book starts by talking about some of the lessons from the 1997 publication and how those have proven to be true over time. The original book eventually turned into a series of books, a board game, and a radio show.

In a sense, Robert had two dads while he was growing up. His real dad was a highly intelligent and well-educated teacher who made a substantial income. However, he was poor. Robert also spent a lot of time with his friend Mike and Mike's dad (Rich Dad). Rich Dad was not well educated; however, he did things differently. He later became one of the richest men in Hawaii.

Robert learned lessons from both dads. He goes on to describe what rich people know about money that the poor and middle class do not. The differing views from each dad helped Robert think critically about the contradicting lessons. One dad told Robert that "the love of money is the root of all evil." Surprisingly, the other dad told him, "the lack of money is the root of all evil." Depending on which of these perspectives you adopt, you will have a very different approach to your finances.

You may have heard the adage that the rich get richer and the poor get poorer. This is because financial skills are not taught in schools. Rich parents teach their kids different things about money than what poor and middle-class parents teach their kids. This knowledge is a huge advantage to make the rich get richer. This book gives you the secrets about wealth that you may simply not have access to until now.

(My parents taught me to get good grades in school so I could get a good job. I thought that was the best way to live before RDPD opened my eyes. I once asked my dad, a highly intelligent physician, if he could teach me about finances so I could become wealthy. He replied that he was unable to help me with that. Thank you, Robert Kiyosaki, for blowing my mind with RDPD!)

One dad told Robert, "You can't afford that!" However, the other dad told him to consider, "How can you afford that?" The second is a question that forces you to be creative in finding solutions. Necessity is the mother of innovation. One approach focuses on scarcity, the other on prosperity. Do you want to struggle with money, or do you not want to worry about your finances? If you look for problems, you find more problems. If you look for solutions, RDPD is solution-focused when it comes to money. One dad taught Robert to avoid risks, while the other taught him how to manage risks. Exercising your brain while examining financial solutions will make it a lot stronger. Being broke is temporary, and you can easily bounce back from it. However, if you have the mindset of being poor, that is eternal. RDPD inspires you to break free from that mindset. It also teaches you to start living like a rich person who is on their way up in life. RDPD is like your own personal (and rich) mentor who is empowering you to become rich too.

(One of my favorite quotes is from another book, Think and Grow Rich: "You become what you think about." Do you want to spend your time stressing out about your finances, or thinking about your financial prosperity?) Having said that, we'll now go into the six main lessons from RDPD.

Lesson 1: The Rich Do Not Work for Money

When Robert was a kid, he asked his dad how to become rich. His dad said, "Use your head," which meant "I don't know." Robert and his friend, Mike, decided to become business partners. They thought of different ideas to make money. After some brainstorming, they were able to come across a brilliant idea. They went around the neighborhood to collect toothpaste tubes, which were made of lead at that time. They cleaned up the toothpaste tubes, melted them down with a hibachi grill, poured them into plaster molds, and minted USA nickels. Robert's dad then explained counterfeiting to them and how it was illegal.

Rich Dad then offered to give them lessons on how to become wealthy through a sort of work-study instead of classroom lessons. They started by working in his convenience store on Saturdays for 10 cents per hour, dusting canned goods in the 1950s. After about four weeks, Robert decided he was sick of working like a slave and told Mike he was going to quit. Mike said that his dad knew Robert would eventually get fed up and wanted to then meet with him. Robert met with Rich Dad, told him that he was greedy, and asked to be treated better.

Rich Dad told Robert that he already sounded like most of his employees. Robert complained that he wasn't taught anything yet since Rich Dad hadn't even talked to him. Rich Dad explained that you remember better by doing, and not by being talked at in a lecture. (For example, you can only learn so much about riding a bike by someone explaining it to you. At a certain point, you have just to do it even if it means you fall off and skin your knee in the process). You can only be shown the door, but you have to walk through it.

Are you going to let life push you around, or are you going to take action and push back? Most people play it "safe" and just quit. However, to succeed, you will need to fight for it. Robert realized that Rich Dad was right. Rich Dad had 150 employees. They all, at the time, only asked for paychecks but never asked to learn what Rich Dad knew about money. Robert learned a lesson to see how he, himself, could change instead of blaming others. The learning needs to start within you. Most people think that perhaps their financial problems will be solved by making more money through a raise or a second job. However, the true problem is the erroneous way they think about money. Building assets is significantly better than increasing income. Income from your job stops when you're not working. Assets deliver cash flow that happens, whether you work or not, even while you sleep. With a job, you work for money. With assets, the money works for you.

Rich Dad said that if Robert accepted the 10 cents per hour and had not gotten angry, he wouldn't have been able to help Robert. Robert's dad got an education and a high paying job but still had money problems. This is because the school didn't teach him anything about money. School teaches you how to work for money as an employee. You'll forever stay as an employee if you work for money. If you want to learn how to make money work for you, you need to learn from someone who knows how to do it. When you work for money at a job, you don't even get to keep all of it. This is because the government takes out taxes first. Rich people get to play by different rules.

Robert agreed to keep working for Rich Dad, but for free instead of the 10 cents he was offered earlier. The knowledge Robert was learning was far more valuable than a few dimes. (When I first read this story, I thought, "OMG, the system has hoodwinked me!" I had a college degree but was completely ignorant of how to make money work for me. If RDPD is making you hungry to learn and grow, keep reading!)

Robert didn't tell his dad that he was working for free. Therefore, he didn't have to try to explain things to him. After a few more weeks, Rich Dad explained that most people work hard to earn very little money. They do this while believing in the myth of job security, looking forward to an annual vacation, and obtaining a meager pension after decades of work. Most people fall for this trap, never realize that they are in a trap. They never look for how they can get out of it.

The lives of most people are controlled by fear and greed. Money motivates people to work hard. Most people are willing to trade their time for a price. They wake up each day, work, pay their bills, and repeat. Rich Dad called this the "Rat Race." Their fear of not having money drives them to continue participating in the Rat Race cycle. The money they earn doesn't soothe their fears or desires. However, they keep on working, hoping that it will do so. Even people who say they aren't interested in money still work for it.

To break out of this cycle, start by doing your own thinking. Robert's dad often told him to stay in school and get good grades so that he could find a good job. This is the normal financial advice that most people give. When a rich person needs money, they first think to determine whether a job is the best solution to help them in achieving their long-term goals. Rich people become the master over money instead of being controlled by it through fear and greed. To get out of poverty, you first have to free yourself from the ignorance and fear that traps you in it. School teaches important trades that the world needs. However, it does not teach financial intelligence. Schools teach how to trade your time for money but not how to control its power.

Children spend their money on toys. Adults also spend their money on toys like a new car or a big house to impress others. The more money most people make, the more of it they spend. This keeps them trapped in the Rat Race.

A lot of us live our lives worried about bills or chasing a bigger paycheck. That is not living life to the fullest. You need to manage your emotions, or they will do your thinking for you.

Robert worked a few more weeks for free at Rich Dad's store. He was sad that he didn't have money to buy comic books like he did when he was making 10 cents per hour. Then he saw the storekeeper throwing away old comics. He got permission to take them for free as long as he promised not to sell them. Robert and Mike then opened their very own comic book library. Mike's sister worked in it and charged admission to kids who could look at the comics for 10 cents. Robert and Mike averaged $9.50 per week and paid Mike's sister $1. Eventually, they landed in trouble with some bullies, and they had to shut the library down. However, Rich Dad was proud that they had learned how to make money work for them instead of the other way around.

Life teaches you lessons by pushing you around. If you don't push back, you might spend your life blaming other people for your problems. You will be waiting for things to get better on their own magically. Playing it "safe" is actually risky because that means you are not in control of things.

Rich Dad had 150+ employees, but Robert and Mike were the first people to ask him how to make money. The knowledge that Rich Dad had to offer was significantly more valuable than any wages that he paid his employees.

Lesson 2: Why Teach Financial Literacy?

When Robert was 47, he retired because he was making money from his assets. It didn't matter whether he worked or not. If you plant a tree, you need to take care of it for years. Then one day, it will be able to continue to flourish without you. You need to create a system of assets that work like this.

There is a story from 1923, where the top leaders and richest businesspeople met together in Chicago. Many of these people died broke. It's not known what really happened, but the Great Depression may have had something to do with it. Today is a time where things change at a lot faster rate than back then. It's important to focus on flexibility as well as your financial education to be able to handle the inevitable ups and downs. Robert says that we are now in the Information Age, where people are getting rich, making websites and apps that change our lives.

We've all heard of sports stars and lottery winners who made millions and then lost it all. It's not about how much money you make. It's about how much money you keep. (If a poor or middle-class person makes millions of dollars, their status remains the same. Being rich is not about your bank account balance; it's more of a mindset.) To build a skyscraper, you first need to dig a solid foundation, so it doesn't fall over. Rich Dad gave Robert and Mike a strong foundation for their future wealth.

Rich people build a portfolio of assets. Poor and middle-class people buy liabilities that they mistake for assets. To become rich, you need to know the difference between the two and then acquire assets. An asset makes you money. However, a liability costs you money. It's that simple. Does something make cash flow into your pocket, or out of it?

Everyone has expenses in their life. A poor person makes money from their job and then spends it all on their expenses. A middle-class person makes money. They have liabilities like a mortgage and car loan, and their liabilities increase their expenses. That is where they spend their money. A rich person, on the other hand, has assets that bring in money through cash flow. That is used to cover their expenses, whether they work or not. Getting a high paying job isn't enough to get you out of the Rat Race. If you don't have assets that bring cash flow to cover your expenses, then you are still in the Rat Race.

The common life of hardworking people has historically revolved around getting good grades in school, getting a good job, getting married, moving into one apartment together to live cheaper, and saving up for a dream home. They then have a house with a mortgage and lots of credit card debt. When their income increases, they increase their expenses as well. That further traps them in the Rat Race. They incorrectly believe their home is their greatest asset. However, in reality, it is their biggest liability. They think that their only way out is to make more money. They should instead learn how to spend their money more wisely. Money won't solve their problems, but financial intelligence will.

Rich Dad was willing to do things differently from the crowd. He surrounded himself with highly qualified bankers, attorneys, brokers, and accountants, etc. He took their advice, but still forged his own path to greatness. If you wish to be financially free, then you, too, will need to do things differently than the crowd. You need to carve your path to greatness. The rich get richer because the way they handle their money is much different than how the poor and middle class does. The income for poor and middle-class people is mainly through their jobs. The rich mainly make their money through their assets.

When you work at a job, you make money for others before yourself. You first make money for the shareholders of the business, then for the government by paying taxes. Then you make money for the bank by paying your mortgage and other debt. Working harder doesn't help, but working smarter does. R. Buckminster Fuller said, "Wealth is a person's ability to survive so many number of days forward." If you stopped working today, how many days could you possibly survive? If you have an asset that makes $1000 per month and your expenses are $2000 per month, you have half of a month of wealth. With sufficient assets, you could survive indefinitely.

Counting on a pension, a 401(k), or Social Security for your retirement is a terrible plan. These are not in your control. However, you can control the assets you build, such as a business or real estate.

Lesson 3: Mind Your Own Business

Ray Kroc founded McDonald's. In 1974, he spoke to an MBA class at the University of Texas at Austin. He asked the students, "What business am I in?" They laughed and told him he was in the hamburger business. Ray laughed and responded that he was not. This was because his business was that of real estate. This is because the location of each franchise was the key thing to make McDonald's successful. His words are reflective of McDonald's success today. As of 2017, this hamburger chain owns more real estate in the world than anyone else.

If you are mindful of your business, you will make it grow and flourish. Rich people focus on their assets while everyone else focuses on making earned income, as explained above. The first way helps you achieve financial freedom. The other keeps you where you are. With school, you tend to become what you studied. For example, if you studied cooking, you would become a chef. If you studied the law, you then become a lawyer. However, the mistake people made is they work in someone else's business instead of working on their own business. You would work to make someone else's business flourish and make that person richer, not yourself. If you mind your own business, you help yourself to become rich.

People who say "I just need a raise" or "I'm going to get a second job to make extra money" are focusing on staying in the Rat Race. They are making other people rich instead of themselves. If they use their extra money to buy assets, they would then be on the right track. However, spending their money on things other than assets does not help with their financial freedom at all. If you are ever downsized by losing pay, hours, or your job, then you will realize very quickly that your house and car are not assets. This is because they do not make you money. If you get in a tight spot financially and need to sell the car you bought for $20K and cellphone you bought for $1K, you will only be able to do so for a fraction of their original costs.

Robert's advice is to keep your day job, for now. You should keep your expenses down, get rid of unnecessary liabilities, and start to buy assets that make you money. Assets could be businesses that don't require you to be present. These could be stocks, bonds, or cash flowing real estate. These could be notes or royalties from any intellectual property, and any other things that produce income. Robert buys real estate because he likes buildings and land. Also, he likes stocks of small startups as well. You should find an asset class that you enjoy building as well. Your investment path will be easier if you love your assets.

Think of each dollar that you invest as an employee that you put to work that would make you more dollars. When your income from assets grows, only then should you use that cash flow to indulge in luxuries if you like. Poor and middle-class people tend to buy luxuries with their earned income. Even worse, they buy those luxuries on credit.

Lesson 4: Understanding the Power and Taxes of Corporations

Using corporations to pay fewer taxes is the biggest secret of the rich. England and America did not originally have regular taxes. They were just an occasional thing to raise money during war times. Income tax did not become a permanent thing until 1874 in England, and 1913 in America. The poor and middle class want the rich to pay more in taxes. The educated, well-paid middle class pays taxes to provide for the poor because of corporations. The tax laws give incentives to business owners and investors so that they create more housing and jobs.

Even when there are laws to tax the rich, they use their financial knowledge, money, and power to find legal ways around those laws. Understanding and using corporations give the rich a huge advantage with their taxes that the poor and middle class do not have. By owning corporations, rich people get to pay their expenses first, and then they pay taxes on whatever is left over. Poor and middle-class people's paychecks get taxes taken out first, and then they have to live on what is left. They just don't have the knowledge, power, and resources to protect themselves from taxes as the rich do.

Start playing the game smarter. By owning businesses, real estate, and other investments, you too can protect yourself from taxes like the rich. As a young adult, Robert worked by selling Xerox machines. He worked hard to sell as many Xerox machines as possible to invest his earnings in cash-flowing assets. This allowed him to get out of the Rat Race and live off of his investments alone.

Financial intelligence is made up of four main parts. Firstly, you should be able to read and understand numbers. That is vital to building an empire. Secondly, investing involves finding creative strategies to make money. Thirdly, understanding markets allows you to know the supply and demand of your potential investments. Finally, knowing the law allows you to avoid lawsuits. You can legally use your income to build your empire instead of seeing it evaporate through taxes.

Lesson 5: The Rich Create Money

You may have heard the following sayings: "carpe diem, seize the day," "go big or go home," "the squeaky wheel gets the grease," and "just do it." You don't just need to have financial intelligence to make your investment dreams come true. You also need to be bold and take action. There are many start-up companies, especially with today's technology. Their founders have created empires. Entrepreneurs such as Steve Jobs, Mark Zuckerberg, Bill Gates, Jeff Bezos, Larry Page, and Sergey Brin did what it took to achieve their goals, and so can you. You have to create your own luck and take responsibility for your own financial education.

Robert invented a game called CASHFLOW® to teach people how money and investing work. It is a fun way to learn how assets and liabilities impact your income and expenses. It is a reflection of real-life and teaches you how to get out of the Rat Race. The more times you play it, the more you can understand how the rich handle finances. You will learn that you need to take advantage of the opportunities that come your way. (I own the game and highly recommend it!) You can play it online at www.RichDad.com.

Rich dad said that the poor and middle-class work for money. The rich, however, make money. Money itself is not real, though. It is whatever we all agree that it is. By training your mind, you can create wealth for yourself. This is what Robert has done, and so can you.

In 1989, Robert bought a single-family house for $45K in Oregon and then rented it out. He only made about $40 per month from it. However, a year later, the market was improving. He then sold it for $95K. He used a 1031 exchange to reinvest the profits, tax-free, into a 12-unit apartment building for $300K. Two years later, he sold it for $495K and used the profits, also tax-free, to buy a 30-unit building in Phoenix. That provided him with $5K per month in cash flow. That $875K building would later sell for $1.2M.

The Phoenix economy of the early 1990s was terrible. People bought $100K houses that were soon just worth $75K. Robert and his wife, Kim, started buying those houses. They did not pay $75K from a realtor for each of them. Instead, they bought them in foreclosure at the courthouse steps for $20K or less. They then sold them for $60K. This made them $190K in cash-flowing assets in a single year. That, in turn, paid their bills. It took a total of 30 hours of work to make this happen.

Robert and Kim also like to purchase stock in private companies just before they go public. For example, they might purchase shares for 25 cents each. Those might be worth $2 each in six months, and then up to $20 each later. With this method, they have turned a $25K investment into $1M in less than a year. While this all might be hard for some people to believe, it is true. By understanding how money works, you can make it work for you and reap in huge profits on your investments.

Lesson 6: Work to Learn Instead of Working for Money

Robert was once interviewed by a reporter who stated that she was inspired by him and that she hoped to become a best-selling author like Robert. He had read some of her articles and saw how talented she was. She said that her novels didn't sell even though people said that they were excellent. She asked Robert for advice, and he recommended her to take some sales training. She was offended because she hated salespeople. She refused to become one of them. Robert said that he was a best-selling author, but not a best-writing author. In fact, Robert admitted that he was a terrible writer.

Being smart and skilled in your trade isn't enough to become wealthy. It's no surprise that people at all educational levels struggle financially. It takes more than just hard work to become financially free. If that reporter had taken a job working for an advertising agency, even for a pay cut, she could have learned valuable sales skills. This would help her to become both a best-selling and a best-writing author. Many people can cook a better hamburger than McDonald's. However, what sets McDonald's apart is its highly effective business and marketing strategy.

Schools teach you to memorize information and not to make mistakes. However, the best way for people to learn is through experience and by making mistakes. Through real-world experience in something like sales, you will learn much faster and better than you could otherwise. Learn directly from people who have actually done what you want to learn. Rich Dad recommended that Robert should know a little bit about a lot and then hire specialists to work for him. Robert spent his time learning international trade, sales, people, business styles, leadership, accounting, marketing, and various cultures.

JOB stands for "just over broke." Even if you are working for free, aim to do work where you can learn valuable skills that you can apply to your investing. Robert recommends working for a network marketing company because they often have good training.

Plus, you will learn how to overcome your fears of failure and rejection. (I used to be deathly afraid of public speaking and talking to strangers. However, my experience in the field of network marketing helped me to manage my fears.)

Rich people groom their children to understand the overall operations of the business, not just how to specialize in one narrow field. The main skills you will need to learn are how to manage cash flow, systems, and people. If you do learn a specialized skill, let it be sales and marketing. Your life will be easier when you become better at negotiating, communication, and handling rejection.

Overcoming Obstacles

The main difference between rich and poor people is how they manage their fear. Even if you are financially literate, you might still get held up by your own fear, cynicism, laziness, bad habits, and arrogance. You need to see the joy of being rich is more important than avoiding your fears. It's perfectly normal to experience fear. How you handle that fear will make all the difference. If you are so afraid of losing money that you are paralyzed by it, then you will never invest in anything. Frank Tarkenton, a former great NFL quarterback, said, "Winning means being unafraid to lose." To learn how to ride a bike, you will need to be willing to fall down in the process, perhaps even many times.

To become rich, you have to be willing to lose money, make mistakes, and learn from those experiences. Winners are inspired by their failures. This is why they are not afraid of failing. Losers, on the other hand, are defeated by their failures. John D. Rockefeller said, "I always tried to turn every disaster into an opportunity." Your next step is to focus your energy on one course until you achieve success.

We all have cynical self-doubts such as "this won't work," "I'm not good enough," and "what if I lose everything." Whether these sorts of things come from inside your head or someone else, you should think of them as just noise. If you allow that noise to control you, you will have a significantly harder time achieving financial freedom.

Robert's friend, Richard, once started to buy a $65K investment townhouse for only $42K. Richard's neighbor, who was not an investor, told him it was a bad deal. Richard backed out. A few years later, that same townhouse was worth $95K. It also brought in great rents. Richard allowed the noise of his doubts to cloud his judgment. To this day, he still has no investments. Be wary of taking investment advice from people who aren't investors.

The busiest people can also be the laziest. They work long hours, watch lots of TV, or spend a ton of time on their hobbies. They use those to avoid working on their relationships, health, and finances. To cure laziness, it just takes a little helping of greed. Poor and middle-class parents teach their kids that greed is bad. They teach them to be content with what they have. However, by wanting more, you are inspired and motivated to take the action necessary to get what you want. Saying, "I can't afford it," shuts down your drive and permits laziness. On the other hand, saying, "how can I afford it," inspires you to be creative and take action.

Getting Started

Opportunities surround you at all times. Most people don't know how to see them. Learning how to find great deals is similar to learning to ride a bike.

It's a little wobbly at first, but then gets easier. The world teaches us how to work for money. What's important is to learn how to make money work for us.

Awaken the financial genius within you with the following ten steps:

1. Find a very strong reason to drive you to become financially free. This could be a combination of things you want and others you don't want. Robert didn't want to work all his life and be tied down to a job as an employee. He wanted to travel the world and live a great lifestyle.

2. Make choices daily that help you get closer to achieving your goals. Are you spending your time on things like watching TV and playing golf? Should you instead spend that time on financially educating yourself and finding opportunities?

3. Choose your friends very carefully. Surround yourself with people who can mentor you. This way, you can learn things that will help you towards financial freedom. (I've heard it said that your network is your net worth).

4. Continually learn different financial formulas. The formula for the poor and middle class is to trade their time for money. Learn things like how to buy foreclosed properties, and trade on the stock market, etc.

5. Pay yourself first by using money to invest and save. Use your remaining money to pay your bills. You may not have enough for the bills at times. In that case, motivate yourself to find ways to create more income. However, if you pay your bills first, you can easily trick yourself into being complicit with where you are in life. Keep your expenses low and avoid

buying unnecessary doodads that you don't need. Spend wisely. It's hard to earn money but very easy to spend it all.

6. Pay your team well. This includes your real estate brokers, stockbrokers, attorneys, and accountants. This will motivate them to help you make more money while saving you time.

7. When investing, ask how quickly you will get your investment money back. An annual return on investment (ROI) is a measure of how much of your money you get back each year. Robert likes to invest in a stock. He pulls out his original investment amount once the stock increases. He then enjoys owning the remaining stock for free.

8. Spend your earned income on assets, and then use the cash flow from your assets to buy luxuries. If you use your earned income or credit to buy things like a new car, then you are only further trapping yourself into the Rat Race.

9. Decide on who you want your heroes to be, and emulate them. Robert's heroes include people like Warren Buffett.

10. Give value first to other people. You will then see it come back to you in multitudes. If you want to make sales, help other people with their sales. If you want to expand your network, help others expand theirs. (My own real estate business was going incredibly slowly until I started making the effort to find people whom I could help with their businesses).

If a ten-item to-do list isn't enough, Robert recommends the following. Stop doing things the way you are doing them. Start doing things differently instead. Find new ideas and information to help you. Find a mentor or coach who can help you along your path. Educate yourself by taking classes, reading books, listening to podcasts, and attending seminars.

Also, make a ton of offers on real estate to find a few good deals that go through. Jog or drive through a targeted neighborhood to search for potential bargains. Network with other investors. Thinking big and taking massive action will help you in achieving tremendous results.

Conclusion

The three types of income include ordinary earned, portfolio, and passive. If you follow the advice that most people give, you go to school, get good grades, and find a secure job. If you want to be financially free for life, you'll need to do what other financially free people have done instead.

Your first step is to understand how they think, which has been the focus of RDPD. *Think and Grow Rich* by Napoleon Hill is another great book that can help you with this. The sequel to RDPD, *Rich Dad's Cashflow Quadrant,* focuses on the different ways you can make money. *Rich Dad's Guide to Investing* goes into detail about the portfolio and passive investing. It's up to you to do what it takes from here with education and action.

"To be successful, you must be willing to do the things today others won't do to have the things tomorrow others won't have." - Les Brown

Additional Reading

Rich Dad's Cashflow Quadrant: Rich Dad's Guide to Financial Freedom by Robert Kiyosaki

Think and Grow Rich by Napoleon Hill

Chapter 2: Real Estate Basics

The ABCs of Real Estate Investing: The Secrets of Finding Hidden Profits Most Investors Miss by Ken McElroy

Introduction

If you want to be a successful real estate investor, then seek out insight from successful real estate investors such as Ken. He owns a large property management company and has developed commercial properties that are worth millions. Whether you are new to real estate investing or are looking to up your game, Ken's experience and insight can help you get on the right path toward success.

Real Estate Myths

Some real estate investors seem to have all the luck. However, luck does not play a factor in success. Ken started working the grind of property management over 20 years ago to learn how to achieve financial freedom. He made many mistakes in his learning process along the way. But he found that through hard work and determination, he was able to overcome his challenges and take advantage of the opportunities that came his way. With a little common sense and good focus, you too can make other people think you are "lucky" with real estate.

If you think you already have to be rich to start investing in real estate, then you're in for a nice surprise. If you find good deals and network with other investors willing to invest with you, you can buy properties with none of your own money. When you work together with other investors, you can obtain real estate that you could have never purchased on your own. Communicating with them and treating them well will result in having many people wanting to invest with you.

Some people believe they have to start with small deals because there is too much risk with larger properties. A 50-unit building may be safer for you to buy than a single-family house or a duplex. This is because the loan for the single-family house or duplex is secured by your personal finances. The loan for the apartment building is secured by itself and how well it performs. Furthermore, you have more control over the profits with a larger property than a smaller one.

Many people see flipping and "no money down" deals as the main path to success. While you can make good money flipping, it takes a lot of work and comes with added risk. If you buy a property with no money down, it means that you will likely have higher mortgage payments with bigger interest rates.

If you're not skilled at business or negotiation, you don't know anything about real estate, and you don't know anyone in the real estate business, you can still invest in real estate. You will gain the skills, knowledge, and network over time just by working on your real estate business. Don't allow fear to keep you from getting started. It's okay to be afraid as long as you are willing to take action.

What is Your Goal?

Setting a goal is your first task with real estate. What is it you want to achieve through real estate? It should be SMART, which stands for specific, measurable, attainable, realistic, and timely. Perhaps you want to become your own boss within a year, buy two properties per year for the next ten years, or earn $5K per month within the next two years. If your goal is too vague, then you won't know whether you ever achieve it. If your goal is out of your reach, unrealistic, or doesn't have a deadline, then you may never achieve it.

One goal-setting program is called Strategic Coach. It helps you create a life plan by following certain rules. These include things like making your future better than the past, and your gratitude bigger than your level of success. Another great program is called Setting Family Goals, which helps you find the right balance between marriage, family, and your business.

It's good to have an accountability partner who will help you stay focused on your goal. Write down your goal and tell it to everyone. Break it down into smaller milestones, so you know you are making progress. You may need to change your daily behaviors to align them with your goal. Be ready to do whatever it takes to stay focused and persevere to achieving your goal. Your goal may change over time, which is okay.

Building a Team

To truly succeed, you cannot do it all on your own. (My biggest mistake when starting, was thinking that I could.) You need a team, plain and simple. A team of experts can help you make better decisions, avoid costly mistakes, find more and better opportunities, make more money, and achieve your goal faster than you could have ever done by yourself. The team you build will be the basis for your future success and network. Join a real estate club to network with other people as they are a great place to meet prospective team members and find investment opportunities.

Your team needs to at least include an attorney, accountant, real estate broker, and a property management company. Your attorney and accountant will help you set things up correctly and legally to protect you and your assets. Your broker and property manager will help you find great deals. Your property manager will also help keep your properties profitable. Among others, you will also need a good mortgage broker to lend you money, investors to help you buy deals, contractors to inspect and repair your properties, and an insurance agent to keep you protected.

You may or may not choose to include family members on your team. This is a personal preference as there are both good and bad aspects of going into business with family. The same can be said about whether you want to have partners. Good partners communicate with each other, share the same values/vision, and hold each other accountable. Keep networking until you find both good team members and partners.

Choosing a Market

There are many ways to find properties that you will want to buy. Those properties and the information about them are available. You just need an effective research strategy, which could even be fun. This comes down to using the available resources to get an insight into an area. You can do this by talking with people, touring a neighborhood, looking online, and traveling around. This could even mean taking a tax-deductible vacation to an area where you want to buy properties.

Your research to find deals is done on three levels. The first level is preliminary work that can be done in your home. That is where you can choose some cities where you might want to invest and research on them. Examine things like their population growth, the supply of rental properties, public transit access, unemployment, and job diversity. The second level is best done by going to one or more of these cities to network with who will become part of your local team. Choose team members who can confirm whether your first level findings were accurate and help you narrow your search to a smaller submarket. The third level is where you take a deeper dive to analyze any potential submarkets in depth.

If you don't research a property and its market before you buy, you might get tricked into buying swampland. The market and submarket you choose will matter more than a specific property.

Going with your gut instinct on your real estate choices isn't the best way to go. Instead, rely on the numbers and accurate data to make your business decisions.

Choose a market where there is a high demand for real estate and a low supply. You can tell if a market has high demand if occupancy rates are high and the number of move-in specials is low. Also, consider how many new units are being built since they will soon impact the supply. Other indicators for a growing demand include an increasing number of jobs, population growth, and the location.

When a market has an attractive persona to it, such as Venice Beach, CA, more people will be attracted to living there. Such personas create a boom for real estate investing. Look to see if there are new roads, stadiums, casinos, military bases, or colleges as they will also drive population growth. The available jobs should be diverse. If the main employer or industry in a market goes belly up, then so will the demand for real estate.

The location of a market and a specific location of a property within the market are both quite important. You are better off buying properties that are easily visible from main roads. They should be in an area that is attractive to people. Narrow down your focus to a specific submarket that has as many of the above qualities as possible. Become an expert in your chosen submarket(s) and stay up-to-date since markets are always changing.

Finding a Property

Think of finding a property as you would approach online dating. You sift through online profiles until you find one that interests you. Check out that property's profile and pictures. Ask any mutual acquaintances (property managers and brokers) about their thoughts on the property. You should personally see the property and its surrounding area. Spend some time and money to get to know the property better. And if everything works out, you get into a serious relationship with the property (by buying it). However, you don't necessarily need to buy the most beautiful property on the market.

If you research a property and decide you want it, then it's time to contact the owner. It's not difficult to find their contact information on the internet through tax records. Gauge whether they would be willing to talk about selling their property. Ask for things like the rent roll, operating expenses, and occupancy rate so you can determine how much you can offer based on the numbers. If they are hesitant to give you this data, say that you can at least give them a risk-free idea on the worth of their property. If they are not interested, ask if you can stay in touch in case anything changes. In Ken's book, he gives you a script to follow on how to talk with owners about selling their property to you.

You will get information about the property from the owner and/or listing broker. They may have their numbers put into a document called the pro forma. Trust but verify the accuracy of this data. You don't want to discover any costly details after your purchase is completed. It may even be worthwhile to have someone, such as a broker, go through property listings for you to narrow it down to the ones that match your investment criteria. Ken has his broker look for properties that fit specific criteria. These include a minimum number of units, good visibility from major roads, located in specific submarkets, and are owned by people motivated to sell.

You can use a real estate broker to help you find properties. You can find good deals that are listed for sale, as well as great off-market deals. After all, everything is for sale at the right price. The majority of properties you try to buy will not go through. It's a numbers game to first find properties that match your investment criteria and might be a good deal. Then, you would find owners who are willing to sell for a good price. Finally, you need to make sure everything is in good order for the sale.

If you find a diamond in the rough with lots of potential, you can do quite well with it. However, you need to verify that such a diamond is not actually a cubic zirconium. The numbers will tell you the truth about a property. 95% of the time, Ken makes offers on properties without personally visiting them. His offers are solely based upon the numbers and having a local team member tour the property. However, he always inspects every unit in a property before its sale is finalized.

Don't worry about a seller's asking price because the numbers will tell you what you can actually offer for it. There are five steps to use the numbers to determine a property's value. You want to do these as fast as possible so that you can get the property tied up to prevent another potential buyer from snatching it away from you.

1. Verify the income of the property as the seller's pro forma may not tell the whole story. Found out the actual income from the previous trailing 12 months (T12) and not just what the seller is projecting the future income will be. Look at the list of the types and numbers of units, scheduled rent, actual rent collection, vacancy, turnover rates, and other income such as parking fees. Income verification is especially true with commercial properties because their value is based on their cash flow.

2. Verify the property's expenses. It's worth paying a property management company to help you determine what the expenses will be. The expenses include mortgage payments, insurance, taxes, repairs, maintenance, utilities, property management, and advertising, among others.

3. Calculate your net operating income (NOI) by taking the total income minus expenses. Mortgage costs are not included with the expenses in the NOI calculation.

4. Calculate the capitalization (cap) rate and property's value. The cap rate is found by taking the NOI divided by the purchase price. A local real estate broker can tell you what the going cap rate is for a type of property in the market. Then take the NOI divided by the cap rate to determine what your maximum offering price can be.

5. Calculate what your loan payment and your cash-on-cash (CoC) returns will be. You can find out what your loan payment will be if you know what the sales price will be. You will also need to know your interest rate and the down payment you need to pay to get the loan. Either an online mortgage calculator or a mortgage broker can help with that. Minus your loan payment from the NOI, and you now know your projected profits. The annual profits divided by your down payment will equal the CoC.

Making an Offer

Once you have the numbers ready to make your case, you can make your offer based upon them. If your seller's pro forma overestimates the worth of the property, show them the facts and numbers. This will help them understand that you're offering a fair price. Start by sending the seller a letter of intent (LOI), which is a proposal to purchase the property. It should include the purchase price, down payment amount, time required for due diligence, escrow amount, and financing contingencies. You can find sample LOIs and other forms at www.KenMcElroy.com.

The seller might accept your LOI or make a counteroffer. You may need to go back-and-forth until an agreement is made. It's possible that the numbers aren't right, or you and the seller can't come to an agreement on the price. In that case, it's perfectly fine to walk away from the deal. If you and the seller both sign a final LOI, then the property is off the market. You will then need to get a purchase and sales agreement signed that covers the various details of the transaction.

You will need contingencies in the contract, which will allow you to back out of the deal if certain things end up going wrong. A loan contingency allows you to back out if you don't get the loan you needed. A due diligence contingency requires that you receive the documents and information to verify that the numbers for your LOI are correct.

Due Diligence

Due diligence is when you examine a property in-depth with meticulous attention and effort to see if your previous quicker assessment was accurate. Examine every document about the property so you know it can follow your business plan. Inspect every unit, so you have a full understanding of the property's condition and its tenant base. You are looking to see how you can add value to the property by fixing it up and/or reducing expenses.

During Ken's due diligence, he has discovered various problems, Those included drug dealers, squatters, units in terrible shape, holes in the roof, and falsified rent rolls where units were vacant even though they were supposed to be rented. He even found a boa constrictor on the loose. Poor due diligence puts you in danger of finding your own nasty surprises.

Depending upon the property, the length of time for due diligence is usually between 10 and 30 days. Use that time effectively. Audit the books and files to do things like comparing every lease to the actual tenants and income. Review the public records to find any issues with zoning, fire code violations, building permits, or environmental concerns such as asbestos. Look over any service agreements for parking, alarm systems, landscaping, etc. Have a professional inspection done so you have an idea of when things like the roof or HVAC will need to be replaced.

Ken looks at due diligence as an Easter egg hunt. He's looking for the secrets about the property. Finding those has saved him many thousands of dollars. If you find issues with the property or its finances during the due diligence period, you can do two things. You can walk away or renegotiate things if you had the proper language in your sales contract. Tactfully present your findings to the seller if you believe any changes to the sale need to occur, such as lowering the purchase price. If you don't find any surprises during your due diligence, then you can at least rest assured that everything was as you expected.

Putting It Together

Consider how you will operate your real estate business. Make a plan with your team, especially your accountant, property manager, insurance agent, and contractor. Their insight will help you maximize your profits, prevent costly mistakes, and achieve your goals faster than you could on your own. A good plan focuses on increasing income while decreasing expenses. Both will improve the profitability and value of a property.

Adding value to a property can make you a ton of money. You need to figure out how you can increase property value. There are some ways to do that. Can you upgrade the inside or outside to get higher rents? Is there an old tennis court that could be converted to garages or a dog park? Are there systems you can put in place to improve the property's efficiency? Can you get bids on things like insurance and landscaping to get better value? Can you reduce utility costs by installing energy-efficient lightbulbs or low-flow toilets? Can you hire an on-site property manager for less than an outsourced one? Use your creative mind to find solutions to the property's problems. Fixing those problems Will in turn increase the property's value.

Increasing income and decreasing expenses will have a profound impact on the worth of your property. If between those two, you increase the NOI by $10K per year on a property with a 5% cap rate, then your property will be worth $200K more. A solid business plan is necessary to make this happen.

The rents you collect will be the main part of a property's income. The potential income is what a property would make if every unit was rented. You can also make money from parking fees, laundry, late fees, and charging utilities to tenants. There are also various expenses for which you should plan. These include payroll for any staff, administrative costs such as for an attorney or accountant, marketing costs, taxes, insurance, utilities, capital repairs to replace the roof or upgrade units, and property management.

Managing the Property

Property management is a make-or-break factor for real estate. If you buy a property right but manage it poorly, then you could lose your shirt on the deal. The key action here is to follow through on your business plan while staying on budget. There are various property management software programs that can help you with the entire process.

You might choose to manage the property yourself or oversee a property manager you hired. Regardless of which you choose, you'll need to know what it takes to properly manage a property. A good property manager's job is to solve the daily problems, oversee any staff, handle the maintenance, advertise the open units to attract good tenants, leases out those units, screens potential tenants, provide 24/7 customer service to tenants and treats them properly, collects rent, increases the cash flow, ensures the laws are followed, pays the bills, manages the budget, and evicts tenants for nonpayment of rent or lease violations.

If you decide to hire a property management company, know that they vary a lot in quality. Some might overcharge you, not have enough experience, have insufficient policies and procedures, fail to properly train their employees, be unlicensed, and decide not to perform background checks on their employees and/or the tenants. Screen potential property management companies and check their references. You need to set up your expectations from the beginning, which should be realistic.

Treat your property manager with respect, and they should do so in return. However, you may sometimes have to fire your property management company. The reasons for this include if the property is performing poorer than expected, if operations are not improving, or if the property is performing so extremely well that you think you can manage it effectively yourself.

There is a domino effect where some bad property management decisions can lead to bigger and bigger problems. If you don't do background checks on tenants, then you can attract the wrong crowd. Drug deals or sex offenders could move in and make good tenants decide to leave. Your tenants are your customers. Be responsive to their needs to keep them happy. Be very thoughtful before you allow tenants exceptions from following the rules. For example, do not waive late fees because that can lead to tenants being late with rent more often. You should not be lenient with them. Have enough reserve money to cover the unexpected repairs that inevitably occur.

Selling vs. Holding

While Ken likes to buy and hold properties for cash flow, many people like to sell. This way, they can either keep the money or buy a new property. If you decide to sell a property, you will want to sell it for the highest price and with the best terms. Prepare for this as part of your business plan.

Maximize your income and minimize your expenses so that you have a high NOI, and therefore a high property value. Your actual

NOI will help you calculate the wholesale price, whereas your potential income and NOI will determine the retail price. You are better off with having higher rents with some vacancy than to have low rents and 100% occupancy. For example, suppose you have a 20-unit apartment building that is 100% occupied but, it has a 10% cap rate, and the rents are $35 below market rate. This means you are missing out on $8400 in annual cash flow and an extra $84K in the sales price. It's silly to leave money on the table like that.

The second part of increasing the sales price is to reduce expenses. Some of these you will have more control over than others. When Ken prepares a property for sale, he likes to run things leanly by reducing staff, cutting back on landscaping visits, minimizing advertising, and raising his insurance deductible. This way, there is a lower insurance payment.

Keep your property manager and real estate broker in the loop to help you with the sale. Before the sale, you should decide whether you prefer to pay the capital gains tax or if you want to do a 1031 tax exchange. The tax code 1031 allows you to defer capital gains taxes indefinitely if you follow all of the various rules for it within a specific timeline.

Conclusion

This is another great book from the Rich Dad Poor Dad series. Therefore, you can feel confident that it has quality information without overburdening you with trivial details. Ken prefers to invest in apartment buildings instead of other types of real estate. For him, cash flow is king because of the financial freedom it gives him. As you will see in my other chapters, there are many ways to successfully invest in real estate. The lessons in Ken's book ring true for all approaches in real estate investment.

Additional Reading

The Advanced Guide to Real Estate Investing: How to Identify the Hottest Markets and Secure the Best Deals by Ken McElroy

The Millionaire Real Estate Investor by Gary Keller, Dave Jenks, and Jay Papasan

Chapter 3: Creative Financing

The Book on Investing in Real Estate with No (and Low) Money Down by Brandon Turner

Introduction

No matter how much money you have, if you keep investing in real estate, you will eventually run out of your own money. If you want to keep investing, you need to be creative when it comes to financing strategies. Brandon lays out a ton of great options to buy real estate with or without using your own money. The most powerful part of real estate is leveraging other people's money to make yourself money. Having the creative financing options in your toolbox that Brandon describes in his book will help you with this.

Creative Real Estate Investing

When you go to get a pizza, you can either exchange your money for it or face potential criminal charges. If you want to buy $1000 worth of gold or stocks, you need $1000. Then perhaps the gold or stocks will be worth even more in the future. However, with getting real estate, there are other legal options to buy it without your own money. Instead of using your cash to buy real estate, you can use your knowledge, time, and creativity.

Brandon started investing in real estate when he was 21 and had no money, credit, or any idea what he was doing. He was forced to educate himself and discover creative ways to find funding for his real estate ventures. He made a lot of mistakes and learned many lessons. He shares them with you in his book to help you become successful.

Regardless of how much money you have, you are not able to buy all the real estate using only your own money. That's where creativity comes in to play. It will help you get the number of deals, income, and cash flow that you want to achieve, regardless of which approach to real estate investing you choose to take.

Author and radio show host, David Ramsey, advocates only for buying properties when you can pay 100% in cash. Buying real estate with money from the bank or other investors has a risk to it. However, the risk can be managed if you have a little know-how. Brandon attributes *Rich Dad Poor Dad* as the inspiration to find ways to afford things instead of being in the "I can't afford" mindset.

Do you want to retire as a millionaire after working for 40 years behind a desk, or would you rather retire as a millionaire sooner? Brandon prefers to do things differently from the average person so that he can retire young enough to enjoy it.

Following are four main rules to follow with creative real estate investing:

1. Find better than average deals. This allows you more wiggle room to use less of your own money while making more profit.
2. Be extremely conservative with your approach and plan for the worst-case scenarios.

3. Be ready to make sacrifices of your time, energy, creativity, and profits. This will enable you to find ways to make each deal work.

4. Have a cushion while you creatively invest so that you can handle the various problems that might occur.

Many infomercial gurus talk about making no money down deals. While these exist, the gurus make it seem like real estate is easy money. They also may make it seem like a way to get rich quick. It is neither. However, it is a solid way to build wealth over time. Each chapter goes over a different approach to invest without using much or any of your own money. Some of these are easier than others. However, it's good to have investment strategy options. Think of these different approaches as tools for your toolbox. Depending on the project you are doing, you might need to use one specific approach or a combination of different approaches.

Owner-Occupied Real Estate

This is an inexpensive way to get started in real estate investing by buying a personal residence that is also a rental property. This is often referred to as house hacking. The property could have anywhere from one to four units. It could still be considered residential instead of commercial. You can do this with as little as $0 as a down payment, get a lower interest rate, have easier financing, and get qualified with a lower credit score. *Rich Dad Poor Dad* talks about how your personal home is a liability and not an asset because it costs you money instead of making money. However, if you rent out or flip your home for a profit, then it becomes an asset.

Brandon's first property was a four-bedroom house where he rented the extra bedrooms to his friends. He fixed it up before selling it for a $20,000 profit nine months later. (For example, my first property was a triplex where I lived in one unit and rented out the other two. The rent covered the mortgage, taxes, insurance, repairs, and utilities. That literally allowed me to live for free!)

Only you can decide if a single-family or multifamily home is right for you. Perhaps you live in an especially expensive area, have a lower credit score because of some past mistakes, or may not have the income or savings to be approved for a home loan. In that case, this might not be the right time for you to buy a property on your own. However, there are some programs to help make it easier to purchase an owner-occupied property.

The Federal Housing Authority (FHA) has a popular loan insurance program for people in the lower and middle classes. It allows you to only pay 3.5% of the purchase price as a down payment. There are some rules about this, though. You have to pay a mortgage insurance premium (MIP) until the mortgage is paid down to be only 78% of the property's value. The MIP has a 1-2% upfront fee along with a monthly fee of about $100 for each $100,000 in the loan. The property has to be in decent shape as well. You can only have one FHA loan at a time. (For example, if you are married, you can have one in your name. You can then have the second one in your spouse's name. If you refinance the FHA property into a conventional loan, you can then get a new property under the FHA).

The FHA offers a subset type of loan called a 203(k) loan. That gives you money to both buy a property and rehab it with FHA approved contractors. The FHA would need to inspect the repairs to make sure they were done satisfactorily. The 203(k) loan down payment is still 3.5% of the purchase price. However, it requires more paperwork and red tape than the regular FHA loan.

The United States Department of Veteran Affairs (VA) offers a loan program to USA veterans. Veterans can pay as little as $0 for the down payment with this program. Unlike the FHA loan, there is no MIP with the VA loan. The United States Department of Agriculture (USDA) offers a similar program. However, that's only for rural single-family homes being purchased by low to moderate-income people.

Partnering with Others

While you have your strengths, you also have some weaknesses. You can benefit from having partners whose strengths complement your weaknesses and vice versa. With real estate investing, you might be short on money, time, knowledge, creativity, ability to find deals, ability to do the labor, or a network.

If you create your persona or brand as a real estate investor, you will start to attract other people who are also interested in real estate. Your brand consists of both you and your product. Market yourself as an investor with a good reputation, knowledge, and experience. Your honesty, consistency, and focused efforts matter here. Your real estate deals are your product and need to be awesome.

All of this together will help with building your brand and finding partners. Brandon recommends the following four ways to put together partnerships and has used all of these ways to make a deal work.

1. Full equity partnerships are when perhaps one person funds the down payment and the rehab costs. Another person then manages the property. The two people split the profits of how they choose, maybe 50/50.

2. Down payment equity partnerships are when perhaps one person funds only the down payment. Another person then manages the property. Either another person funds the rehab costs, or maybe the property is already in great shape. Then the investors split the profits of as they see fit.

3. Private lending partnerships are when one investor loans money with a fixed interest rate and term to another investor. That investor buys and manages the property.

4. Credit partnerships are where one investor has good credit that they use to get good terms on the loan. The other partner(s) in the deal handle other aspects of the property.

Using a partnership to get a portion of a deal is better than not being able to get the deal to work. Beware of the potential pitfalls of having partners. Those include clashing personalities, trust issues, reduced profits, complications in taxes, stressed relationships with friends and family who are partners, and expectations that are not realistic. It is best to use an attorney to set up a partnership correctly. Only you can decide if partnering with someone is the right move to make.

Home Equity

Home equity means that a property you already own is worth more than what is owed in liens, such as a mortgage. For example, perhaps your home is worth $150K, but you only owe $100K. This means you have the other $50K as the home equity. A home equity loan is like a second mortgage that uses your home equity as collateral.

You can either have a regular home equity loan or a home equity line of credit (HELOC). In a regular home equity loan, you get all of the money upfront. You then pay it back according to the terms of the loan. A HELOC is similar to that, but you can take out as much or little of the set dollar amount at any time. With a HELOC, you still have to pay back the loan.

It's much easier to get a home equity loan for your personal residence than for an investment property. However, some banks do offer business lines of credit. These are secured against the equity of multiple investment properties. To find out if a bank does home equity loans, you just have to ask them. Banks usually only lend up to 90% of a home's value. Some loans have adjustable rates that will increase or decrease at various times. Make sure the investment is still a good deal if the interest rates on your adjustable-rate loan were to go up high.

You can use a home equity loan to invest in a new property where it could cover the down payment, cost of repairs, or perhaps even the entire property. (I only recommend using a home equity loan if the investment property you are using it for will pay for more than the loan payments. Otherwise, it's not profitable.)

Hard Money Loans

Hard money loans are those that come from private lenders or businesses. They are usually for a short term (6-36 months), have a high-interest rate (usually 10-20%), charge closing costs, and are based on the investment value of a particular property. They are easier and quicker to get than traditional loans. Some people use these as a short-term solution during a house flip before selling. Other people use these to buy a property and do a renovation on it. They use it before refinancing it into a lower interest mortgage at a bank and keeping it as a rental property. Most banks want you to have a property for at least six months before you refinance it.

If you are looking for a hard money lender, the *BiggerPockets Hard Money Lender Directory* or an internet search may be a good place to start. You can also ask other local investors for recommendations on the best local hard money lenders.

For a hard money lender to give you money, they have to feel like it is a secure investment that will allow them to get their money back plus interest. They might be willing to give you enough money to cover both the cost of the property and repairs if there is enough value in the property to cover everything and more.

Generally, a hard money lender will not lend out more than 60% of what a property would appraise when it is in good condition. This may not cover all the money you need. In that case, consider if doing another creative option described in the book to get the additional money would be the right option. Hard money is a great short-term solution. Since it is so expensive, be sure that the financial numbers are in good order for you to make money from using hard money.

Private Money

Private money is an amazing thing in real estate. It's where other investors give you their money in exchange for a portion of a property's profits. Private investors are not professional lenders. Otherwise, their money would be considered hard money. A private investor is someone who wants to invest in real estate but may not have the time or interest to do it by themselves. Maybe, they earn a high income or have money sitting in the bank. It's also possible they have money available in a retirement account like an IRA or 401K.

As of 2010, 22% of Americans had at least $100K saved up in their retirement accounts. You can find lots of people looking to get good returns on their money by investing in real estate. It's just a matter of matching what you are doing in real estate with what a particular investor wants in an investment. For example, if you only do short term flips, then find those people willing to fund flips for a quick return. You have to find the right match.

Many people start by obtaining investment funding from their family and friends. You can network with potential investors at real estate clubs/conferences, BiggerPockets.com, or Chamber of Commerce meetings. You can also blog about your real estate ventures, or do public searches for people who already fund other real estate deals.

Brandon recommends creating a high-quality information packet to market to potential investors. This includes your business name, contact info, goals, description of how your business works and uses private money, your track record, referrals from other investors, and expectations for everyone in the deals. (When talking with potential investors, think of it as offering awesome opportunities, and not so much of a sales pitch.) Brandon's book includes a script on how to address concerns from potential investors. It also has interviews with several people who raise money from private investors.

Make sure that the details of the agreement between you and a private lender are clear and legally documented. Since raising private money can be complicated, it is highly recommended that you first consult with an attorney who will ensure that you are following all of the laws.

Lease Options

So far, you've learned about buying real estate with little to none of your own money. Lease options, however, allow you to invest in real estate without actually buying any. A lease option or "rent to own" is where a homeowner rents a property to a tenant. Then, the tenant has the right to buy the property at a certain price within a certain timeframe IF they choose to do so. The lease option is used when a tenant can rent a property that they have an interest in buying but first need to save up for the down payment. Either that or they want to build their credit to be approved for a loan. To have exclusive rights to the option to purchase the property, the tenant usually has to pay an upfront option fee of around $2-5K. That can be used as part of the down payment.

Most lease option investors make money from being the homeowner. It is where they make money off the option fee, rent, and purchase of the property. It's possible to go through a few lease option tenants before finding one that chooses to go ahead with the purchase. A bonus of the sale is that there is no six percent real estate agent fee to be paid, thus increasing profits.

You might consider signing on to be the tenant of the homeowner with a lease option. You could then sublet the property for a profit (with the owner's permission). This way, you keep the extra cash flow you earn. You can also sell your option to another person. This would allow them to purchase the house. For example, if you have the option to buy the property for $200K. However, you later end up finding someone who will buy it for $250K. Therefore, then you get to keep that extra $50K as profit.

There is something called a lease option sandwich. This is where a homeowner lease options a property to you. Then you turn around and lease option that same property to someone else for a profit. You can charge a higher option fee, higher rent, and higher purchase price than what the original homeowner charged you. If your tenant does not end up buying the property, you could find another buyer. You can also ask for a lease extension from the homeowner, buy the property yourself, or simply walk away without buying the property at all.

To do the lease option sandwich successfully, you need to secure a longer lease period from the homeowner. Also, keep them informed about what you're doing. Screen potential tenants well, and connect your tenants with a mortgage specialist. This specialist can help them with the purchase and arrange to pay your rent directly to the bank to cover the homeowner's mortgage. This creates a legal record of your option contract at the county administration department. Do not apply your tenant's rent toward their future down payment because that's potentially illegal. At the same time, don't take advantage of your tenants.

A master lease option (MLO) is a next-level approach where a tenant pays all of the taxes, insurance, and maintenance fees. They then sublet the property to other people. This is used often with larger properties. It is similar to seller financing but does not include a title transfer. An MLO is a great way to buy large multifamily properties with little to none of your own money.

Nearly all mortgage paperwork includes a due-on-sale clause. That is where the bank can demand the entirety of the loan be paid back at any time. This happens when you are doing a lease option from a homeowner. When their bank demands the loan to be paid in full, and the homeowner cannot pay it, you as the tenant might be out of luck. While this is a potential risk, Brandon has never heard of this ever happening. However, please pay attention to whether the mortgage strictly forbids lease options.

Seller Financing

Seller financing is amazing! It's where the current property owner owns 100% of a property and they sell it to you. Then, they act as the bank by loaning the mortgage to you as well. The owner can sell with owner financing while still owing money on their mortgage. In that case, they either need to pay it off or run the risk that the bank will demand that the due-on-sale clause be honored immediately.

The terms of the mortgage are really up to what is mutually feasible to you and the seller. It could include no or low down payment, easier financing, and negotiable interest rate and payment dates. You can use seller financing to buy properties that the bank would not finance for whatever reason (perhaps it is in a state of disrepair). Also, the transaction won't show up on your credit report unless the seller reports the loan to a credit reporting agency.

Seller financing is a great way for sellers to still get monthly cash flow from their property. They can do so without having to deal with tenants or do any work. The seller could get a better return on their money with seller financing as compared to other forms of investment. This also lets the seller avoid a potentially huge tax bill that would otherwise be due after the sale.

You can also do partial seller financing if the seller owes some mortgage that they don't have the cash to pay off. For example, there may be s a $100K property that had $50K left in the mortgage. You could then get a bank loan for most of the $100K. Then, you can have the seller give you a second loan through seller financing for the rest.

To find sellers willing to do seller financing, you need to first ask if they are willing to do so. Real estate clubs are a great way to meet such sellers. Look for words in the property's advertising that include words such as "owner will carry" or "owner financing." You could also do direct mailing through companies like ListSource.

Wholesaling

A real estate wholesaler is a middleman who earns fees by connecting the seller of a property with the purchaser. They do this by finding good deals, negotiating the price, getting the property under contract, and then selling that contract to another investor for a profit. Successful wholesaling takes more time and effort than you might expect. Interacting with successful wholesalers in BiggerPockets Wholesaling Forums is a great place to kickstart your wholesaling journey.

Brandon gives an example where a homeowner named Clarence is motivated to sell his home. However, he is unable to because it needs repairs he can't afford to do. Beth is a wholesaler who runs the numbers and offers him a lower price. After some negotiation, Clarence agrees to sell at the lower price. They sign a contract that either Beth or one of her associates will close on the house in six weeks. Beth had already met an investor named Jackson who looks at the house and is willing to pay $10K more than the amount that Beth and Clarence had negotiated. Jackson pays Beth a nonrefundable $2K deposit. When the sale closes, Beth receives the additional $8K as profit.

Essentially, Clarence had a problem, and Beth was able to solve it for him. Also, that's what wholesaling is all about. Find motivated sellers, figure out the problem that they are facing, and create a solution for that problem. Be ethical in your approach to wholesaling, and do not prey on people who are in a vulnerable situation. You can wholesale with no money, but it's easier if you spend some money on marketing and general expenses.

There are several ways to find deals for wholesaling. One way is called "driving for dollars." That is where you drive around a neighborhood looking for properties in disrepair and finding the contact info for the owners in the public record. Using direct mail can be costly but allows you to contact more owners than you could from driving around. You can also use search engine optimization (SEO) to direct people to your beautiful website that describes how you can solve their real estate problems. "Bandit signs" are those small roadside signs that say something like "We buy houses for ca$h." However, these are often illegal to use. Renting billboards would be a legal, although more expensive, version of bandit signs. You can find properties listed on the MLS. Those would cut into profits a bit since a real estate agent would be involved. Searching Craigslist for some "for sale by owner" (FSBO) properties is a solid free option. Furthermore, you can look for FSBO yard signs or in dedicated FSBO listing services. Another way is to ask people called "bird dogs" to find deals for you. You then pay them a finder's fee for deals that go through.

Wholesaling is more of a job than investing. However, the amount of work needed for it can be reduced if you have good systems in place. Most wholesalers aim to make at least $5K per deal. Brandon recommends it as a way to earn money and also gain a real estate education that can be used in other investment approaches.

A wholesaler needs to still sell properties at enough of a discount so that another investor will be willing to buy them. This is where a little math comes in handy. First, determine the after-repair value (ARV) of a property by checking on how much comparable properties in the area have sold (comps). You initially require just a ballpark figure. You can get that yourself by comparing the average price per square foot of very similar properties. Public records can provide some information about a property, including its recent sale prices. If you build a relationship with a real estate agent, they may assist you by doing some comps for you. Websites like www.Zillow.com or www.Trulia.com can give you estimated prices as well. The smaller the area you focus on, the better you will get at determining the ARVs there.

When determining whether a property is good for flipping or wholesaling, many people use the 70% Rule. This entails that your maximum allowable offer should be no more than 70% of the ARV less your fee and the cost of any repairs/upgrades. The 70% Rule is more of a general guide and may vary depending on the deal and market. A fixed cost method is a similar approach that focuses more on the investor making a specific dollar amount in profit per deal.

Estimating the cost of the rehab/repairs is essential in determining the profitability of a deal. You should have a good understanding of the neighborhood and who the ultimate buyer will be. There is no need to rehab a property better than what is needed. Take a slow and detailed tour through the property while taking pictures and videos that you can later show the investor. Make detailed notes of the problems through the property. Then, condense that list into categories. Finally, break it down to figure out a rehab price for each of those categories. There's no shame in asking for help on this from the BiggerPockets Forums, a local contractor, or even a local investor. This all gets easier through experience.

Once you determine the ARV, cost of the rehab, and maximum allowable offer, you need to negotiate with the seller to get down to that price or lower. Build rapport with them, listen to them, learn what their problem/motivation is, and show how you can realistically help them. Be willing to walk away from the deal if needed. There are many books written about the fine art of negotiation that cover this in greater detail.

Once you both agree on a price, get a signed contract in place right then and there. Putting down earnest money, even as little as $1, helps seal the legality of the contract. Make sure there is a contingency in the contract. That contingency would allow you to back out if you cannot find a qualified buyer.

It helps to have a handful of investors ready before putting in offers. That way, you can focus on the kinds of deals that match their investment criteria. You can find these investors through several methods. These include Craigslist, real estate clubs, real estate agents, hard money lenders, the public record that shows who is buying properties, court auctions, ListSource, or BiggerPockets.

Once you have an investor ready to buy a property, you should have them pay you a nonrefundable fee of $1-5K. Then assign the contract to the investor, so they are listed as the buyer of the property. Your wholesaler fee will be listed on the closing paperwork, which the seller can see.

If the bank owns the house due to foreclosure, assigning the contract is usually not allowed. You would then need to do back-to-back closings. That situation occurs when a wholesaler uses a hard money loan to buy the property before turning around and selling it to the investor a few minutes later. The fees for this sort of transactional lending is usually around 1-3% plus closing costs. This is because it is a low risk to the hard money lender. If you do back-to-back closings, be sure to include these extra transaction costs to your calculations.

Additional Reading

Raising Private Capital: Building Your Real Estate Empire Using Other People's Money by Matt Faircloth

45-Day Investor: How to buy an investment property with nothing down in 45 days or less by Kevin Amolsch

Chapter 4: Single-Family Houses

Building Wealth One House at a Time by John Schaub

Introduction

Many people, including John, have made millions of dollars by investing in single-family homes. By treating others fairly in your real estate ventures, you can build a good reputation for yourself. That eventually will help attract future deals to you. Investing in single-family homes helps create affordable housing for families. It can also give you control over your retirement that can change your life for the better. It's not very complicated. It can be done with very little education, money, or time. John's book teaches you how to control your retirement by investing in single-family homes.

Making Money with Single Family Homes

Most people remain poor because they are held back by the fear of purchasing their first property. Investing gets easier after the first house. While there is some variance from year to year, rental prices for single-family homes go up over time, similar to home prices. Like most real estate, you make your money when you buy if you buy right.

John can make more money with less work with single-family homes. This is more than he can with other kinds of real estate. This is because the tenants tend to stay longer, typically five or more years. This results in lower maintenance and vacancy costs. The worth of a house is not wholly based on the rental income. You can still make money from an empty house due to appreciation. (Focusing only on appreciation tends to be common in places like California and New York. There, the rental income does not keep up with prices very well.) The national average annual home appreciation is 5%, which can result in great returns when you have low down payments.

Single-family homes are easier to buy because they require a lower down payment as opposed to commercial properties. Banks are also more willing to give out loans for houses. Houses have fewer vacancies than commercial properties as well. If you need to sell a house, there are also more home buyers as compared to commercial property buyers. That makes it easier to sell. You benefit when you sell to someone wanting to live in the house instead of selling to an investor. You also get the best possible sales price.

Expensive homes can appreciate quickly during an economic boom. However, they depreciate quickly during a recession. Lower-priced homes tend to be more stable and remain occupied. John recommends investing in multiple houses as opposed to apartments. This is because it diversifies your investments in multiple neighborhoods and price ranges. If you need cash, you can always sell one house. If you own an apartment building, you'd have to sell the whole thing.

Research the area where you want to buy houses. Much of the information you need is available in public records. Those show what properties have sold for in the past, and are selling for currently. It also shows which neighborhoods are performing better. The higher rate of appreciation for an area is always better. The other things to consider could include population growth, an increasing number of families, public facilities such as schools, and the inflation rate of the US dollar.

Buying Right

It's important to have a plan for the kinds of houses you want to buy. Furthermore, it's vital to stick to that plan. Don't just buy any old house that you see. The criteria to consider may include the house's age, amenities, location, price, size, and the type of tenants it will attract. Additional criteria include the quality of the neighbors, property taxes, expected maintenance costs, and cash flow. With most things, including houses, it's best to buy low and sell high. You will get a higher profit margin with rent on cheaper houses. However, they tend to come with bigger problems and have little appreciation. Then inversely, you get lower profit margins and fewer problems, but more appreciation with more expensive homes.

Plan out your investment strategy and purchase homes that fit with your goals. You don't want the best or worse house on the street. This is because you won't make as much money as you would with a "normal" house in the area. Make sure a house you buy has the number of bedrooms, size of the yard, etc. that your ideal tenants will want. At the same time, make sure to rent to the kind of tenants who will take care of the house and pay rent on time.

Buying houses without using your own money is also a great strategy. This can be done in two ways. Firstly, you can do so by using money from other investors. Otherwise, you can if the seller doesn't have a mortgage on the property and they do seller financing. Find houses that have been on the market for over six months. Then, you'll find that sellers will be more willing to do a seller carried loan with no down payment.

In general, when you find a seller with problems that you can solve, you can create a win-win situation. They get to sell their house and solve their problem, and you end up with an awesome deal. Just be sure to rent or sell them. This way, you won't get stuck paying mortgages on a bunch of empty houses. If you have better financing for your mortgage, the cash flow you can have from renting a house will be even better.

Buying houses that are in good working order and keeping them that way will save you money (and headaches) in the long run. Houses wear out over time, so it's the lot they're on which appreciates in value. It is better to buy in neighborhoods that are on their way up in value.

Working with Real Estate Cycles

Real estate bubbles are caused when people speculate that profits are going to continue to rise. When the 2007 bubble was at its peak, people were able to buy real estate without any down payment and borrow more than the price of the house. This led to a lot of foreclosures when prices started going down. Investors were then able to buy millions of houses at deep discounts and rent them out for incredible profits.

Unfortunately, it's difficult to know the precise future of the market. However, there are six things to indicate that the market might be nearing its peak.

1. Getting financing for deals is simple.
2. Everyone is investing in real estate.
3. Home prices are increasing faster as compared to rents.
4. Buyers are overleveraging their houses.
5. Developers are overbuilding new housing, and over speculating in both land and houses.
6. Buyers can only make money on properties if they appreciate it. This is because the rents don't cover the mortgage and other expenses.

When the next market crash comes, you can make a lot of money if you are prepared for it. You can prepare for a crash by having a good understanding of your local market's prices and rents. You can also keep cash reserves in the bank, knowing where to find additional investment dollars, renting to tenants with diverse employment, and embracing change when it occurs.

Finding Hidden Opportunities

John finds it best to invest in the town where you live. This is because it's easier to oversee the property, market, and property management company. It's easier for you to find properties to buy as well. While you can find good deals on the market, you can find better ones off-market. Drive around town looking for empty houses, houses that need some work, and are in nicer neighborhoods, houses owned by people who reside out of town, and houses in foreclosure.

Normally, 90% of the houses for sale are not good deals. You want to find the sellers who are motivated to sell because you can help solve their problems. Once you have identified a house that meets your investment criteria, ask the owner why they want to sell, and whether you could assume their existing loan. Furthermore, ask how much they owe on their loan, what will they do if they can't sell the house, how long the house has been for sale, and how much they paid for it. From there, determine the seller's level of motivation to sell and the profitability of the deal for you. The best buyers use negotiation and are prepared to make counteroffers for; however, the seller may decide to respond.

Pricing a House

Know what you can pay for a house before you make an offer. This will depend on whether your investment plan focuses on cash flow, appreciation, or both. You could pay for an appraiser to determine a house's price. However, that takes money and time. If the house is not on the market, it's easier to start by making a low offer on the house and to see how the seller responds to it.

You will pay under the retail price if a house is distressed, in foreclosure, or in a short sale. Look at prices similar homes have sold for in the area (comps) and what the trends are in neighborhood home prices and length of residency. The price to offer depends on a few factors, it could be whether the market is going up or down. If your investment focus is cash flow, determine whether a house at asking price will earn you at least a 4-6% return on your investment. You can also look at the price to reproduce a property to see its potential worth.

Funding Options

If you use a loan to buy a house, then you need a way to pay the mortgage. Ideally, you will want the rent you earn from tenants to be more than the mortgage payment and other monthly expenses. This means that the rent rates can determine how much you can pay for a house. The higher the rent, the higher the mortgage and the purchase price you can afford.

To find out the rent rates, look at other similar rental houses in the area to see how much rent you can reasonably charge. You can do this by looking on Craigslist or by calling landlords in ads while pretending to be a potential tenant. When real estate prices increase, and interest rates decrease, more people buy houses. This means rents will remain stable or could drop. However, when interest rates go up, fewer people can buy. This means rent prices will go up. Over time, rent prices will increase, and so will your income.

It works best to have a long-term loan with a low-interest rate. This way, you can borrow more money. As long as your tenants are paying rent, they are covering the mortgage payments. John has a 10/10/10 rule that he follows. He does not pay more than 10%

down for a property so that he can purchase more properties. He does not get loans with interest rates higher than 10%, so that doesn't cut into profits too much. Also, John buys houses at prices for at least 10% below market value to ensure his profitability.

Whatever you do, avoid loans that are shorter than ten years, have a variable interest rate, have a negative amortization with payments less than interest only, or require a personal guarantee that puts your personal assets at risk. Furthermore, avoid loans that are more than the worth of the property, thus overleveraging you. (These mistakes got many people in deep trouble during the last recession.)

It can be a good strategy to own real estate free and clear of a loan. This can increase your cash flow from a house. However, you get a better return on your investment by using less of your money and more of other people's money.

You could buy a $100K house with $100K in cash. If it has a net income of $8K, then you earn an 8% return on your money. However, you could buy four similar houses with $25K down each with 6% 30-year loans. That would net you more than 10% return on that same $100K. Also, that doesn't include the returns you get from the loan pay down or appreciation.

John loves seller financing, where the seller acts as the bank. This is because you, as the buyer, then don't require the services of a bank. Also, if you end up not being able to make the mortgage payments, you just give the house back to the seller. If you went with a bank, it might go after your personal assets.

Using Other People's Money (OPM)

John started out without a steady income and could not get approved for a bank loan. This turned out to be an important part of his success since he had to use creativity to purchase houses. With bargain deals, the sellers need to sell immediately. Banks take longer and sometimes too long to process a loan. They also won't loan you more than 80% of the purchase price on an investment property. Plus, it's tough to get a bank loan for real estate when prices are low during a recession. This means you need alternative funding to close good deals quickly. It's handy to use a mortgage calculator. You can get it for free online to determine the interest rate and the loan amount you can handle for a deal to work.

John has used one creative solution when a seller has an empty house for sale. That solution is to offer to take over their mortgage payments and then pay the seller the equity when John later sells the house. For example, there is a house worth $200K-$250K and has a $150K mortgage. John will take over the mortgage and pay the seller $50K when he sells it later. This solves the seller's problem of making payments for an empty house. This works because John then rents the house for more than the mortgage payments and other expenses.

One strategy for buying multiple houses is to refinance the first house to buy the second. Then, you can repeat the process for the third house and so forth. However, be cautious with this approach. It increases your debt and the risk of potentially losing your property. Do not put yourself in a position where a refinance puts you into a negative cash flow situation. You're better off using the cash flow from one property to purchase a second property.

Many people want to make money passively. They are also dissatisfied with the return on their money in the bank or the stock market. You can show them that investing with you is a safe way to get a better return on their investment. Make a list of people in your social circle and family who could be potential investors. This could include people such as business associates, family members, your accountant, your lawyer, contractors, or other local investors. Then find a good deal and put it under contract with a "subject to" clause. This will allow you to line up money from potential investors. If your people say no, ask them if they know anyone who might be willing to invest. Just be picky about who you partner with on a deal. This is important as that can matter more than the deal itself.

Using other people's money (OPM) is great. This is because you can make it, so you don't have to repay it until the house sells. There are no payments on it, it allows you to make a larger down payment, and it means that you can buy more houses with less of your own money tied up. (If you have a more positive track record making money for your investors, the easier it will become to get more OPM for future properties.)

When using OPM, clarify your role and how the profits will be handled. Never make any guarantees of profits because you can't predict the future. You never know if the market or the property will have a catastrophe. You will need to make everything legal. You'll need to either use a joint venture, tenants in common (TIC), trust, corporation, or limited liability company (LLC). Whichever you do, make sure to use a good attorney to get everything in order.

Real Estate Contracts

Using a contract is necessary when buying/selling real estate. It helps to keep a record of the agreement. Plus, it protects you if you ever need to enforce things in a lawsuit. ALWAYS read a real estate contract before you sign it. This is because that will potentially save you time, money, and headaches. Contracts and clauses can vary widely, so pay attention to the small print. You can always renegotiate things that seem unfair to you. Practice reading and filling out real estate contracts to get a feel for them. If you are using a real estate agent, it's a good idea to use their contract as it should be more in your favor.

On a contract where you are buying, list your name as the buyer, followed by "and/or assigns." This will give you the right to assign a different buyer if you decide to wholesale the property. It's in your interest to give as little earnest money as possible. This way, it is not tied up. You will want to make the sale subject to acquiring a loan. This will give you the option to back out if you don't find suitable financing.

Always make the sale contingent upon a clean title search and inspection. Keep in mind that you can certainly renegotiate if new things come up during this process. When there are major repair issues, you can either have the seller take care of them before the sale. Otherwise, you can ask for a discount on the price or walk away from the deal. It is better to walk away from a bad deal instead of getting stuck in it.

There will be closing costs involved. These include title insurance, appraisals, loan fees, and realtor commission, etc. Get to know your local laws and customs as to which closing costs the seller and buyer pay, respectively. If the seller had a loan on the property, the loan will either need to be paid off during the sale. Otherwise, the seller could take over the loan, or the seller could take the seller's equity subject to the loan/liens. "Subject to" means that the loan is still in the seller's name after the sale, but you are paying for it. You can get good deals with subject to loans if the seller is trying to prevent a foreclosure from going on their record.

Making Offers

After you have done your math, find out what the seller wants and/or needs. Talk with all of the decision-makers together and ask why they are selling. You need all of the decision-makers there. This way, you can get the sales contract signed. Think of yourself as a problem-solver. Your goal is to discover the seller's problems and show how you can solve them. This could mean offering a quick losing or money to help them relocate. If they have other obligations like credit card bills or medical bills, you should have them list those out. You can offer to take care of the payments of those things in exchange for a smaller sales price.

If you are going to do anything with real estate, then you will need to unleash your inner negotiator. The better you become at negotiating through practice, the better money you will make. Be fair in your negotiations and create win-win agreements so that both parties benefit. At the same time, this will ensure that the other party doesn't try to back out of the deal. Ask the seller to be fair with you as you are with them. When you negotiate fairly, you build a good reputation that will bring you deals in the future as well.

Ask the seller the price they want for the house before you offer anything. You can guesstimate based on the valuation of the house at the time. If it's a good price, buy it. If it's too high, it's time to negotiate. Your first offer should be at a low enough price so that you know you will make good profits. It may take some back and forth. Remain silent after you make an offer. That usually leads to the other person making a good concession.

Start the negotiations covering the things that don't matter to you, knowing it is okay to lose on those items. Point to those concessions once you get to the items that are important to you. You can find more info about the negotiation from John's "Negotiation Secrets of a Professional Buyer" course at www.JohnSchaub.com.

If the seller has time to find other interested buyers, the price might increase. You need to ask them if they are ready to sell their house right away or within a couple of hours. They need to know that your offer is only good for that day. Have a contract ready to be signed as soon as they agree to the sale terms. (I have a friend who keeps fillable contracts in his car. This way, he can take them out as and when needed.)

To get your offer accepted, it's best to keep it simple. This way, the seller understands it. You could make an offer where you pay all the closing costs. In that case, you can tell the seller how much they will profit, and they will like that. If you offer to buy the house "as is," then the seller won't have to do any work. They would likely be willing to sell the house for a lot cheaper. Always get an inspection so you can renegotiate a lower price if needed. It's a good idea to walk through the house on the day of the closing to ensure it is ready for you.

Using Real Estate Agents

You can find some great deals through real estate agents. John recommends that you should inform an agent if they bring you a deal that follows your criteria, you will make an offer on it. Make sure to describe to them in complete detail what it is that you want in a house.

If you don't already have an agent and you see a listing for a house you want, it is best to call the listing agent directly. If they represent both you and the buyer, they get a bigger commission. Therefore, they will try very hard to make it work out for you to buy the house.

If you use an open listing when selling a house, your agent only gets a commission if they sell it instead of you or another agent selling it. You can also use an exclusive right of sale. In that case, your agent gets a commission regardless of who sells it within a certain timeframe. Preferably, this timeframe is no more than 90 days. Using the exclusive listing is better when selling. This way, there will be more agents showing the house to more potential buyers. Treat agents fairly as they will help you buy and sell more houses.

Buying and Selling

Flipping houses isn't as easy as it sounds. It takes a lot of work and skill to make short-term profits. Your profits are determined by how many houses you flip as well as how quickly you flip them. When you stop working, so does your income. The best thing to do is to buy and hold a house in a good location. That will bring you easier long-term profits from the cash flow.

Follow these five steps to make good money with buying and selling homes:

1. Determine the price range of homes that sell quickly in your target area.
2. Find out which neighborhoods have a good supply of those homes available for sale.
3. Research the properties that you think might be considered as good deals.
4. Decide your minimum profit that you are willing to accept after repairs, such as 10% of the purchase price.
5. Keep a journal to track the details of each house you buy. This way, you can improve what you do each time.

Knowing the right time to sell can be tricky. However, it helps to pay attention to the state of the local market. You need to pay attention to the following. Are houses selling quickly and for high prices? Is your house getting good rental income and keeping great tenants? Is the property easy to manage because it's close to you and in good shape? Decide when to sell based upon the factors that are most important to you.

When you sell a house for profit, you normally own the government a capital gains tax on your profits. You could use a 1031 exchange to use the profits to buy a new property. In that case, you can defer that tax potentially indefinitely. Another good tip is that if a buyer wants to buy your house while they sell their smaller house, you can potentially accept that smaller house as a down payment for them to purchase your house. That way, you can make money on both transactions similarly to a car dealership when you trade-in your car.

Lease Options

When you are buying a house, you can get a better deal when the seller needs to sell quickly. When you are selling, you can maximize your profits by using a short-term lease/option. This is where the buyer pays an option fee and monthly rent. At the same time, they work on getting financing together for the purchase. The option fee and portion of the rent go toward the purchase if it goes through. Around half of John's lease/option buyers go through with the purchase.

The three variables you work with for-profit include the option fee, rent price, and sales price. Typically, the higher the sales price you ask, the lower the option fee and rent need to be. You may have to adjust these based on which factor is most important to you. If the buyer backs out, you keep the option fee. However, it's a nice thing to refund part of that if the tenant took good care of the home.

The purchase price is determined at the beginning of the lease. If the house appreciates during the lease, the buyer will get that benefit. This is because you already agreed on a lower price. Limit the lease term to one year, so you don't give too much away in case the house increases in value. You can always offer a one-year extension at a higher price if needed. In the meantime, you'll still be collecting rent.

Buying (Pre) Foreclosures

You can find great deals by helping people avoid foreclosure. You can do this by buying their homes at a discount. However, you will need to know the complicated laws involved to make it work. When starting out, use a good attorney to help you through that process.

Homeowners and mortgage lenders tend to not like foreclosures. It destroys the homeowner's credit, it's traumatic for them, and it forces them to move out and find a new residence. Mortgage lenders also dislike foreclosures because they don't want to be a property manager, and they might lose money on the sale. When you create win-win situations with foreclosures, you set yourself up to get referrals for other good deals.

There are a few ways for you to find homeowners facing foreclosure who need your help. Look at public records to see who has a second mortgage with a high-risk lender. (You can sometimes buy a second mortgage from the lender for pennies on the dollar or even get that lender to refinance the house with great terms.) Offer a finder's fee to lenders who bring you deals. You can get people looking to sell to call you by using postcards, bandit signs, or other advertising. Hire someone to "bird dog" for you and find you deals that match your criteria. You could also drive/walk around neighborhoods you like to find distressed properties that could be good deals. (This is called "driving for dollars.")

When talking with owners who are facing foreclosure, explain the consequences they will face when the foreclosure happens. Listen to learn their motivation and willingness to work with you. Also, show them how you can solve their problems. Be very cautious about renting the house back to the sellers. This is because they might still be in a tight spot financially. Create a solid plan with them for rent payments if you decide to go that route. If the local laws permit it, you can ask them to provide a large security deposit. This will ensure they leave the house in good condition when the rental period ends. It can actually be good for you because it means you won't have a vacancy or turnover expense.

Buying a house at the foreclosure auction is risky, but could also be lucrative. The owners might still be in the house, and they might not leave it in good condition. (Or there might be some surprise liens on the house.) If the bank wins the house at auction, it becomes real estate owned (REO). John loves buying REO house in good condition at a great discount. This is because they can be immediately rented.

Attracting and Keeping Good Tenants

There are a few traits found in the best tenants. They pay on time, take care of the property, stay there forever, and never call you except when necessary. They are looking for houses in a safe neighborhood, are clean and maintained, have enough space/bedrooms/yard, have privacy, have fair rent prices, and are not being sold. Your focus should be on owning rental houses that match these criteria.

Get to know the fair housing laws as well your local single-family landlord laws, and then follow those laws. Learn what you and your tenants are each responsible for in a lease. When there are problems, solve them quickly to prevent legal issues. Set the security deposit higher than a month of rent if your local laws allow it. When it's harder to find good tenants, decrease the rent. However, make sure your standards aren't compromised.

Before renting a house, it is very important to make sure it is clean and in good condition for the new tenants. Meet the neighbors and give them your contact info. This way, they can call you if they notice any issues. Determine how much an average tenant will need to make to cover rent plus their other bills, such as utilities, groceries, etc. Tenants usually can't spend more than 30-40% of their income on rent. Set your rent to be a little below market rate to attract good tenants, but then raise it a little each year when appropriate and feasible.

Advertise a rental opening on the internet, with a sign out front, and/or by letting the neighbors know so they can refer a friend. Your ads should include the rent rate, security deposit, location, size of the house, and include good professionally made pictures. Be ready to answer your email and phone. If the house is vacant, you can ask potential applicants to drive by it and look in the windows before you schedule a tour. One good way to save time with tours is to hold an open house.

If someone wants to rent the house, have them complete an application. You can also have them pay either an application fee or a small refundable deposit. Check out their car too. This is because their car's condition inside and out is a good way for you to judge as to how they will treat your house. Call their references. Verify their income. (And always do a background check to see if they have any criminal history, major financial problems, and/or prior evictions.)

Do not give your new tenant the house keys until they have paid the deposit as well as the first month of rent. Complete a move-in inspection to take note of any pre-existing issues. This way, you can compare the initial state of the house to when they move out.

If you self-manage your properties, maintain good boundaries with your tenants. This way, they don't expect you to work every night and weekend for non-emergencies. Tenants will sometimes think something is an emergency when it is not such as a slow drain. Be fair but firm while you train them to follow the rules and policies. This is because they may push the boundaries at times.

If tenants are not paying rent on time, you should then immediately issue a pay or quit notice. That is the start of the eviction process. They will usually pay you then. If not, discuss with them to figure out a payment plan. If that doesn't work, offer to pay them part of their security deposit back to move out immediately. This usually works better than an eviction (and is called "cash for keys").

Becoming Debt-Free

Owning a house free and clear means that you're not using the power of leveraging other people's money to maximize your profits. However, if you want to pay off your mortgage sooner, use your rental income to pay down the principal balance. You could also either refinance or sell some of your houses to pay off other houses. It doesn't hurt to ask your lender for a discount when you are going to pay off a loan sooner than you had planned. They may be willing to accept a lower amount to get their money back now instead of waiting.

Conclusion

John's book lays out ways to become financially free by investing in single-family homes. The key to making this happen is to take action. Once you have your first house that cash flows, you will have the confidence necessary to keep going. Because real estate goes up in value over time, you will eventually make money even if you have to wait things out through a recession. Buy houses that have good value for bargain prices, and then hold onto them. Sell off any houses that don't make you money. By using the insight in this book, you can create greater wealth than the vast majority of your friends and neighbors.

Additional Reading

Easier Than You Think: An Expert's Guide to Single-Family Real Estate Investing by Mike Hanna

First-Time Landlord: Your Guide to Renting out a Single-Family Home by Janet Portman, Ilona Bray, and Marcia Stewart

Chapter 5: Small Multifamily

Investing in Duplexes, Triplexes & Quads by Larry Loftis, Esq

Introduction

Investing in small multifamily rentals with two to four units can be a sweet spot for many investors. They provide the benefits of having multiple units without being too big to handle. Plus, they can be purchased with residential financing as opposed to commercial financing. These sized properties can be either great long-term investments or a good jumping-off point to get into larger multifamily properties. In his book, Larry provides detailed advice on how you can be successful in investing in duplexes, triplexes, and quads.

Investing in Real Estate

Real estate is the best way to build wealth. Regardless of the market, you can make money in real estate. Appreciation comes quickly when prices are increasing. When the market is down, you can get some great deals on properties. Larry sees two- to four-unit properties as the fastest and safest way to invest your money into real estate.

You can make money a few different ways in real estate. Cash flow is the money that you keep each month from rents that exceed the expenses. Your property can appreciate over time due to inflation and increased demand. You can also force appreciation by doing something to increase income/rent or decrease expenses (which is called "value-add").

The tax benefits of owning real estate are amazing. They can make it look like on paper that you are losing money despite making boatloads. As you pay off your mortgage over time, you build up equity in your property. Being able to invest with other people's money allows you to leverage your own money to buy even more real estate.

The gross rent multiplier (GRM) is the price of a property divided by the annual rents. If a property costs $100K and brings in $10K annually, then $100,000 \div 10,000 = 10$ GRM. A GRM between 7.5 and 16 is good, depending upon the market. However, buying at a higher GRM can work if the area is appreciating quickly, or if you find a way to increase rents and/or decrease expenses.

Residential Multifamily

Residential real estate is any property with one to four units. Residential multifamily has two to four units. Commercial residential real estate has five or more units. When deciding in which type of real estate you want to invest, ask yourself if you are comfortable with it and how profitable, safe, simple, and time consuming it is. There are MANY options from which to choose in real estate.

Investing in single-family homes (SFH) is easier to get into as compared to some other types of real estate. If you have an SFH that is vacant, it has 100% vacancy. The cost and time needed for managing and maintaining four houses are more than that of a single quad with four units due to economies of scale. Since there is more competition for buying SFH than multifamily, SFHs will get less bang for your investment buck.

Flipping can be a good way to make short-term profits. You need lots of cash to do flips and a willingness to handle the fierce competition. To maximize your profits, you have to do flips as quickly as possible. Otherwise, you are paying for the mortgage out of pocket. You need some skill to be successful in flipping (because it's harder than the TV shows make it appear). Flipping also prevents you from using all the tax breaks that buying and holding allows.

Foreclosures can have small margins. This is because there is heavier competition now than there used to be. They tend to need more work than non-foreclosures. You also need to be able to buy a foreclosure in all cash. Pre-foreclosures, on the other hand, are when you help a homeowner avoid foreclosure by taking their equity away from them.

Vacation properties can be great because you can use them yourself when they aren't rented. However, they might give you a negative cash flow during the off-season, surprise you with unexpected expenses, and can make it hard to force appreciation if it's a condo.

Properties with two to four units are easy to finance with good loan terms. This is because they are considered residential and can be bought with a lower down payment than commercial properties.

(I bought my first triplex with only 3.5% down!) This means you can buy more real estate and have a better return on investment (ROI). Small multifamily properties have a similar price tag to SFHs but provide more income. If you have a vacant unit, the other occupied unit(s) can help cover your expenses. An SFH is all or nothing with vacancy. It's easier to rehab multifamily because you can do so on one unit at a time. Also, multifamily is more cost-effective to manage per unit that SFHs.

Creating Wealth

Leverage is the most powerful tool in real estate. The less of your own money you put into a property, the higher the return is on the money you have in the deal. (If you own part of a property where you only use the bank's or other people's money, then your return is infinite.) Real estate appreciates an average of around 7% annually, which is the icing on the cake.

Depreciation is where the IRS says that parts of a property lose value over time due to use. This includes things such as the roof, appliances, carpet, etc. With a residential multifamily property, the worth of something is divided by 27.5 years, and that amount is a tax write-off annually for that time. (Different things can depreciate faster, resulting in larger tax write-offs.)

The "Rule of 72" is a formula to show how long it will take to double your money. To calculate it, you first take 72 and divide it by the rate of the ROI, which gives you the number of years. If your ROI is 10, then $72 \div 10 = 7.2$ years. That is the number of years it will take to double your money. (When you combine the cash flow, appreciation, depreciation, and tax benefits, then real estate becomes a vehicle that multiplies your money at warp speed!)

If you have $200K, you could buy a $200K property in cash. However, if you buy properties with a 10% down payment, then you could instead buy ten $200K properties. As long as the income still exceeds the expenses, you will be set up for success with all of the properties cash flowing and appreciating simultaneously. (Even if a recession happens that drops real estate prices, you will gain that back over time. That is, as long as you can hold onto your properties for long enough. Buy properties that will cash flow even during a recession.) It's hard to time the market to know when it is the best time to buy or sell.

Rehabbing a property can provide you with a large increase in equity. You can do a cash-out refinance to take out your equity tax-free. By investing that into more real estate, you are really leveraging your money.

Wealth cannot be created from earning income at a job or saving in a retirement account. It takes investing to do it. This is how rich people do it. That's how you need to do it too. Real estate investing has created more millionaires than any other means.

Investment Strategies

There are three main investment options: buy and hold, pyramiding, and refinancing to buy more. For example, you can buy and hold onto a property long term. In that case, you will avoid transaction costs and capital gains tax from a sale. Furthermore, you can pay off the mortgage to own the property outright. However, this approach takes a lot of time. It can also be a financial hardship if it takes too much time to see the real profits, or if your ROI is smaller as compared to short term flips. You may also realize that you might not be using leveraging your money for maximum profits.

Pyramiding is when you sell a property and reinvest the profits into a bigger and better property. This creates better leverage for your money. It also gives you a value-add opportunity with the new property. You might have some time in between properties where your money is just sitting there. You might have a tax liability unless you do a 1031 exchange. There are also transaction costs to consider in this scenario.

You can combine these two methods as well. That can be done by refinancing a property you own, keeping it, and using the money you pulled out (tax-free) to purchase more real estate. This allows you to benefit from the appreciation, tax benefits, and cash flow of multiple properties while at the same time avoiding the capital gains tax. Banks don't usually allow you to refinance more than 80% of a property's value, thus leaving some equity untapped. You might be able to get a second mortgage to use some additional equity.

Using Real Estate Brokers

Using a broker or is the most common way multifamily properties are sold. This is beneficial because they may have insight into the local market at the same time giving your property a lot of exposure on the multiple listing service (MLS). You could use a real estate agent who works under a broker. Agents will vary in their market knowledge and sales skills, so be picky in who you decide to hire. Referrals are the best way to find a good broker or an agent who specializes in multifamily.

The commissions for brokers are usually between 5-7%. If the buyer and seller have different brokers, then the commission is split between them. If your market has buyer-brokers, then they either work at a flat rate, or they will split their part of the commission with you. Larry recommends using a commission broker because they are incentivized to get you a higher sales price. He especially likes companies such as RE/MAX, Coldwell Banker, and Keller Williams.

How to Find a Property

Look for properties with the following criteria: contain multiple units, located in good areas, and are fully occupied, have a value-add opportunity, have decent taxes, and will have positive cash flow. The MLS is a national network that shows you tons of potential deals. You can search for it for free at www.Realtor.com. Just select the search option for multifamily. You won't find all the info you need here, so tell your broker the MLS number of a property you like. This way, they can bring up the full listing.

You can drive around the area where you want to invest (which is called "driving for dollars" which is the same sort of idea as "dialing for dollars" where you call homeowners). Look for properties that are for sale by owner (or vacant or for rent) and then give those addresses to your broker. You can also look through the local newspaper, commercial websites such as www.Loopnet.com, and property magazines. Look for ads where the seller might be motivated to sell fast.

How to Determine the Value of a Property

Looking at a multifamily property's income is the best way to valuate it but does not provide a perfect picture. Looking at comparable sales (comps) shows you what prices similar local properties have sold for within the past six months. The final option is to valuate a property based upon what it would cost to replace it if it burned down. (That is called a replacement cost.) Construction costs can vary widely.

The GRM is the way investors tend to valuate properties. A GRM of 8-11 is a good range. 20+ is a hot area and is a seller's market. Below 6 or 7 is a bad neighborhood to avoid at night. You can have a better cash flow in a bad neighborhood, but that also comes with higher risks. GRMs vary widely depending upon the area and market conditions.

Each valuation method is only one metric and doesn't give the whole picture. Other metrics to consider may include the price per square foot, the capitalization (cap) rate, which is the net operating income divided by the purchase price, and the margin of safety, which is 100 minus the operating and debt service divided by the gross potential income.

Doing Due Diligence

Once you find a property that looks good on the surface, it's time to really analyze it. Ask for the annual property operating data (APOD) statement to see the income and expenses. This would be more useful than the pro forma, which shows the property's numbers with rosy colored glasses if everything went perfectly.

Trust the APOD, but also verify the numbers. Look at the leases, the taxes form the county assessor, estimate what your taxes will be at the new purchase price, and then see if the units have separate utility meters. If there is only one meter, it will make a difference whether the residents are paying for utilities or if you will be.

Calculate your debt service coverage ratio (DSCR) by dividing the net operating income (NOI) by the mortgage payment. Lenders have different requirements with DSCR, but they are usually around 1.25. This means that if your mortgage payments will be $1000, then you need an NOI of at least $1250 for the lender to feel comfortable with the deal. (If your DSCR is too low, you can increase it by making a bigger down payment.)

After you have a property under a purchase contract, ALWAYS hire a professional property inspector. They will provide you a list of the things that need to be repaired. They will also inform you of how urgent each repair will be. (This could potentially allow you to negotiate for a lower price or reasonable concessions.) Follow them around during the inspection if they allow it.

How to Make an Offer

A contract is needed to make your offers legally binding. There are real estate gurus who will offer you a generic real estate contract. However, they will then try to upsell you to their program for a state-specific contract. Larry, who is a lawyer, strongly advises you to do instead what most investors do. He advises using the standard contract that is from the state bar or the local board of Realtors for free. Use an attorney for complicated or commercial deals.

In your purchase contracts, Larry advises against adding clauses "and/or assigns" or "subject to inspection and partner approval." The first allows you to sell the contract to another investor in case you decide to pass on it. (Essentially, this is what's called wholesaling.) The second gives you an out if you need to back out. Both clauses can be damaging to the agreement.

Gurus, who tell you that sellers will usually give you 100% seller financing, probably haven't ever invested in real estate themselves. However, you might be able to get some seller financing sometimes. You will also need to put at least 0.5-1% down right away as a good faith escrow deposit. This is to show that you are serious about the purchase.

In your contract, you should make it specific that you will get all of the personal property. That includes things like the appliances. Give the seller an offer period of two days and a closing date 30-35 days from that time. Keep in mind that everything is up for negotiation. The more motivated the seller is to sell the property, the better deal you can get. Don't be afraid to walk away if the numbers don't add up for you to make the deal work.

Closing a Deal

Your first closing can be scary because of all the documents and not knowing what to expect. The closing usually involves the buyer, the seller, a title company or closing lawyer, and any brokers involved. The people on your team will ensure that things go smoothly.

There are five categories of closing costs, which can sometimes be negotiable. Lender fees run around $1450+ and include an appraisal fee, underwriting fee, tax service, and an origination fee. The title charges for the title policy cost around $850. Government and recording fees are non-negotiable. Those will cost around $1500 for a $250K property. Additional settlement charges cover the survey and cost around $270. Prepaid expenses are put into escrow to cover three months of taxes and one year of insurance. (Prices are in 2006 dollars.) Also, there are broker commissions to be paid of 5-7%.

If you can time the closing to occur on the second or third of the month, then you will get a large check of the prorated rents for that very month. You won't have a mortgage payment until the following month, which means that the first month is very lucrative for you.

Property Management

When a tenant leaves, it's a good time to rehab their unit or at least paint and clean it. You can make other improvements to allow you to increase the rent. You will, at the same time, be able to attract great tenants who pay on time and keep things in good order. You should be very selective with potential tenants. This will give you fewer headaches in the future. Screen potential tenants by talking with them and trusting your gut instinct. Have them fill out an application, provide job and income verification, and pay a deposit that is at least worth one month of rent.

Make sure to follow your local laws regarding disclosures, deposits, leases, etc. Decide whether you want to charge for things like pet fees, utilities, or late fees (depending upon what your local laws permit). To get more information about property management, read a good book on it (such as my chapter about it).

Legally Avoiding Taxes

A good way to get started with investing is to buy a property with two to four units, live in one unit, and then rent out the others. (This is called "house hacking.") This allows you to homestead the property and pay less in tax. Plus, you can keep a close eye on the property and tenants a lot easier since you are also living there. If you live in the property that has four units or less for two of the past five years, then you can avoid the capital gains tax completely on the first $250K in profits if you are single and $500K if you are married.

If you sell a property after owning it for less than a year, you will have to pay a capital gains tax on profits you earn. This will be taxed at your normal income tax rate. Holding onto the property for over a year reduces that down to 15% on your profits. (It is often better to hold on to it for at least a year and then sell it if possible.)

If you hold onto the property for at least a year, then you can do a 1031 exchange to defer the 15% capital gains tax. 1031 exchanges do have very specific rules to follow. You have to keep all of the net sales proceeds with a 1031 exchange agent, identify up to three "like-kind" properties you are considering buying within 45 days of the sale, close on one of them within 180 days of the sale, and apply all of your escrow money to the sale. If you don't follow all of these rules, you would just have to pay the capital gains tax as a consequence.

Next Steps

Take action. Buy a property that has two to four units with 0-10% down, live in one unit to live rent-free, and rehab the property to increase rents. Then, you can refinance after one year or sell after two years to access your equity tax-free, and repeat this process. If you don't want to live in the property, then buy one or more quads in a high-appreciation area with a 10% down payment. Rehab them to increase rents, sell or refinance them after at least a year, and then use 1031 exchanges to buy better quads or properties with even more units.

If you are broke, use a buyer-broker who is willing to split their commission with you. Also, you can use a mortgage broker who can give you a great rate to fit your credit score. Buy a triplex or quad, close on the second or third of the month, to get some cash back at closing. Put a 0-5% down payment, use an interest-only or adjustable-rate mortgage to have lower payments if needed. Then, close later in the year to pay fewer taxes for that year. Live in one unit rent-free, rehab when you can to raise the rents, and then refinance after a year to be able to keep buying real estate.

Continue to educate yourself by reading books, joining real estate clubs, and attending seminars. (I also recommend networking with other investors and hiring a mentor.) It's up to you to take control of your financial freedom!

Conclusion

Even though this book was written during the boom leading up to the 2007-2008 recession, the lessons are still valid regardless of the state of the economy. This chapter is near and dear to my heart since my first property was a live-in triplex that I had rehabbed after paying a 3.5% down payment. From my first-hand experience, I can say with confidence that Larry knows what he is doing regarding small multifamily properties.

Additional Reading

The Complete Guide to Investing in Duplexes, Triplexes, Fourplexes, and Mobile Homes: What Smart Investors Need to Know Explained Simply by Edith Mazier

How to Make Big Money in Small Apartments by Lance Edwards

Chapter 6: Wholesaling

If You Can't Wholesale After This: I've Got Nothing for You by

Todd Fleming

Introduction

Whether you plan on getting into wholesaling or not, this book teaches you how to find off-market deals at great prices. This is valuable knowledge to have, regardless of the kind of real estate you want to buy. Todd shows you how to wholesale even if you have no money and/or bad credit.

Todd started a real estate company to teach people how to become financially free. You can find out about it at www.TheKingdomRealEstate.com.

He learned from his parents to take action now instead of waiting. If you don't take action now, you will be plagued with the dilemma of "what if" you had. If you feel stuck in your J.O.B. (just over broke) in the rat-race trap, then it may be time for you to do things a lot differently.

The Right Mindset for Wholesaling

Todd had this very epiphany one day while working in his cubicle at work. He then decided to take responsibility for his future. He eventually quit his job to live off his savings while figuring out his next steps. He was not a reader but began reading three to four books per week. These include books such as *Rich Dad Poor Dad*,

Think and Grow Rich, and *Third Circle Theory*. He learned the secret to becoming wealthy begins with having the right mindset for it.

After failing at investing in the stock market, he switched to the real estate business as a realtor. After failing as a realtor, he met a real estate investor who said he could invest without a license or even any money. The investor explained to him that through his online training program that this could be done through wholesaling. Todd was desperate to make it work for him immediately because he only had $11 to his name by this point. Within a few weeks, he was able to complete his first deal.

It takes more than just knowledge to find success in wholesaling. You must also think big, take massive action, and do not quit or get stuck when you find yourself in analysis paralysis. Plus, you can't do all of this by yourself. Your network is your net worth. The people around you impact your success or failure. It is important to surround yourself with people with the same success mindset as yourself. You need to avoid the negativity that is rampant in the news and on social media. Be self-aware of your emotions and how you are presenting yourself to others.

Commit to having a mindset of abundance. By helping others and finding solutions, you will find opportunities all around you. However, if you have a mindset of scarcity, you will only find problems and other limitations. The law of attraction states that whether you are thinking positively or negatively, you will attract more of that to your life. Therefore, it's best to think positive.

Wholesaling

Essentially, wholesaling is a perfectly legal method where you get a discounted property under a sales contract and then sell the property to another investor for a profit. For example, if a seller agrees to sell their house for $100K and you find a buyer willing to pay $130K. Thus, you get to keep the $30K difference as profit. Regardless of where real estate is in the market cycle, you can still make money by wholesaling. Better yet, you can also do it without using any of your own money.

You can complete a wholesaling transaction through a contract assignment or a double closing. Assigning the contract is when you simply reassign the original sales contract with the seller to a different buyer for a fee. Everyone then knows who paid which prices and also how much you made in between.

A double closing is a little more complex. This is when the property is sold from the seller to you, and then again from you to the buyer for a higher price. Both sales happen simultaneously and use the buyer's money. Each transaction involves separate closing costs, but the amount you profit is kept private. Double closings are sometimes called an A-B-C transaction in that A is the seller, B is you, and then C is the buyer.

Title Companies

State laws will determine whether you have to close a deal with a title company or with an attorney. Both parties do the paperwork, oversee the closing, transfer the money, and do the title search. They will help protect you, the seller, and the buyer in the transaction. You should only give money to the title company or closing attorney and never directly to the seller or buyer.

To do an assignment of contract or double closing, you need a title company or attorney who is skilled with them. Not all of them are familiar with wholesale deals. This is why it is important to get references from other investors for a good title company or attorney. You can also do a Google search or look in the yellow pages, and then call around to find someone who is a good fit for you.

When you call a potential title company or attorney, make sure you talk with the person who makes the decisions. Most won't know what double closings or assignment of contracts are, or they may even mistakenly think that they are illegal. Keep calling around until you find one with the proper experience and understanding to assist you. Always ask to see their "For Sale by Owner" package to see the wording of their purchase agreement.

Finding Buyers

The next step is to line up some buyers since they have the money for your deals to happen. Have a list of buyers handy in advance so that you can move quickly once you find a deal. Ask what criteria they are looking for in a property, and then base your search upon the kinds of properties they are willing to buy. It's always wise to have at least a couple of solid buyers lined up before you start searching for properties. Your buyers do not have to be cash buyers if they have access to other forms of financing. This could be through a bank or with seller financing if the seller is willing/able.

It's easier than you think to find buyers. Search on websites such as www.Meetup.com and www.EventBrite.com to find free or cheap real estate groups. You can also attend your local Real Estate Investors Association (REIA). You can find ads online of buyers looking for wholesalers on www.Craigslist.com or Facebook. Search Instagram to find the accounts of potential buyers by searching for the hashtag #Flipping. You can also ask for references through property managers, title groups, realtors, and insurance agents. If you have advertising money, put flyers and business cards around everywhere. You can also put "bandit signs" on telephone poles and in grassy areas, or direct mailing to tax mailing addresses of buyers listed in the public record who have paid in cash.

Once you find a potential buyer, you should be honest and ethical with them. Aim to build positive working relationships. Furthermore, ask them about their goals and investment strategy. Also, consider where they want to buy, and the price range they are willing to pay, and how they pay for properties, what their perfect deal would look like. You should know whether they are flipping and/or holding properties, how many properties, and what kinds of deals they have done if they are okay with you wholesaling deals to them. Finally, you should know how they want you to contact them.

Finding Sellers

Your next step is to find homeowners with problems that you can help solve. You're not looking to offer your buyers the average house for sale. You are looking for sellers with different problems. These include pre-foreclosure, divorce, probate, bankruptcy, problematic tenants, tax liens, recession, job loss, moving, living out-of-state, losing money each month with the property, deferred maintenance, health code violations, and downsizing. If you find a seller who is more interested in selling quickly, getting great terms, doing it without a realtor, and not so interested in getting top dollar for their property, then you can help them.

To find motivated sellers, you need to put your name out there and then go through the numbers. Just like when you were looking for buyers, you can find sellers with little or no money if you don't have much of an advertising budget. Look through the "for sale" section of Craigslist. Post your ads on different sections in Craigslist ten times per day with the various zip codes for where you are looking. You can also put up free ads for free on Facebook's local buy/sell/trade groups, just only about once each month; otherwise, you could get blocked. Ask permission from each Facebook group's admin before posting your ads there.

Your ads should include three pain points, the solution to the pain, and your contact info. The pain points could include things such as "Need cash now?" or "Want to sell fast?" The solution could be "Quick cash and quick closing." There is a copy of one of Todd's ads on page 46 of his book for reference.

Besides finding buyers at local Meetups and REIAs, you can also find other wholesalers who are willing to split their profits with you if you help them in finding a buyer. Look through the public records at the county courthouse to find homeowners who are experiencing foreclosure, unpaid taxes, property liens, and code violations.

Driving for dollars is defined as the method of driving, walking, or riding a bike around to find houses that look vacant or run down. The names and the tax mailing addresses of the owners can be located in the public record or possibly from a neighbor.

If you have an advertising budget, you can put flyers, stickers, and business cards at various kinds of local businesses. "We buy houses" bandit signs usually work, but are technically illegal in many places. If you are worried that city workers will take down your bandit signs, you can put them up on telephone poles and in grassy areas on a Friday afternoon and then pick them up again on Sunday evening before the city workers remove them on Monday morning.

Sending letters through direct mail is an effective method of finding sellers, but it can also be spendy. Todd's advice for the most responses from direct mail is to use red ink on yellow notebook paper and business envelopes without a return address. Use www.ListSource.com to create your focused mailing list.

Once you find a potential seller, it works best to knock on their door so you can show them personally how you can help them with a solution to their problem. Whether you talk to them face-to-face or over the phone, start by building rapport with them by asking questions and listening. Find out what challenges they have faced with their property, what their goal is, and why they want to sell it. Schedule a time for you to see the property. Take pictures and think about your safety during this inspection.

Maintain clear and honest communication with the seller. Give them a good expectation of how quickly you can close the deal with their help. Tell them either you will keep the property yourself as a rental, fix and resell the property yourself, or sell it to one of your partners if the property is a better fit for them. Explain to the seller that they will still get their agreed-upon price, and more importantly, nothing will change for them regardless of the outcome on your end.

Setting up the Deal

Once you have a willing seller, call one of your buyers to describe the deal. Then, see how much they are willing to pay for it to be a good deal for them. You may need to negotiate down the seller's price to ensure that there is enough space for your profit as well. It's okay if the buyer needs to see the property before making an offer, just be clear that it's not yet under contract and you are the direct contact with the seller.

When negotiating with the seller on a price, it must be done in-person to maximize your success rate. By focusing on solutions for the seller, they will be more than willing to work with you because they believe that you care. Say something like, "I believe this offer is perfect for helping you with X problem." Tell them that you love the property and that to get it into top condition, you can only offer them a certain amount. Explain your offer amount by referencing the problems with the house and what similar properties in the area have sold for recently.

If the seller agrees to a price lower than your buyer's amount, get a signed sales contract and assignment sheet. (Keep some of these in your car ready to go.) If you can't do a contract assignment, then prepare for a double closing by making a separate contract with your buyer. You can use paperwork from your state, title company, or attorney. To protect yourself when something goes wrong, your contract needs to say that the sale is contingent upon your partner's approval. Make sure the seller understands what's in the contract.

Closing the Deal

Contact your closing title company or attorney to let them know about the sale. Clear communication with them every few days will help prevent you from many headaches. Send them the signed paperwork and everyone's contact info. If you are doing a double closing and don't have the cash to close, you can also send them the info for your transactional funding for the first closing.

Keep your buyer informed on the progress of the closing preparation so that they will also be ready and prepared. As long as you followed all of the previous steps, the closing and paperwork will go very smoothly. You will then walk away with a nice sized check. Reach out to the seller to make sure they were completely satisfied since they might refer other sellers to you in the future. Also, make sure to follow up with your buyer to help prepare things for the next deal.

Additional Info

Think of your first few deals as more of a learning process. Continually analyze your system and negotiation skills to find ways to make things as efficient and profitable as possible for you. One cool thing about wholesaling is that instead of earning a one-time fee from a deal, your buyer could give you a promissory note with monthly payments that include interest. This acts as a lien on the property if the buyer stops paying you.

Investors will be your main source of repeat buyers. While it is profitable to wholesale to investors, you can earn a lot more in a deal by selling the property directly to a retail buyer. Retail buyers are willing to pay top dollar because they plan to live in the property themselves. It might just take a little longer to close with a retail buyer if they are getting financing from a bank for the transaction.

Conclusion

The book centers on the great questions to ask yourself and others while you are wholesaling. Todd emphasizes the importance of being honest and ethical while following the law. There are many scripts in the book you can use to interact with sellers, buyers, and closing agents to close deals successfully.

Wholesaling can feel more like a job than real estate investing. Many people wholesale with the plan to save up to themselves buy properties that provide them with a source of passive income. Wholesaling gives you the skills to find great deals if you have the money or financing to buy them. Don't let fear and excuses keep you from taking action!

Additional Reading

Never Split the Difference: Negotiating as if Your Life Depended on It by Chris Voss, Michael Kramer, et al.

The Art of Wholesaling Properties: How to Buy and Sell Real Estate without Cash or Credit by Aram Shah and Alex Virelles

Chapter 7: Short Sales and Pre-Foreclosures

Short-Sale Pre-Foreclosure Investing: How to Buy "No Equity Properties Directly from the Bank – at Huge Discounts by Dwan Bent-Twyford and Sharon Restrepo

Introduction

When people discover what Dwan and Sharon do, they ask whether they are taking advantage of homeowners who are stuck in bad situations. Rather, the homeowners are experiencing things like job loss, medical issues, and death in the family, etc. Dwan and Sharon can provide these homeowners with solutions to keep a foreclosure from destroying their credit. This book teaches you how you can find properties other investors have missed and create good deals out of them even when there isn't any equity in them.

When this book was published in 2008, many people were experiencing financial hardships from the recession taking place at the time. However, all parts of the economic cycle will have homeowners who are struggling. Through the school of hard knocks, Dwan and Sharon learned how to be successful with short sales and pre-foreclosures. They became nationwide educators about it and are sharing their experiences and insight in their book.

Getting Started

Fear holds a lot of people back, especially in the beginning. Knowledge can help you overcome your inhibitions. Once you have managed your fears, you can then achieve financial freedom and all of its wonderful benefits. Opportunities are around you all of the time. It's up to you to seize them. You don't find deals. You have to create them instead.

An investor shared a story of how she came across a deal that needed to be done as a short sale. What she did was to follow the steps and scripts and made $25K. Another time, they bought a 4-plex in pre-foreclosure for $535K and then sold it through a double closing for $800K. She netted $210K after expenses on that deal using the system taught by Dwan and Sharon. The seller was grateful for being saved from a financial disaster.

Start by discovering and understanding and what it is that motivates you. It's easy to know that you don't want to be stuck in a job, work for a boss you dislike, lack any real money, not have any vacations, and be worried about being able to retire. Your real motivation will come from setting goals of what you do want and then writing them down. 98% of people don't even do that. Your goals should bring balance to your life. It's helpful to break them down into achievable steps and review them daily.

Treat your real estate business as a business and not just as a hobby. Organize your business so that you have the tools, business plan, and team members you need to succeed. Do not listen to the naysayers who try to convince you to go for job security instead of building your wealth. However, it's often advisable to wait to quit your job until your business is ready to support you.

Short Sales

A short sale occurs when you convince a lender to accept less than what is owed on a mortgage and then label it as "paid in full." For example, if a homeowner is facing foreclosure and has a $200K house and owes that amount on the mortgage, and you negotiate with the lender to accept only $100K, then you just bought that house for half off. If that is something you are interested in doing, then read on!

With wholesales, there has to be enough equity already in the deal for it to be workable. With short sales, you create equity through negotiation with the lender. The trick to short sales is to give convincing explanations to lenders as to why they need to reduce the price and to build a reputable business in the meantime. Build and maintain good relationships with the lenders. (They will work with you more if they know, like, and trust you.)

A bank will be willing to accept a short sale because the mortgage payments are behind, the property is in bad shape or has depreciated. This is because they need to prevent more foreclosures on their books, and they can get some money now, at least. Banks do not want to do foreclosures because they are in the business of lending money and not real estate ownership. Plus, too many foreclosures will make it hard for a bank to wholesale any money from larger banks.

When you are making a short sale offer to a bank, it's as if you are a lawyer in court, pleading your case. Building a better case leads to a bigger discount. Focus on the distress of the homeowner and property, as well as on the situation's hardship. You should always know your exit strategy before making an offer. For example, if you plan to sell a $100K property to a rehabber who would buy it for $65K, then you might start the negotiations at $40K. Work backward from the current market value of the property to know the highest price that you can offer. It's better to start by offering too little than too much as you can always increase your offer.

Finding Properties

When the bank foreclosed on a property and becomes the owner, it's called real estate owned (REO). Contact the REO departments of banks to find out who their listing broker is and then contact them. Use your real estate agent and have them search for listings that include words such as "fire damage," "foreclosure," and "bank-owned."

If a bank is offering a $100K property for $85K, then offer them $50K. Include a detailed description with pictures showing why they should accept this lower amount instead. Show them how other similar comparable properties in the area (comps) have sold for low prices and list the problems with the neighborhood. It's recommended to offer cash for the house, a closing date within 30 days, and no inspection period. The bank will still provide you with a 7-10 day inspection period in the contract. Use this time well by inspecting the property and lining up a rehabber to buy it with a second contract.

Running newspaper ads and "I buy houses for cash" signs can be good sources of leads. Ask pawnshop owners if you can pay them an advertising fee to keep one of those signs in their window. Furthermore, network with people through real estate clubs, local businesses, churches, etc. Send postcards to people listing in the public record as going through foreclosure, divorce, bankruptcy, incarceration, and tax liens. It's a good idea to put a magnetic sign on your car. Call bail bondsmen as they often have property deeds that they are willing to exchange for cash. Just be ready and available to answer your phone as and when they call. You can talk to mail carriers and utility workers who see vacant homes every day. You can also advertise on bulletin boards, billboards, and bus stop benches.

Approaching Homeowners

Your goal here is to create win-win situations with homeowners. Start by finding a homeowner who is facing foreclosure and doesn't have any equity in their home. Explain that you can help them walk away from it with a short sale if the bank is willing to negotiate with them. Ask them how much money they need to move and what their move out day is since they need to move out by the closing date. They may only want to save their credit, or perhaps they may need a little money. Banks don't normally allow the seller to receive money in a short sale. However, you can pay the seller for something like appliances or cleaning, so they get some money back.

It's very important not to be judgmental of a homeowner's situation. However, do listen and understand what their motivation is with the property. When they say what they need, you should repeat it back to them, respond with empathy, and then ask questions to steer the conversation into showing them the solutions that you can offer. Creating solutions that meet people's needs (while making yourself money) will turn into free word-of-mouth advertising that can bring you even more leads.

When connecting with homeowners, wear casual yet professional attire. Do not hide your eyes with sunglasses or a hat that has a visor. Use a similar talking speed (and body language) as the homeowner to show them subconsciously that you are very much similar to them.

If a homeowner says they have already taken care of their situation, ask them what they have done. Then, ask if they are using the loopholes of the foreclosure system to be able to stay in their property longer. They will probably want to know more information. By having a conversation with them, you will build rapport that will help convince them to work with you.

The "loopholes" and options you can help with are as follows:

1. Loan modifications to extend the mortgage length
2. Forbearance agreements for a payment plan

3. Deeds in lieu of foreclosure where the homeowner hands over their deed to the bank
4. Taking over the property with a "subject to" where you take over the current mortgage
5. Referring them to a bankruptcy attorney.

Paperwork for Your Offer

Once you have found a property in distress and a homeowner willing to accept your help, it's time to contact their mortgage lender. To speak with the bank about the mortgage, you'll need the homeowner to sign an authorization to release information. Use a separate one for each lien holder. Keep a phone log of the times you contact the bank.

Next, you'll need to get the homeowner to sign a sales contract. You can get one from your local real estate board. You need to just make sure the wording of it is not one-sided against you. To help protect yourself from lawsuits, switch the contract to be under a company name instead of your name before the closing. Ask the bank for their per diem rate they charge for each day past the closing date you have to go.

A two- or three-page detailed hardship letter written by the homeowner is vital to both explain their distress as well as to ask for a discounted payoff. The issues listed by the homeowner must have evidence to back them up. This needs to convince the bank that they can no longer afford the property. If the homeowner writes that they are planning on filing for bankruptcy, then the bank will be especially willing to work out a deal.

Firstly, begin your short sale package for the bank with a cover letter that justifies your low offer. Request that the bank waives the deficiency judgment to protect the homeowner. Make sure to include any helpful comps of other similar properties sold in the area in the past six months. The bank will want to look at your net sheet that shows how much your offer nets them. A more detailed closing or settlement statement will be used at the time of closing. If they want to see a realtor listing agreement, then they will usually pay the realtor's commission. They may ask you for proof of funds or funding to show that you or your end buyer can afford to buy the property.

If the property has any damage or disrepair, send unflattering pictures of that to show how much pain the rehab would be to undertake. Finally, include a detailed list of repair costs that are needed to bring the property up to the market standard. Since banks don't want to rehab, these costs and the pictures will help convince them to give you the property at a discount.

Approaching the Bank

Depending upon the market conditions, a bank's loss mitigation representative could have up to hundreds of foreclosures being processed at any given time. You should only contact them once you have the signed authorization to release information form. You may have to reach out to them multiple times in multiple ways to get noticed by the right person at the bank. It's best to tell them you are a full-time investor (or a realtor if you have a license) who does short sales, you have a package prepared for XYZ address, and that you want to know the bank's price point for it.

Banks normally keep multiple mortgages in portfolios that are later sold and resold to other banks. For you to buy one specific mortgage, it usually has to be in default. The difficulty of the short sale for a mortgage will vary based upon its particular portfolio. While you will primarily interact with the loss mitigation representative, it's their supervisor, the asset manager, who will ultimately make the decisions about your requested short sale. With some persistence, you can get around 60-70% of your offers accepted.

Negotiating Junior Mortgages

When a property has multiple mortgages or liens, you would have to do separate short sale negotiations for each of them. Second mortgages can usually be bought relatively more cheaply than first mortgages. Also, third mortgages are usually even cheaper in comparison. For these junior mortgages, the homeowner should state in their hardship letter that those mortgages will be wiped out in the upcoming foreclosure process.

You should request the bank to tell you what amount they will accept for the short sale before you start negotiating. If you can't get that number from them, then proceed with your initial offer. Dwan and Sharon usually start with $1K for the second mortgage, and

$500 for the third and fourth mortgages, regardless of their value. Second mortgages can generally be bought for 10¢ on the dollar, and sometimes for even less.

Sometimes, you may find that the first mortgage won't be willing to give you a discount. However, if you can get a good enough deal on the junior mortgage(s), then it could still end up being a good deal. Junior mortgages know that they are in a weaker position than the first, and are usually more willing to work with you.

Legal Points

In addition to finding good deals, you also need to have a thorough understanding of the legal process. The laws about foreclosure are different in each state and could potentially change over time. Participate in your local Real Estate Investors Association (REIA) to become knowledgeable about your local laws. You can also find updates at www.TheIEU.com.

Depending on the state, a foreclosure may go through the judicial process or a deed of trust process. In the judicial process, a bank will file a lis pendens in the public record, usually after the mortgage hasn't been paid for around six months. The homeowner and anyone with an interest in the property are notified and, therefore, have a little time to respond. Else, the bank will move for a default lawsuit and the court hearing. A judgment is then made, and a date gets scheduled for a courthouse auction or sheriff's sale. The highest bidder gets the property. The deed of trust process is similar but happens faster because it allows the sale to occur without the need for a lawsuit.

When a property is facing foreclosure, you have to purchase it from the homeowner as they have the title to it. To buy a property directly from the bank, they would have had to initially buy it themselves at the sheriff's sale. Before that point, you are only negotiating with the bank to release the mortgage for less than what is owed on it. You are simultaneously buying the title from the homeowner for free or very cheaply.

If a property has multiple mortgages and at least one forecloses, it then goes to a sheriff's sale. The first mortgage holder usually bids the exact amount that is owed for the first mortgage to then own the property. If no one bids higher than that, then the junior mortgage holders get nothing. A junior mortgage holder would have to bid higher to buy the property and protect its money. However, that comes with a big risk. This is why they are usually willing to negotiate beforehand for a smaller payoff. (You can bid on properties at the sheriff sale and get great deals. However, by this point, the properties are often in poor condition, and you can't negotiate a lower-priced based upon their condition or comps.)

A title company can help you discover whether there are any hidden mortgages/liens on a property. Dwan and Sharon once had an unfortunate surprise three weeks after they bought a house. This happened when the city tore it down due to a lien that was missed by the bank during a title search. Imagine driving up to your new house and find that it's no longer there! Some of the most common types of liens include a court judgment, certified final judgment, tax lien, mechanic's lien, a lis pendens, or a mortgage.

When You Get a Yes

When a bank has agreed to your offer, you must get it in writing ASAP. Dwan and Sharon had had it happen several times when a representative said yes, they quit or got fired before sending a written approval, and then the replacement rep went back on the original representative's offer. The bank's approval will be contingent upon you following their terms of the transaction. These include a closing deadline and not giving sales proceeds to the homeowner. You can often get an extension for a per diem rate if needed.

If you find a willing homeowner and there isn't enough time to do the short sale before the sheriff's sale, you should then ask the bank to postpone or cancel it in lieu of the short sale. Make sure to get this in writing from the bank. Also, make sure the foreclosure attorney gets a copy, so they don't proceed with the foreclosure. If the bank is not willing to delay the sheriff's sale, the homeowner's only option at the time may be to declare bankruptcy to extend the foreclosure timetable and then work out a sale directly with you. Just be careful not to give the homeowner legal advice on what to do so you can be sued for illegally practicing law.

Exit Strategies

Dwan and Sharon usually short sale properties and then wholesale them immediately to rehabbers. That usually occurs either through a double or simultaneous closing. This happens when the rehabber's money buys the property from you, and that same money simultaneously pays off the mortgage and any other liens. Make sure you use a title company and attorney who understand how this works. They also rehab their properties to sell or just rent them out for cash flow. You'll have to decide which exit strategy is right for you.

With wholesaling, you don't actually take ownership of the house. This is because you reassign the sales contract to another investor. You can wholesale with little or no money. You can also do it with or without also doing a short sale. If you do it without a short sale, negotiate a low purchase price directly with the homeowner. Dwan and Sharon usually also pay a $10 down payment to the homeowner. This is to make it legally binding. If you don't already have a list of investors looking to buy, then make one now by running ads (or networking at real estate groups). You should negotiate a higher resale price with your end buyer and then definitely get it in writing. You get to keep the extra money when the deal closes.

If you decide to rehab and flip a property, start the rehab and sales marketing process immediately after the closing. You can make the most profit selling after the rehab is complete. Make sure to have a plan to keep the rehab on budget and also that you get all necessary building permits. Make the rehab look nice, but don't overdo it beyond what is normal for the area. Great ways to add value to your property include painting, cleaning, landscaping, resurfacing cabinets, replacing appliances, upgrading the flooring in the kitchen and bathrooms, and converting rooms to bedrooms or bathrooms.

Renting out properties after the rehabs is a good income stream in between deals. You will, however, need cash reserves to protect yourself in case of vacancies as well as additional repairs. Some landlords accept subsidized housing tenants through the Department of Housing and Urban Development (HUD) just to have guaranteed rental income. Just make sure you screen your tenants well. Dwan and Sharon like to do "subject to" rentals. This way, they take over the mortgage payments of a home, and the homeowner rents from them so they can continue to live there.

Closings

The closing just consists of signing papers, photocopying driver's licenses, and exchanging the money through the closing agent. Since you will likely bring the closing agent lots of work, you should ask them for a discount on their fees.

After you get the sales contract in place and have given the paperwork to the closing agent, they will do the title search and oversee the final tasks leading up to the closing. It's best to coordinate your purchase and subsequent resale to occur at the same time if you are wholesaling. If you planned on closing in 30-45 days, but if things line up sooner, the homeowner is usually willing to get the headache off their hands that much faster.

At the closing agent's office, both the homeowner and rehabber will be in different rooms while you go between them to sign the papers. You should have a backup plan just in case any part of the deal falls apart. It is best to include a clause in the contract with your end buyer that states that you have to first close with the homeowner before reselling the property. This will allow you enough time to find another property if the homeowner backs out of the deal, which is rare. If needed, you can sue the homeowner for nonperformance and force the closing. That can happen if they don't have a good reason for backing out of your agreement. Dwan and Sharon only allow the homeowner to back out if they found a solution that allows them to remain in their home.

The rehabber who is buying the house from you may decide to back out. However, if you require nonrefundable deposits of $3K or more, then that minimizes the risk. The rehabber will then agree to this if they are a serious buyer. Real estate is a relationship business, which makes it essential to network and maintain good relationships with other people to achieve success.

At closings, Dwan and Sharon prefer assignments of contracts instead of double closing. Both offer the same payouts, but the assignment of contract doesn't cut into your profits by making you pay closing costs. However, everyone knows what you make in an assignment of contract, and it's trickier to get banks to do them. Your assignment fees can average between $25-$100K per deal!

Double closings are indeed legal as long as the closing agent did proper disclosure with all of the parties involved. While the double closing costs money, it will hide your higher assignment fee amounts. A double closing also becomes necessary when the property is REO or done with a short sale. You don't require money to do a double closing since both sales transactions occur with the end buyer's money. You can even set it up so that their money covers your closing costs. It's always a good idea to get title insurance to protect you. That helps in case there are surprise issues with the title.

Conclusion

You don't need a college degree to be a real estate investor or even possess any experience. You just need to be willing to put in the work and have enough perseverance. It's important to commit to your real estate business and track your goals daily.

You need to understand other people's points of view and use creativity to find win-win situations for everyone. It may take you years to get where you want to be, so don't even think of quitting. Continue your education and network with other investors. Also, above all, take action!

Throughout the book, Dwan and Sharon include many additional examples of other people's successes. There are also various sample forms and scripts to help make sense of the whole process. The website they give in the book for downloading the forms is unfortunately no longer active. However, you can either transcribe the things from the book or just do an internet search for other sample forms and scripts. The action steps in this book are described in a way that makes them appear well within your reach. Dwan now has a podcast, blog, and other training opportunities that you can find at www.Dwanderful.com.

Additional Reading

The Realtor and Home Owner's Guide to Short Sales: Step by Step by Loren Keim

Buy & Rent Foreclosures: 3 Million Net Worth, 22,000 Net Per Month, In 7 Years... You Can Too! by Joseph Neilson

Chapter 8: Flipping Houses

The Flipping Blueprint: The Complete Plan for Flipping Houses and Creating Your Real Estate Investing Business by Luke Weber

Introduction

The reality of flipping houses is not like how things are shown in the various TV shows about it. It takes a lot of work and expertise to be successful at it. While it might feel like a job at times, it can bring you great financial rewards if you approach it correctly. Luke has already made all of the common mistakes and gives you the best flipping advice in his book. It's well worth your time to read his full book if you desire to become a successful flipper.

Creating Your Story

When Luke was 22, he bought his first property. It was a rundown condo in Las Vegas. He did some work himself and also hired contractors to fix it up. This project took longer than expected, took more work, and then went over budget. However, he was still able to make $80K on the sale. He then repeated the process until the market collapsed during the Great Recession.

In 2010, Luke and his wife began to cautiously invest again. He was devastated by his father's death in 2012. He then realized that he was working too many hours at his day job to spend sufficient time with his family. He was only flipping one house every other month and decided to take his real estate business to the next level.

Luke began attending real estate seminars, including one that cost him $40K to attend. He realized that it was run by a guru who provided inadequate information that he could mostly have found by searching on Google anyway. Luke learned flipping better just by doing it himself and networking with other investors. Your flipping education will be easier and faster by learning from Luke's experience and mistakes.

Like Luke, you will need your own story that communicates who you are and what you want to others. This will help convince others to work with you on your goals. Use the truth, but paint it in its best light. If you've ever bought and sold any properties, you can say that you are an experienced real estate investor who has flipped homes. If you have some money in the stock market, even if it's only a little, you can say that you are transitioning your investment money into real estate. Having your own story makes it easier to communicate with realtors, contractors, and other investors.

Analyzing Markets

A guru might tell you to invest in a specific area, but fail to explain why you should. Luke recommends starting with a close-by market with at least 100K people, preferably at least 1M, since there will be ample opportunities there. Flipping is easier to do locally, but you can also have success with remote investing. Pick one or two markets and focus your efforts there. A large market with few properties for sale is good for flipping. This means when you find a deal and go to flip it, it will sell quickly.

After choosing a market, find a realtor so you can access the local multiple listing service (MLS). You can search for local realtors on www.Zillow.com. The top results are of realtors who have paid the most for advertising. Start by looking at the last results to find the hungry and motivated realtors who will want to work with a new investor. Email them through Zillow so you can quickly contact 10-20 realtors and then ask them to call you if they are interested in working with an investor.

When a realtor calls you back, ask them how many active single-family homes (SFH) are listed on MLS, how many have been sold in the last 30 days, and the average number of days those were on the market (DOM). They will likely need to email you the answers. Of the realtors who email these numbers clearly and simply, compare their numbers against each other.

Once you determine that you have accurate numbers, divide the active SFH listings by the number sold in the last 30 days. This will give tell you how many months of inventory there are. Less than four months is a great market for flipping. Four to six months is stable but will give you challenges. A market with six or more months of inventory is bad for flipping. If the DOM is 60 or fewer days, it is ideal for flipping. 60-90 DOM is a slower market that could prove difficult. A DOM of 91+ is one to avoid at all costs.

Estimating the Numbers and After Repair Value

The after repair value (ARV) is the most important number in flipping. It's how much you can sell a property for after you renovate it. This is because a property's ARV minus the cost of repairs, miscellaneous costs, and how much you want to make equals how much you can offer for the property. If you are off on your ARV estimation, then your profits might be lower, and you could even lose money on the deal. Don't just hope you will make money on a property. You should know that you will.

There are multiple ways to determine the ARV. A decent way is to ask several experienced realtors who can provide ARVs accompanied by explanations of their numbers. By calculating the average price of all the recently sold neighborhood homes or their price per square foot, it will give you a poor estimate. If you think your property will sell for the same as the highest-priced house in the neighborhood, you will probably end up being disappointed, so it's best to have realistic expectations. Zillow's Zestimates are not as accurate as you might hope. It is better to consult a highly trained appraiser who can give you a forecasted opinion of what they think the property might be worth in two to four months. However, an appraiser's info at best will be as accurate as what the realtor would provide, plus appraisals cost money. Furthermore, one of the least accurate methods is to ask the seller what their property is worth.

The best way to determine the ARV is through comparable sales (comps) of similar properties in the area that have recently sold in the past three to six months. Your comps need to be houses that are in a similar condition, size, and design as what yours will be after the repairs. Use at least three comps less than a mile away that are not on the other side of something big such as a highway or river. You should Look at the average DOM of your comps to see how long it will probably take to sell your renovated property.

It's okay to do an estimate of repair costs when you look at a property instead of getting bids from contractors. This will allow you to put in offers a lot quicker than other investors. You can make a quick estimate based upon the square footage of the house and the extent of repair that is needed. Contractors can get you quotes during your due diligence period after you have the house under contract. If you get a range of costs in a quote, plan on having to pay the higher end of it.

A basic remodel is where you will replace things like carpet, appliances, countertops, and paint. It will cost around $14/sf. A standard remodel involves replacing hardwood flooring, showers, cabinets, and maybe a roof will cost around $18/sf. A "vandalized" remodel costs around $26/sf. This is because you have to replace stolen or damaged copper wires, pipes, mechanical systems, etc. A high-end remodel where you add fancy things like stone flooring and crown moldings will cost you around $32/sf.

Pictures of your comps will tell you what standard to aim for in your rehab. Make sure to not make the rookie mistake of over rehabbing your investment properties like the TV shows lead you to do. That will limit your profits and force you to lose deals, as well. This is because your offers will be too low. You should understand the local market to see what is expected in the end product. Essentially, your flips need to be clean, functioning, and move-in ready.

There is no magic formula for a certain percentage of the ARV because every deal is different. Rather, you need to take into account the various expenses. You should estimate 2% of the purchase price for closing, 8% closing costs at the sale, repair costs, cost of the loan if you have one, your desired profit, and six months of taxes, utilities, insurance, and other monthly costs. This will let you know the maximum amount you can offer for the property.

Deal Flow

There are always deals floating around. The trick is to know where and how to look. The bigger your network, the more deals you will get to see. The MLS is your best resource for finding deals, analyzing a market, and calculating the ARV. Other websites like Zillow or Redfin pull their info from the MLS. Your realtor can set up your customizable MLS search criteria that will email all deals automatically to you.

The best search terms include things like distressed, fixer, fixer-upper, handyman, must sell, reduced, damaged, and short sale. Bank-owned properties are also called real estate owned (REO). REOs usually also have one of the above search terms. REOs that have been on the market for at least 44 days are much easier to buy at a nice discount.

You should ask your realtor to narrow down the search by mapping the boundaries of your search area. Have them search for non-distressed houses that have sold there in the past 90 days and then calculate their average price per square foot. Create an automatic search to find the properties within your boundaries that are for sale at 80% or below the average price per square foot. This will give you a shortlist of the people who are motivated to sell their home quickly.

It's a good idea to be connected with multiple realtors. They can send you pocket listings. These are houses they are selling on behalf of a homeowner, but have not yet put them on MLS. Realtors are willing to do this because it means they will make a 6% commission instead of the 3% due to being the only realtor in the transaction.

Besides realtors, wholesalers are another top source of deals. They find deals, put them under contract, and then sell you the rights to the contract for a fee. They might make anywhere from $1K-$200K+ on a deal. It doesn't matter how much a realtor or wholesaler makes on a deal. Your concern should be the numbers that work out for your profitability.

You should always double-check a wholesaler's numbers to make sure you know the deal will work out for you. Your realtor will run the comps in the hope that you will later sell the house with their help. You need to get back to the wholesaler ASAP to get a good deal before it goes to someone else. You may need to put down some earnest money, which should only be given to the title company for safekeeping. Read all of a wholesaler's paperwork, including their original purchase agreement, before you sign anything.

The best place to find wholesalers is by looking at the real estate ads on www.Craigslist.com. You can also find them on Facebook, LinkedIn, and local real estate groups. The more wholesalers you connect with, the more deals will be sent to you.

You can find deals through auctions, whether they would be in person or online. While they don't allow for a due diligence period, you can usually look at the property beforehand and then calculate your numbers. Take into account that auctions charge up to a 10% fee on top of the sales price. Be very cautious with auctions so that you don't lose out big time. A realtor experienced with auctions can help you with the process.

Houses that are for sale by owner (FSBO) can be good deals. When you see one with an FSBO sign out front or find one online, you should call the owner to ask them about the house and how much they want for it. Tell them that you will do some research and get back to them after that. Find out the ARV and estimated cost of repairs so you can calculate your maximum offering price. You will need your purchase agreement for FSBOs since there is no realtor involved.

Making Offers

Think of your initial offer as the beginning of a conversation. Start a little low, but not too low, so that you can keep room for negotiation. Whatever amount you want to make on a deal, add an extra 25% as a cushion. If you want to make $40K, underwrite the deal to make $50K so that you're ready for any unexpected expenses.

You can get a copy of a residential purchase agreement (RPA) from a realtor. When it's filled out, it needs to include the property's address, purchase price, name of the buyer, amount of the earnest money deposit, and timeframe for both the due diligence and closing. It also needs to include whether the purchase will be in cash or through a loan proof of funds, and any contingencies such as financing or an inspection. Your realtor can put these things into the RPA for you and send it out for electronic signatures online.

It's best to buy properties under the umbrella of an LLC to protect your assets from any potential lawsuits. Real estate LLCs are best if they are based out of investor-friendly states like Nevada, Delaware, or Wyoming. Have a legal expert help you with this.

Offer a larger earnest money deposit than requested as that will help your offer to be accepted. Only pay it to the closing agent so that you can get it back easily. That is only in case you need to back out of the deal during your due diligence. You should keep ten days for your due diligence, once the seller has accepted your offer. That is pretty typical. During that time, it would be best to do your inspections, take at least 100 pictures throughout the property, have contractors and insurance agents give you quotes, confirm the ARV with three realtors, and finally line up your funding.

Luke does not recommend sending out lowball offers as they can cost you deals. Make reasonable offers that sellers will be willing to accept. If you aim to make one offer per day, then you can get more offers accepted than you might be able to do. You can always wholesale the extra deals for which you don't have the funding to close yourself.

Remain in close contact with the title company and lender if you are getting a loan. Be prepared to start on the rehab right after the closing. The longer you hold onto a property, the less money you will make in the flip. Make sure to have your contractors and the utilities scheduled and ready to go.

You should do a final walkthrough right before closing. You don't want any bad surprises such as new damage, missing appliances, or squatters. If you find any issues, you have three options. You can close anyway and deal with it yourself. You can delay the closing so the seller can fix the issue. You can also renegotiate the purchase price to be lower if the seller doesn't want to take care of the problem. Luke once had an issue where the seller accidentally burned down part of the house the night before the closing! Luckily, Luke caught this because he performed a final walkthrough.

Funding Deals

If you don't have the cash yourself to buy a deal, there are other options you can exercise. If you buy a house in really rough shape, traditional lenders may not be willing to fund it. Hard money lenders (HML) will give you the money to buy and fix a property with a short-term high-interest loan. HMLs usually charge you an interest rate between 8-18% and probably with additional fees and/or points (1 point=1% of the loan amount). The period of the hard money loan is usually between 6-12 months.

The quickest way to find HMLs that lend to people in your market is via a Google search. Another investor can also refer you to a local HML. Don't confuse HMLs with hard money brokers (HMB), which are companies that charge you fees to find you an HML. HMBs may advertise a wide range of interest rates and loan amounts, and say that they loan to all 50 states. An HML will have a tight range of interest rates and only loan to a few states. It's better to deal with an actual HML directly than to go through an HMB.

Hard money loans are based upon the property and not your credit/income like a traditional loan. Hard money loans are done in three ways. Firstly, they might give you 65-100% of the purchase price. Secondly, they might give you most of the purchase price and the majority of the repair costs in draws during the repair timeline. Finally, sometimes HMLs might give you 60-75% of the ARV. When you contact an HML, ask them about their interest rates, points/fees, how much they lend based on the loan-to-value (LTV), whether they lend money for repairs, how fast they can close, and also how many deals you have to do with them to get their best rates.

In addition to hard money loans, you can also get private money loans. This is when you get funding from family members, friends, other investors, or various people you meet while you are networking. You can tell people in person or in online ads that you are looking for money partners because you have more deals than you have financing for them. It would be best to prepare a proposal and email them an honest presentation with pictures and a description of the return they will get from their investment. The general rule here is to underpromise and overdeliver to your partners.

Private money can be in the form of loans you pay back, or they can buy equity in the deal. If they want equity, set up the deal as a joint venture where they put up the money, you do the work, and then the profits are split 50/50 or whatever you both agree on together. Make sure your partnership is documented with a legal contract. Keep your partners informed about the progress of the rehab and the later sale.

Gap lending is another option that combines both hard and private money. While an HML will give you most of the money as a first mortgage, a gap loan will give you the rest of it as a second mortgage. This allows you to do the deal with no money of your own. However, it could make you lose money on the deal if it goes over in time or the budget. You need to be considerate of any loan costs as they can quickly cut into your profits.

Contractors

You will need both good contractors and handymen to help you to be successful in flipping. You could do the rehab work yourself too, but they will do it better and faster than you. Also, your time is better spent growing your business by finding more deals, analyzing them, networking, and getting funding.

Your contractors and handymen will benefit from working with you because of the repeat work with bigger projects. You can find contractors and handymen through www.Thumbtack.com, www.AngiesList.com, www.Craigslist.com, Facebook friends or groups, contractor desks at Home Depot or Lowes, real estate clubs, Meetup groups, the Yellow Pages, realtors, or even by looking at other rehab projects. Like searching for realtors, you want contractors and handymen who give you great value because they are hungry for work.

On average, you will need to contact ten contractors to get quotes from at least three of them. Three quotes are necessary, so you can compare them for anything that got missed. Be upfront with your expectations, and make sure to tell them that you are flipping a house since not everyone wants to work on flips. Make sure they can do all aspects of your project. Always be on the lookout for new contractors and handymen.

It's helpful to send contractors pictures of a previous flip you've done so they can see what end product you want. Confirm your appointments with contractors two hours beforehand to increase the probability for them to show up on time. Make sure not to come across as a pushover who will pay retail rates like someone remodeling their personal residence. Shop around to find contractors that understand your vision, price point, and expectations.

Just like with your partnerships, your agreements with contractors need to be in writing. Those contracts need to state that the contractor is responsible for the people they bring to the property, paying subcontractors, insurance, and the progress of the project for payment. Furthermore, they need to state the draws, start/end dates, and that any additional work/charges that need to be signed off by you. Don't get tricked if a contractor tries to charge you for additional work that wasn't planned or agreed upon in advance. Always double-check their work before you make payments, which should be done in draws during the project.

Selling Properties

Once you have finished the rehab, it's time to sell so you can get your profits. Choose a realtor who will do widespread marketing beyond just using the MLS. They don't also have to be the same realtor you used for buying the property. You normally pay 3% of the sales price as a commission to your realtor and another 3% to the buyer's realtor. Your realtor should do the work to earn it by negotiating effectively and listing the price based upon accurate data. It's better to list the house for a little below your desired asking price to start a bidding war.

Luke always has his realtors pay for professional pictures to highlight the house's qualities. Have electronic lockboxes installed that track the showings other realtors do with potential buyers. There should be a sign in front showing that the house is for sale. Once the house is listed on the MLS, check over the agent's full report to review it for accuracy and descriptive language to make it sound more appealing. Luke does not recommend letting your realtor do an open house as it's additional wear and tear on your house. Plus, open houses are rarely effective at selling it.

Your realtor may recommend that you "stage" the house by having a professional company put in nice furniture to make it more attractive to potential buyers. If you do choose to stage it, look over the staging company's work beforehand, keep the furniture small to make rooms look large, limit clutter, be ready to sell the furniture with the house if needed, and use fake TVs and such in cheaper homes but go for the real stuff in higher-end homes. The furniture needs to complement the house.

If there are showings but no offers, lower the price every two weeks. If the market really starts to sink, lower the price to the bottom end of the pricing range to get it off your hands. Don't make the mistake of deciding to keep a property you planned on flipping. You normally do better upgrades on a flip than you would if you had planned on keeping it as a rental from the start.

Closing Deals

You know you have done well with your rehab and advertising if you get offers within two weeks after listing a property. The sale contracts a potential buyer sends you is the beginning of the sales conversation. You should never take it personally when you receive lowball offers and complaints about the quality of the rehab work as it's part of the game. Luke is usually okay with agreeing to do up to $1000 in repairs. He would need specific reasons for anything more than that.

Ideally, you would want a buyer who pays you cash or is preapproved for a VA loan or a conventional loan. FHA loans create extra challenges, such as you having to pay the closing costs. The higher the earnest money deposit amount and the sooner the closing date, the better it is for you. Have the buyer use your title company, who will then give you a discount if you have a title insurance binder policy with them.

Luke does not like buyers whose purchase is contingent upon the sale of their current home unless there are especially favorable circumstances. These include different factors. It could be that the buyer's property was appraised for more than yours, the due diligence is already done by the buyer of your buyer's property, or if the buyer agrees that you'll get to keep their earnest money in case they back out after their due diligence period. The due diligence should not be more than 12 days long.

It's a good situation if you have multiple offers at the same time. Use a multiple counteroffer form to inform your potential buyers that you have multiple offers. Have your realtor negotiate with one buyer at a time so they can find the buyer with the best price and terms for you.

Your buyers will have one of two types of home inspectors. Some inspectors are laid back. Others see the worst-case scenario in every potential issue. The second kind includes those that could kill a deal. It helps if your realtor or contractor will be present during the inspection to help things go smoothly. Luke is usually okay with agreeing to do up to $1K in repairs. He would need specific reasons for anything more than that.

If your buyer is using a loan, then the bank will require an appraisal to be done on the property. The bank won't loan out more than the appraiser says the house is worth. Have your realtor meet with the appraiser to judiciously give them a list of all the completed improvements along with the comps that prove the ARV is accurate. If the appraisal comes in low, then ask the buyer to come up with the difference. You can also submit a rebuttal to the appraisal. These steps could make a difference of thousands of dollars or more in profit for you. You can always renegotiate other parts of the transaction if needed.

Check over the final paperwork before the closing date to review it for accuracy. Ask your title company to wire you the funds instantly because a check could sometimes take 7-10 days to clear. Finally, share your success on social media since investors, realtors, and wholesalers want to know they are working with a successful wholesaler.

Investing Remotely

Luke started off in real estate by investing in local properties because there was a comfort in being able to drive over to see them and check the rehab progress. As he expanded, he began investing in properties in other markets. Each market comes with its own rules, challenges, as well as benefits. To be successful at remote investing, you need a solid, knowledgeable, and hungry local team. However, they won't have as much urgency as you to ensure that you make a profit.

Realtors, contractors, and HMLs will make money on your deals even if you do not end up making any. If one of them tells you that a deal is a slam dunk, ask them why then they aren't buying it themselves. It's better to find a local investor who knows the market and wants the knowledge and experience they can gain by working with you. If needed, you can also give them 5-10% of the profits to help them be committed to maximizing your profits.

Put ads for these hungry investors on Craigslist as well as Facebook. Once you shortlist candidates, interview them to learn their real estate story and whether you feel comfortable about working with them. Trusting them is key since they will be overseeing your contractor, realtor, and landscaper, etc. Train them on your process and expectations. You may sometimes have to travel to your remote investments to handle certain issues. Only you can decide if the rewards are worth the additional risks that come with remote investing.

Using Social Media

Most of you are already on a social media platform such as Facebook or LinkedIn. But are you doing it with the purpose to help your real estate business? Before Luke does anything like make a phone call or post on social media, he thinks about what his purpose is with it to make deliberate and thoughtful actions. He sets alarms for the amount of time he thinks he will require to achieve his specific tasks on social media. Otherwise, it can be a black hole that swallows up too much of your time.

The tasks he does on social media include things such as posting pictures/videos of his flips or search for wholesalers and investors. Your social media needs to help drive your business by telling your real estate story, goals, and vision. Your mission statement needs to be stated loud and clear. People will look you up and decide based on your posts and pictures, whether they will be interested in doing business with you. Your network is your net worth. The bigger and better quality your network is, the better off your net worth is too. Your business will grow as you expand your network with solid connections.

If you think that some of your friends and family won't be supportive of your real estate ventures, then that may be very true. Some of them will laugh at you or be mean to you about it. You should never let their negativity distract you. (I unfollowed everyone online who was negative.) Some people will encourage you to strive toward your dreams. Success can happen to you, so surround yourself with the people who will help you succeed.

Conclusion

Your life won't change until you start doing things differently. Luke's book describes in detail the actionable steps to take so you can be successful in the field of real estate investing. He brings to life the advice I always give to new investors. Network with others, including other investors, realtors, contractors, wholesalers, and lenders, etc. Educate yourself by reading books, listening to podcasts, going to real estate clubs/Meetups, and have a mentor, etc. Also, the third most important step is to take action. If you are serious about flipping houses, read this full book, and use it as the launching point for your business. You can make it happen!

Additional Reading

The Book on Flipping Houses: How to Buy, Rehab, and Resell Residential Properties by J. Scott

The Book on Estimating Rehab Costs: The Investor's Guide to Defining Your Renovation Plan, Building Your Budget, and Knowing Exactly How Much It All Costs by J. Scott

Chapter 9: Flipping Land
The Land Flipper: Turning Dirt into Dollars by E.B. "Seth" Farmer

Introduction

Flipping raw land is, in several ways, easier than flipping houses or other properties. While you still seek out ways to add value, you likely may not have to deal with as many contracting headaches. When you own a plot of empty land, you (hopefully) don't have any tenants to manage. By following Seth's steps, you will have a much clearer path to creating wealth with flipping land.

Why You Should Flip Land

Anyone can make a living in real estate, but you have to work very hard to become wealthy with it. You can start by flipping land even if you don't have a lot of money. You can buy cheap lots, clean them up, market them, sell them for a profit, and repeat. There is low overhead involved with doing this business. All you need is access to a computer, phone, and some other incidentals.

There are so many TV shows about flipping houses that it's become a craze these days. However, there are no shows on the air about flipping land. There is a ton of opportunity with land flipping due to the lack of competition. Flipping houses requires a ton more work than flipping land does.

Unlike most houses, it's relatively easy to divide a tract of land into multiple parcels to sell for a greater profit. For example, you could buy a ten-acre plot for $100K. You could then divide it into five plots with two acres to sell for $30K each, and walk away with $50K in profits. The worth of an acre of land will vary widely based upon its location and potential use.

Raw land doesn't require the maintenance that a house does. You won't face issues such as leaky roofs, rusty pipes, and tenants. You will have some upkeep, though, such as clearing brush and watching out for trespassers. Natural disasters cause less damage to the land than they do to buildings. Land value tends to remain steady during the ups and downs of the housing market. Also, you can easily leave a plot of land unattended while you are waiting to sell it.

Finding the Right Land

The most important factor with the land is its access to the roads. Paved roads are a lot better than gravel. Land that has a road through it or is on a corner is very much ideal. Easy access to clean water and other utilities will also make the land easier to flip. Land that is good for homebuilding is on a hilltop with drainage and some trees, but not too many of them.

Just like flipping houses, you can get a great deal on an ugly plot of land in a great neighborhood. You can then easily increase the value of some land by clearing brush, mowing the grass, hauling away junk, etc.

Find land in an area where the local laws are favorable to land flipping. You can use a real estate agent or a broker to search for that land. However, you will have to pay them commission, and they might not have a good understanding of raw land. If you want to search online, you may find local Facebook groups, www.Craigslist.com, www.LandWatch.com, and www.FSBO.com to be good resources. You can also look in local newspapers, the "real estate owned" departments at banks, asking neighbors, or even just by driving around looking for empty land that can be easily flipped.

Once you find a potential piece of land, contact its owner. Build some rapport with them. Ask them for their asking price and also for their permission for you to walk around the lot so you can inspect it. Do not tell them or give them any hints that you plan to flip their land for profit, but do say that you're an investor and be very vague about it.

Advertisements for raw land usually have inaccurate information. Therefore, you will need to research the land by looking on Google Earth for a satellite image. The county clerk of courts will have public records about the land. Get a topographical map of the area to know if the land is situated in a flood zone. Talk to the neighbors to find out the history of the parcel. Also, walk around it to get a feel for it yourself after you acquire the owner's permission. If the land seems good for development, it's now time to move onto the next step.

Government Officials

A county courthouse is a place you may need to visit if not all of the necessary public records are online. While you're there, the sheriff's office would be able to help you verify whether a property's taxes are current. There tend not to be sheriff's sales on lots like there are on houses. However, if you pay a property's delinquent taxes at a tax sale and the owner doesn't redeem the property within three years, then you can buy the land for pennies on the dollar.

The clerk of courts is in charge of maintaining the county's records. At their office, you can find out if a property has any liens or judgments against it. That would make a sale more difficult or expensive. When you're looking at records of plots, most of the USA is divided into boxes through the township system (PLSS) six miles tall by six miles wide. Texas, on the other hand, is on the Spanish system of metes and bounds. That system looks at angles and distances from a point in space.

With the PLSS, those 36 square mile boxes are ideally subdivided into one square mile sections, each of which contains 640 acres. A perfect section has 16 plots that each has 40 acres. The legal description of a plot of land describes where it is relative to a nearby township. You can get the hang of this slightly confusing system through some practice.

The tax assessor assesses properties to determine their worth and the taxes owed to the county. Since they mail out the property tax bills, they know the addresses of all the local property owners in the area. Seth has previously looked through those public records to see which property owners lived out of town. He then drove by those properties to find the neglected ones and then contacted those specific owners to offer them solutions. Now, he just looks up all the owners by section and asks them directly if they are interested in selling their land.

Negotiation and Contracts

When negotiating, do not be the first person to say a price. Listen to the seller to first understand their needs, problems, and asking price. Find out how you can help the seller get what they want out of the deal. Once you have settled on a price, you can then negotiate other incidentals, which can be in your favor.

Be ready to then discuss a list of problems that you have mentally prepared about the property. This can help the seller become more willing to make concessions to you. The nuclear option is to make a lowball offer. This could offend the seller and destroy the deal, but you can sometimes be surprised when they accept it. It's a risk versus reward approach, so choose wisely.

Once you have made an agreement, get it on paper to make it legal. Many states provide standard real estate contracts that you can use. In your contract, an inspection period of 15 days should be enough time to complete any additional research, including a land survey if needed. Have your closing scheduled to take place 15 days after that. If you need a loan to buy the land, make sure to include a clause that the sale is contingent upon the financing. It's normal to put down a deposit between $1K-5K as earnest money. It shows you're serious about the deal.

Some plots of land will have minerals. Do not let the seller reserve any of the minerals that are on the land's surface. This includes ones like iron ore or coal. It might be okay for the seller to reserve the subsurface minerals, such as oil or natural gas. This is as long as they don't leave things like oil rigs or pipelines lying around. If there is nothing in the contract, then it means the seller is selling you both the land, as well the mineral or other resources like timber. Don't mention minerals unless the seller does so at first.

Ask the seller for the disclosure form and the most recent survey to know what you're getting with the land. A new survey can cost thousands of dollars. You can negotiate with the seller regarding paying for the survey if you believe it is needed.

Sometimes you can find a seller who is willing to do seller financing. This means you don't have to go through a bank. You can negotiate the terms directly with the seller. With seller financing, the entire acreage is mortgaged together. However, if you include a partial-release clause that allows you to get part of the land released from the mortgage. Furthermore, if you pay a certain amount extra, then you can start selling off pieces to people willing to buy those smaller portions of the acreage. If you're smart, you will also include a clause that gives you a discount for paying off the mortgage early (when you flip the land).

Financing

If you happen to have an extra $50K lying around, it's not too hard to turn it into cash flow that is worth much more. Seth knows a guy who bought a $50K plot of 20 acres and sold two ten-acre plots for a total of $100K with $20K down payment and $80K in notes with a 10% interest rate. (He turned $50K into $147K over ten years.)

If you don't have that much money to invest, then you can ask sellers for seller financing. If they don't want to do it at first, then help them understand how it works. Also, they may change their mind if months pass without anyone else wanting to buy their land. You can offer terms with a balloon payment so that they know they won't have to wait for too long to get their full amount.

Sellers will prefer a down payment with a seller financing deal. Some land flippers have had success with putting down payments for land onto their credit cards. They then sell the land for a profit before the high credit card interest rates take effect.

Suppose you buy a plot of land with seller financing. Someone else comes along and wants to buy it from you, and that too with seller financing. As long as your mortgage terms didn't have a due on sale clause, you can do a wraparound mortgage. This is where you sell a property where you still have a mortgage that you owe on it. The end buyer makes mortgage payments to you, and you make your mortgage payments to the original seller. You get to pocket the extra money if you sell for a profit and then charge the end buyer a higher interest rate than what you are paying to the original seller.

If you have no money at all to invest, don't worry. You still have options. You can raise money from family and friends or network with other investors. You can also get a loan from a local credit union or bank, find deals for other investors for a fee, which is known as bird-dogging. Or you could work for a real estate developer.

People Who Can Help You

- You will need a good title company, which is also called an escrow company or an abstract company. They will research the property and prepare the necessary legal documents required for the purchase. They also help prevent nasty surprises from happening.
- If the title company's lawyer does not act as the consulting attorney, then you will need to line one up yourself. They can provide any legal advice with a purchase.
- A surveyor will show you where the boundaries of your property are. They can also help you divide a property up in case you want to sell it in smaller portions.
- A dirt person is someone who not only knows how to run heavy machinery, but also has the expertise to fix things like the drainage on your land.
- A certified public accountant (CPA) can help you structure your business so that you're not overpaying your taxes.
- Make friends with mobile home dealerships in the area. When you have some lots to sell, they may know of customers who will be interested in buying them from you.
- Connect with the local utility companies. You may sometimes need to pay to have utility lines connected to your newly purchased land.

- Network with local politicians and community leaders. Try to convince them to approve your subdivision plans through what's called the platting process.
- Get to know the neighbors, so they will call you if they see anyone trespassing or dumping garbage on your land. The more connections you build, the better.

Fixing up the Land

Once you have bought some land, it's time to get it ready to sell for a profit. If you plan to do the fixing up yourself, it will come in handy to have the proper tools. A pickup truck with a toolbox can haul your things as well as cleared brush. Multiple machetes with files to sharpen them will help you clear brush quickly. A tractor with a brush cutter will get the job done a lot quicker. A 200-foot tape measure or distance wheel will help measure distances. Have colorful flag pins to mark barriers on the land. Chains can help you if you get stuck somewhere. Your smartphone with GPS and a compass will come in handy. A laser level will help you determine if there will be drainage issues. Also, a four-wheeler will allow you to get around a large lot easily.

Have a plan before you get started prepping your land so that you are set up for success with its resale. Walk the land with your dirt person and surveyor to inform them about your plan and get their feedback. From there, get your platting plan approved by the county so you can legally divide up the land into even smaller parcels. A local attorney can help you follow the local regulations with this.

The most basic thing you can do to improve the salability of land is to simply just mow the grass. Also, pick up any trash, clear brush from the bottom of trees, and trim unsightly limbs. If it is necessary, build a pond or culvert for drainage. Double-check that you aren't going to hit any utility lines before you start digging. You may need to have a new gravel road put in depending upon how you end up dividing the land. Also, make sure to get any needed permits for your work.

Selling Your Land

Seth does not recommend selling your land through a realtor on the MLS. This is because you will be more passionate and knowledgeable about the land flip than them. You will also be more effective at selling your land as opposed to having a realtor sell it.

There are many different ways for you to market your land. Advertising in newspapers can help you find retirees who want to move out into the countryside. For sale by owner (FSBO) signs and onsite information boxes can catch the eye of any neighbors who have interested family or friends. Facebook works well to attract young blue-collar couples and immigrants who just want their piece of the American Dream. (For them, it would be their dream house they will build on the land.) Also, learn Spanish and post signs/flyers to connect with immigrants. Craigslist and Landwatch are good ways to find other investors who will buy land from you. Sending mailouts to people living in trailer parks can help you find those people who are wanting to move out of their park and into a quiet rural area.

In addition to Landwatch and Craigslist, Seth recommends another website called Zillow. You can post flyers or index cards on the bulletin boards at hardware stores, gas stations, grocery stores, laundromats, etc. after you acquire permission to do so. In your ads, put "Land for Sale" as well as your phone number. Sending flyers to people in mobile home parks is the best way you can advertise.

Next, be ready to answer the phone. There will be some people who will call but won't buy, so you will have to be patient to find that one right buyer. Listen to the people who call. Ask them for their email address so you can send them info. Ask what they want in a plot of land so you can see if what you have at hand matches their needs. Ask how they heard about you, so you know which ads were effective. Ask what their plan is for financing. Finally, ask if they will drive by the property before you meet them for a full showing.

In your email package, make sure to include a location map that makes the property easy to find. Since your land won't have an address yet, include the neighbor's address in case a potential buyer will use their GPS to find their way. Add a simple version of the survey plat with any landmarks as well as your sales prices. Pictures and Google Earth areal maps go a long way. Also, it is helpful to email a one-page info sheet that has details like directions, prices, lot sizes, local schools, financing options, and mineral rights. Even if someone doesn't buy from you right now, keep their contact info. Then send out mass emails when you had additional plots for sale.

Do your best to screen people over the phone before scheduling a showing. (The more information you know about potential buyers, the better it is for you to judge their seriousness in buying your land.) You will sometimes be stood up, though. Call an hour or so beforehand to confirm an appointment. At showings, be friendly and interested in the potential buyers. Always ask them to close on the deal, and then play it cool once someone says yes. Move quickly to get a signed sales agreement and deposit before you take the lot off the market. You can then send the title to your title attorney to make the final arrangements.

Conclusion

This book makes land flipping seem within reach, even when you don't have a ton of investment capital. The idea of having no tenants and minimal expenses is clearly an awesome benefit of flipping land. If you have additional questions, you can email Seth at thelandflipper@gmail.com or go to www.TheLandFlipper.com. You can also take his educational course at www.LandFlippers.com, and use the code 23BOOKS for 25% off of it.

Additional Reading

The Land Flipper on Owner Financing by E.B. Farmer

Investing in Vacant Land: It's Not What You Think! by John Pehrson

Chapter 10: The BRRRR Strategy

Buy, Rehab, Rent, Refinance, Repeat: The BRRRR Rental Property Investment Strategy Made Simple by David Greene

Introduction

This is a great book written by David Greene, who wrote another book I have reviewed within these pages titled *Long-Distance Real Estate Investing*. The BRRRR strategy is like combining the best parts of flipping and the buy-and-hold approaches. It's a very simple idea with powerful results. However, to be successful with it, you need to understand the nitty-gritty details that David explains in it on how to make all the pieces work together.

The BRRRR Method

The power of real estate is using other people's money to make you money. If you had bought a cash flowing rental property 30 years ago, the rent payments would have paid off the mortgage quite easily by now, and the property would have appreciated in value at the same time. If you reinvest your profits into buying more cash flowing real estate, then you can create a ton of wealth for yourself and your family.

The age-old way of investing is to put a down payment on a property, get it rent-ready, and then save up for your next down payment. Your initial investment money remains parked inside of a property. This process is SLOW and linear.

This book will show you how to do that through the BRRRR method, which can accelerate your investing at a compounding rate. You start by buying a property at a discount for cash and rehab it so it is worth more rent it so it cash flows, refinance it based upon the higher value to pull out your money, and use that money to repeat the process with more real estate. You can reuse your investment money repeatedly to buy more and more properties.

One metric of success in real estate is your return on investment (ROI). A 10% ROI means that you are getting back 10% of your original investment in profits annually. Some people include things like appreciation in their ROI calculation. However, David is only talking about the cash flow when he says ROI. It's the cash flow, and not the equity, that will help you through the tough times. To get a better ROI, you can either decrease how much of your money goes into the deal, increase income, or just decrease expenses.

By leveraging other people's money, you can maximize your ROI. This gives velocity to your money and real estate investing. With BRRRR, you are no longer limited to your ability to save up for down payments. The BRRRR method will also make you a better investor because you will be able to find, analyze, and buy more deals through the expanded experience and the network you obtain. Educating yourself and networking with other investors will also help propel you faster and further than you could ever achieve on your own.

Buying Right

Buying right means that you purchase real estate at a low enough price that you can make a profit on it. This is the key to succeed with BRRRR. Instead of just lowballing everyone, your goal is to create win-win situations where you can make money by solving a seller's problems.

A seller could be either experiencing market, personal, or property distress. Market distress is when a whole area is facing a downturn. Personal distress includes things like job loss, divorce, medical problems, or even death. Property distress is when the property is in rough shape.

A quick metric to have a good guess of whether a property will cash flow is if the monthly gross rents are at least 1% of the purchase price. This is known as the 1% rule. To know how much you can pay for a property, calculate what its after-repair value (ARV) will be. If your purchase price, expenses, and repairs add up to 75% of the ARV, then you will know that you both make money on the deal and will be able to refinance out your investment. If a property has an ARV of $100K and needs $25K in repairs to get there, then you should offer a maximum of $50K to buy it. This is because your purchase price plus the rehab costs would equal to 75% of the $100K ARV.

Properties with 1-4 units are considered residential and are valued based upon how much other comparable nearby properties (comps) have been sold for recently. Properties with 5+ units are commercial and are valued based upon how much profit they end up making.

Being able to find great deals is essential to your success. Have clear criteria in what you are looking for in a deal. If you have any fear when considering a deal, you should focus on what the math tells you about it. If the numbers show you that you can buy the property for less than what it's worth and that it will cash flow, then the deal is probably a good one.

Home sellers prefer buyers who can buy in cash. This is because cash means fewer contingencies that might keep the transaction from going through. This can also shorten the closing time from 30 days down to about ten or less. Cash offers even give you access to deals that traditional financing won't allow you to have. (If you don't have enough cash yourself, you can just use a hard money loan or cash from other investors.)

You make your money in real estate when you buy. If you don't buy at a right enough of a price, then you could be putting yourself in danger if anything else goes wrong. You are better off waiting for a good deal instead of getting stuck in a bad deal just for the sake of buying something.

The real estate market goes in up and down cycles. When you buy right, your property will be better able to handle a potential downturn in the market, giving you options. However, if you overpaid for a property and if it is not cash flowing enough, you may be forced to take a loss with it. Prevent this by analyzing the numbers and buying right in the first place.

Finding Deals

If you do anything enough times, eventually, you do become better at it. BRRRR gives you the repetition in real estate investing that you need so you can become a master at it. When you break things down and focus on the most important next step (MINS), your goals become a lot more achievable.

You don't have to do all the work and searching on your own. Find your "Core Four" team members in each market wherever you search. An awesome real estate agent can find and negotiate deals on your behalf. A great lender will be creative to line up favorable financing for you. A good contractor will find ways to save you money in your rehabs. Also, an incredible property manager will run your property a lot more smoothly and refer great deals to you.

The reason David identifies these as your Core Four is that he learned through his failures that they are essential to success. Plus, your Core Four can give you access to their network of other rock star people. Costco has such cheap prices because they buy and sell in bulk. Similarly, you may be able to negotiate discounted deals with your Core Four and other team members because you will be doing business in bulk with them. This is because everyone makes more money together when more business is done. This way, everyone in your Core Four benefits along with you. It's a very good win-win situation.

Wholesalers can bring you good deals, but they tend not to have as good of networks as your Core Four. A bad wholesaler provides inaccurate information. This can cost you expensive mistakes that a realtor could have helped you prevent. An easy way to tell the difference between good and bad wholesalers is the accuracy of their comps.

Find people who will help you find deals by networking. Ask around to find who is a good realtor, contractor, wholesaler, etc. Their experience from their repetition in the business will be a tremendous help to you. You should find ones that are top producers and align with your investment strategy. First, add value to others by helping them with what they need, and then they will reciprocate it back to you. www.BiggerPockets.com is a great way to network and find good people.

Learn how to recognize (and appreciate) talented people. The talented people you find will know other talented people that they can connect you with as well. Talented people push you, know what they want and also how to communicate it, look for solutions instead of problems, continually improve, and add value to you. If your Core Four are real estate investors themselves, then they will be even more skilled at helping you succeed.

Other methods of finding deals include sending direct mail to owners, going to auctions, looking at tax liens in the public record, "driving for dollars" to find vacant or distressed homes, or hiring someone to be a "bird dog" and find those properties for you. Create a website showing that you buy homes and utilize search engine optimization (SEO) to bring people to it. Connect with divorce attorneys, probate attorneys, funeral homes, and companies that handle bankruptcy to find motivated sellers. A customer relationship management (CRM) software will be useful for you to keep track of all of your contacts.

Rehab Like a Boss

After buying right, rehabbing right is the next most important thing. While you don't have to do a big rehab to be successful with BRRRR, it works better with a bigger rehab. To have a great rehab, you need a rock star contractor. When David is looking for a new contractor, he will pay five contractors $50 each to put in a bid on a rehab project. Then he hires the best one who will save him many times. Add value to your contractors and treat them well so they will be motivated to do the best possible work for you.

Other investors can be a great resource to find awesome contractors for yourself. However, they aren't always willing to share their contracts in fear that you might steal them. The trick is to get other investors to like you. The book, *How to Win Friends and Influence People* by Dale Carnegie, can help you with this.

To save on money with a rehab project, you should consider using an unlicensed handyman for some of the easier jobs. Handymen are cheaper than contractors, but they may not be able to perform the tasks that require specialized skills. It will also save you money by being able to understand contractor bids and then be willing to ask questions when something on the bid seems off.

Contractors are either focused on working for people living at their primary residence or investors rehabbing investment properties. The first kind does great work but only for top dollar. The second kind of contractor specializes in doing good work cost-effectively. They are harder to find but are worth it to keep you on budget.

When you have found a contractor you like, confirm how long they expect the rehab job will take, and then give them a little extra time. Offer them a 5% bonus if they finish within that time, but say that you will deduct 5% for each week they go beyond that. This will help motivate them to stay on schedule. If they do a good job, create an efficient system with them to make future jobs go smoothly.

"Upgrade hacking" is where you can get the best bang for your buck with rehabs. Sometimes using top-grade materials doesn't give you such a good return. However, using top materials in key places such as the bathroom or kitchen can get you higher rents, lower vacancy rates, and a higher ARV. Better materials look nicer and will last longer than cheaper ones. You should consider upgrades like nicer tile, granite countertops, and stainless-steel appliances.

There are success patterns in real estate investing and rehabbing that you will get to know through experience. You will get much better at seeing how you can add value to a deal. One such way is to add square footage to a smaller property, for example. If the property has extra space that you can convert into extra bedrooms and/or bathrooms, you are sure to add value to it. Other good upgrades include painting, replacing carpet with laminate flooring, updating cabinet exteriors, and adding individual utility meters for each unit in a multifamily property. Furthermore, it will include installing air conditioning, replacing an old roof, installing low-flow toilets, and cleaning up the landscaping.

To manage your rehab process, you can either do the oversight yourself or delegate it to one of your Core Four members. Another member of your Core Four, such as the property manager, can check in on the contractor. They can also double-check that the rehab is going according to plan. They can also take pictures and videos of the rehab on their smartphone to send to you. David sends the rehab money to the contractor in 25% draws as the job progresses so he can help keep them on track.

Renting Your Property

Before you start finding renters, you need to know how much to charge in rent. It will become your main source of income in real estate. Secret shop your competition to see what other places are charging in rent as well as providing in amenities. You can get a ballpark idea when you are analyzing a property before you buy it. David loves using www.Rentometer.com because it provides an easy way to get an initial rent estimate. www.BiggerPockets.com/calc has calculators that can do much of the deal analysis for you as well. However, to get even more accurate estimates on rental rates, you can ask other local investors, your property manager, and your realtor. Also, you should consult with your property manager about their thoughts on a property before you buy it.

Many factors will impact the value, rentability, and rental rates of a property. You need to check if the property rehabbed to the expected quality level for the area. You need to make sure if people want to move to the area for things like jobs or school districts. You need to assess if people in the area are making enough income at their jobs to afford the housing there. You need to see if the property is in an area that is considered to be up-and-coming. Furthermore, you would need to see if the local climate is considered desirable. Other things to consider would be to see if there are more units available than needed, or if there is a shortage. You need to make sure if the market is so hot such that there is a short turnaround time for homes to sell and also apartments to rent. Finally, see if the rents in the area are increasing at least 5-10% annually.

Buying real estate in the path of progress will help ensure that you will make profits with increased rents as well as equity. For example, San Francisco is becoming increasingly more expensive for both buying and renting. Some of the areas around the San Francisco Bay Area are also expensive. More and more people were willing to live an hour away in Sonoma and commute. That includes even Oakland, which has a history of high crime rates and is showing a steep increase in property values and rent. Oakland and Sonoma became in the path of progress. This is all caused by economic growth in the area.

You need to be very picky about choosing your tenants. A bad choice in one can be a very expensive mistake. If you buy near a hospital, then you can rest assured that well-paid professionals will be interested in renting from you. If there is a pride of ownership in the area such that people take care of their properties, then you are less likely to have problems there. You should treat your tenants well for taking good care of your property. Buying near good schools also helps attract good tenants for those properties.

The lower the vacancy you have, the better it is for you. Sometimes lowering rent is a cheaper option for you than letting that unit remain vacant for too long. You can always raise the rent later to market rate when a tenant renews their lease. When you are a good attentive landlord in the first place, you are more likely to have less vacancy and better rents. You get better rental rates for leases that start in the summer due to that being the peak time. If you have to start a lease with a new tenant in the winter, you can adjust the end date so that it occurs in the summer. (However, some landlords prefer to have leases the end at varying times of the year.)

You will need to decide if you will self-manage your property or plan to hire a property manager. It's cheaper to self-manage, you have more control, and you know you will take good care of the property. However, this involves some more time and energy on your part. By using a professional property manager, you get to leverage their time and experience. This way, you can focus on growing your business instead of just maintaining it. It's not easy to find a good one, though.

Referrals are likely the best way to find good property managers. These referrals could come through trusted sources on your network or even the forums on www.BiggerPockets.com. (I've used both with success.) Once you do find a property manager who has a great reputation, you should determine if they are a good fit for what you need and if you are a good fit for them as well. You should ask them what they like about their work and how their systems work. Trust your gut, whether they seem to be good communicators, knowledgeable, and honest. Also, ask for referrals from other investors with whom they work.

Refinancing

Before buying a property, you should make sure you are pre-approved for a refinancing loan so that you know you can pull out your investment money for the next property. If you wait to get pre-approved, then you might have un unhappy surprise, which would mean that you can't pull out your money whenever you want. You may need to shop around with multiple lenders to get pre-approved and to find a lender with favorable terms. Some lenders are better than others at working with investors, so you need to choose wisely.

The pre-approval letter will give you an idea of how much you can borrow and also the expected terms of your future loan. The terms will include the interest rate (which can be higher for refinancing than purchasing), and how long you have to wait after purchase to refinance the property. They will also include the loan to value (LTV), which is the percentage of the property's value that you can get mortgaged, the closing costs, and the rate buy down fee that you can pay to get a lower interest rate. LTVs of 75-80% are pretty common with investment properties.

If you are an out-of-state investor, then you may need to use a local credit union instead of a bank. Depending upon how much cash a bank has in deposits, they may be more or less lenient at giving out loans. If you are unable to get pre-approved for a loan, then this is not the right time for you to start doing BRRRR. When you do find an awesome lender, it really helps to build and maintain a good relationship with them.

You are not limited to doing the BRRRR strategy with only your own cash. There are different types of loans that are good for investors.

- A conventional loan is a generic loan that is insured by Fannie Mae/Freddie Mac. It requires a down payment of 3-25%, depending on whether it is a primary residence or rental.

- Federal Housing Administration (FHA) loan must be owner-occupied, have low down payments, and would require extra mortgage insurance. (An FHA 203(k) loan allows you to mortgage the cost of the home purchase and rehab together with only just a 3.5% down payment. You can only have one FHA loan in your name at a time. However, you could have one in your name and one in your spouse's name if you are married.)

- Department of Veteran Affairs (VA) loans are only for people who have been in the armed forces. Those can be done without any down payment.

- Portfolio loans are when you need to finance more than ten properties together. Normally, you can only have up to ten mortgaged properties in your name at a time. (If you are married, you can have ten under your name and then ten others under your spouse's name.)

- Hard money loans are short-term high-interest rate loans that are offered by a private lender. They can allow you to get into a property with the plan of selling or refinancing it soon.
- Private financing is when another investor loans you money for a deal.
- Seller financing is when the seller plays the part of the bank and then mortgages the property to you.
- A home equity line of credit (HELOC) is a low-interest second mortgage on an existing property. You use them similarly to a credit card. That is where you only pay interest on the amount that you use.

Mortgage insurance is required if you have a mortgage of more than 80% of the purchase price. One way around that is to do an 80/10/10 where you get a first mortgage of 80%, the second mortgage of 10%, and a 10% down payment. The 10% loan is normally a HELOC.

If you owner-occupy a property, then you can qualify for an FHA or VA loan that you could not if it was strictly an investment property. When you live in a part of the space and rent out the rest, it's called "house hacking." (My first property was a triplex where I got an FHA loan, lived in one unit, and then rented out the other two units to live cheaply.)

In October 1981, mortgage rates were at 18.45%. They are at an incredible low in 2020, which makes money a lot cheap to get. The government purposely reduces the interest rate in an attempt to stimulate the economy. This also then helps reduce the risk of real estate investing. The more you leverage other people's money (OPM), the greater the return you will get on your own money. It also means that money is working for you instead of you working for money. (But if you over-leverage your real estate, then you may put yourself at risk in case anything goes wrong.)

You may be asking yourself whether you should flip a rehabbed property instead of refinancing it. They both would give you back your investment money plus some if you have played your cards right. Refinancing has many great benefits over flipping. It provides you cash flow, continued appreciation, and ongoing tax benefits. It also further saves you from paying the extra taxes, closing costs, and commissions, which cut into your profits. The money you pull out during a refinance is then tax-free until you sell the property!

Using Systems for Success with Repeating

Once you have done this process the first time, you can focus on becoming better at it through the four E's. You can make the process more efficient through simplicity, effective with a much higher rate of success, expeditious with a faster speed, and employability by delegating more of the tasks. The more you work at improving the four E's, the better you will get at it.

If you try to do it all on your own, chances are that you will do everything terribly. The Pareto Principle, also called the 80/20 Rule, states that 80% of your results come from 20% of your efforts. Therefore, you should spend your time and effort on the top 20% of things that give you the most results, and then delegate the rest to your Core Four and others. Don't assume your team knows what you want. This is why clear and consistent communication with them is an absolute must.

The thing that will set you ahead of all the rest is persistence. You will have to go through the grind with the numbers to find yourself good deals, good people, and good people who then find you good deals. You have to be persistent through the challenges you will face and learn from your failures.

Improving your systems will help bring you success, find more opportunities, make things a lot easier for you, and allow you to scale your business to make it bigger. Real estate is not a way to get rich quickly, but it most certainly is a solid way to build wealth slowly over time. It's like planting a fruit tree that you have to take care of for years until it matures and then gives you a bounty of fruit each year.

Compound interest is a beautiful thing when it works in your favor as it does in BRRRR. David's website www.GreeneIncome.com has a compound interest spreadsheet that shows how your money can multiply at a faster rate over time when you invest it wisely. Working with other people on your real estate ventures will help your money to multiply even faster.

If you are waiting for the stars to align perfectly before you take action, you will then be waiting a long time. You have to make the most out of the opportunities you do have. To build good systems, you need to connect with great people and communicate your expectations to them. It is best to create checklists for the different pieces of your system that other people can follow on your behalf. Furthermore, if you can learn how other successful people's systems work and incorporate that into your system, you will give yourself a HUGE advantage.

Conclusion

In David's book, he goes through several different examples and stories that help you understand his messages a lot better. He also includes scripts you can use when you contact people who you want to join your real estate team. If you are looking to be a successful BRRRR investor, then I highly recommend that you read his original book and then connect with other successful BRRRR investors on www.BiggerPockets.com.

Additional Reading

The Real Estate Rehab Investing Bible by Paul Esajian

The Book on Estimating Rehab Costs: The Investors Guide to Defining Your Renovation Plan, Building Your Budget, and Knowing Exactly How Much It All Costs by J. Scott

Chapter 11: Property Management

The Book on Managing Rental Properties by Brandon and Heather Turner

Introduction

This is another fine book from the BiggerPockets series. The website, www.BiggerPockets.com, is known as "the real estate investing social network, marketplace, and information hub." You can join for free and choose to upgrade to a paid premium account to benefit from additional access and content.

This book covers how to make more money while working less as well as how to have fun while you do it. Whether you are new to being a landlord or are just looking to increase your efficiency and profits, you can find solid value in this information. Heather and Brandon made tons of mistakes as property managers. Therefore, you get the benefit of learning from their experiences. This book gives you the tools, systems, and insider information to be a successful landlord.

Being a Landlord

Being a landlord or property manager entails a few things. It means that you protect and grow a real estate investment by finding and overseeing tenants, who are your customers in your business. Make no mistake, real estate is a business, so you have to treat it like one. Effective management of a property is a critical ingredient for its success.

You have two options. You can either self-manage your property or hire a professional property management company. Hiring out for this will likely cost you 8-12% of collect rents and sometimes up to one month of rent for each unit that gets rented out by a new tenant. Usually, the higher quality of a property and the greater number of units, the lower the percentage of rents you'll have to then pay to the property management company. This is because the larger, better-quality places are relatively easier and cheaper per unit to maintain. Furthermore, you will have to pay for repairs and upgrades, whether you or someone else is managing the property. Having said that, hiring a property management company does have its benefits. If you do choose to use a property management company, then you will have more time to do more valuable work, such as finding and investing in new properties.

There is A LOT of variance in the quality of property management companies. You would need to do good research to find the best one in town. This book will give you an idea of what it takes to be a good property manager. This will then help you know what to look for in other companies. You will need to supervise them on some level to ensure that they are treating your property right. It's best to pay them well to keep it in good shape.

8 Business Attributes of a Successful Landlord vs. Someone Who Only Does It as a Hobby

1. Implement good systems with repeatable processes: Just like Starbucks has systems, you also will thrive using an effective and repeatable process. That will allow you to make better decisions, free up your time, improve tenant satisfaction, and also help with financial stability.

2. Strive for continuous improvement: Your job is to find ways to help things run smoother, efficient, faster, and making more profit at the same time.

3. Be firm but fair: If you are "too nice," it will cost you. By all means, this does not mean that you have to be rude to your tenants. It means you have to be very clear about boundaries and rules while being respectful to them. Therefore, your tenants will become better tenants.

4. Outsource and delegate when appropriate: If you're like me, you can probably figure out how to do various repairs by yourself. However, it takes time and specialty tools to do much of the work. I find it more cost-effective instead to hire professional contractors who have all the tools and can do the work quicker and better than me. You can even delegate out the maintenance and repair calls, bookkeeping, advertising, cleaning, signing leases, and pretty much

everything else. As long as other people can do something reasonably well, it is best to delegate it! If you try doing everything yourself, you're only going to burn yourself out. When you have an attitude of delegation, you save yourself time, energy, and stress.

5. Maintain good control of the finances: You should pay close attention to where all the income is coming from for your business. Accountability is very important. You have to keep a watch on every dollar going for expenses. It is best to keep up with an organization system for all of your financial transactions. It is better to make this a habit, and you'll be thankful when you need to look back at the details, such as during tax time or an audit.

6. Focus on customer service: If your income comes from being a landlord, then your tenants are your customers who would pay for your car, food, and other bills. Your customers will NOT always be right, but you must always be respectful to them during your interactions with them. Also, you need to be responsive when they need help or have questions. By keeping your tenants longer and staying on top of the maintenance, you will save yourself tons of money.

7. Know and understand the property management laws: It is your responsibility to know and follow all of these. Otherwise, it could end up costing you big money. This falls into three categories.

a. Fair Housing Laws: You can discriminate to only accept tenants who can afford the rent. However, you cannot discriminate based on things such as race, color, gender, sexual orientation, handicap, or national origin, etc.

b. Landlord-Tenant Laws: Every state has its own rules that cover things like security deposits, evictions, due dates, maintenance, and more. You need to pay attention to those. Failure to do so may cost you as well.

c. Local Laws and Codes: These come from your city and county, and tend to be stricter even than federal laws.

8. Ask for help when you need it: Inevitably, you will encounter problems that you would have no idea of how to solve. However, that's all perfectly fine! You don't have to go at it alone. The best property managers are the ones who reach out to get help on an ongoing basis. There are 28 million real estate investors in the USA, and many of them are willing to help you. A good place to start is by joining the community at www.BiggerPockets.com.

The 7 Steps to Take Before Signing Your First Lease

1. Look at asset protection options such as a Limited Liability Corporation (LLC) or Limited Partnership (LP). This

separates your personal assets from your property's assets just in case you ever get sued.

2. Get good insurance, which also protects you from losing everything in a lawsuit or any other catastrophe.

3. Set up checking and savings accounts for the property to keep your personal finances separate from that of the property. This helps with bookkeeping and proving your LLC or LP is a separate entity from yourself. This makes you look more like a legitimate business.

4. Get the forms and documents ready that you will need. These include a rental application, acceptance letter, deposit receipt, denial letter, lease agreement, rules, and regulations. These also include pet addendum, a move-in/out checklist, lead-based paint disclosure, move out instructions, notice to enter the property, notice to comply with the lease, notice to pay or vacate, and any other locally required forms.

5. Make a company policy binder that outlines how you do everything. This way, there is a standard system for you and anyone helping you to follow.

6. Get to know the neighbors and ask them to inform you immediately if anything weird happens at the property.

7. Set up your bookkeeping with something like Excel or QuickBooks, or you could just hire a professional bookkeeper.

When you buy a property that already has tenants, you have to abide by their pre-existing leases. When those expire, you can replace them with your lease if the tenant decides to stay on. Before you close on a new property, look closely at the leases, so you know what you are getting into and whether the rents on the leases match what the seller said they were. You can also get an Estoppel agreement with each tenant. This means that the tenants confirm the lease terms before you close on the property.

Before a tenant moves in, you must ALWAYS get a security deposit equal to at least one month of rent from them to cover things like repairs (beyond normal wear and tear) or any missed rent. Double-check your local laws on what is allowed with regards to deposits. Tenants should pay you their deposit with a money order or cashier's check so you can be assured that the check won't bounce.

Fair Housing Laws

Being a landlord does not permit you to be mean to people. Following the federal Fair Housing Laws will not only protect you from lawsuits, but it also means that you are probably not a total jerk. It is illegal to discriminate against people based on things like their race, color, religion, sex, national origin, familial status, or disability. (It is recommended to review the specifics of your local Fair Housing Laws as well.)

There are some exceptions to needing to follow these laws.

1. If you have a 55+ community, at least 80% of the units must be occupied by people aged 55 or older.

2. If you are the owner and live in a unit in a single-family house, duplex, triplex, or a 4-plex.

3. If you own less than four single-family homes and do not use advertising or a listing broker.

4. If your religious or private organization only rents to a specific population, such as the congregation members or women escaping violence.

To be compliant with Fair Housing Laws, you should be knowledgeable about the laws, treat everyone equally, avoid making assumptions, be consistent, be thoughtful about your wording, and keep good records. (When I consider potential tenants, I mainly want people who will pay the rent on time and not be full of drama.)

Advertising Your Vacancy

Marketing is the best way to find new tenants. First, think about your target audience. A property near a college will naturally attract college students. Similarly, a 4-bedroom house will likely appeal to families.

It would be better to ask the neighbors what they like about the neighborhood, and then use those positive things in your marketing. For example, is it near any schools, parks, public transit, shopping, restaurants, etc.? In your ads, be careful to avoid discriminatory language that would violate Fair Housing Laws. Good quality photos in your ad can make all the difference in getting people to become interested in renting from you. Make sure your property looks clean and rent-ready inside out.

Using a "For Rent" yard sign is effective, but could alert potential criminals of a vacant house. You can also leave flyers at grocery stores or cafeterias, or advertise for free on www.Craigslist.com (unless you're in New York City). The website, www.Postlets.com, distributes your ads to 20+ websites and advertise on www.Zillow.com (which owns Postlets). You can buy an ad in the classifieds in your local newspaper, and use social media such as www.Facebook.com. You can also offer cash or rent discounts to your current tenants for referrals. When tenants live by their family and friends, they are more likely to rent from you for longer, which reduces your turnover costs. Track the results of your advertising, so you know what your most effective approach is.

Pre-Screening Tenants

It's good to be picky with potential tenants to prevent from having too many damages, drama, financial losses, and other problems. You must consider these questions. Is the potential tenant able to afford the rent and willing to pay it on time? Will they keep the place clean while not bringing drugs and crime to the property? Are they high maintenance, and will they cause you constant stress?

You should use your best judgment about applicants while following the law. The tenants you will want to avoid are entitled, lazy, don't take care of the place, use or deal in illegal drugs, don't pay rent on time, or are overly dramatic. Avoiding these tenants is much easier than dealing with their aftermath. They're not worth the rent they give you.

The pre-screening starts at the first contact between you and an applicant. You are looking for verifiable proof that a rental applicant meets your minimum qualifying standards. No screening process is ever 100% accurate. However, you can at least get a good idea about someone before deciding on whether you will accept their application.

You should consider the following to be included in your minimum qualifying standards, which will help prevent some problems from occurring. Their current income should be three times the monthly rent so that they can also afford their other expenses in life. A potential tenant needs to have good references, especially from their previous landlords. Bad credit, prior evictions, and violent felony convictions are huge red flags that you can easily find through a background check. Brandon and Heather prefer to see credit scores of at least 600. They like to use www.Rentprep.com and www.MySmartMove.com to do their background checks. (You must ALWAYS do background checks, or you will regret it sooner or later.) Make sure you follow all of the local and federal laws when screening tenants.

In your ads, on the phone, through email/text, and in person, you should be clear and upfront about your policies, rent price, deposit needed, the application process, and what utilities would be included. If you do not allow smoking inside the property, you must mention that in your ads to reduce the number of calls you get from people who are looking for a place where they can smoke inside.

When you meet an applicant in person, you should pay attention to how they dress, how they conduct themselves, whether they are clean, and the condition of their car. How they take care of themselves and their car is a good indicator of how they will also take care of your property.

If you accept Section 8 applicants at your property, the Department of Urban Housing and Development (HUD) will pay for some or even all of their rent. The property has to meet the HUD standard of habitability. That includes basic things like having heat and windows that can open. With Section 8, you can make a little more money, but you may have extra cleaning and repairs to do in between tenants. (Most investors tend to either love or hate Section 8.)

After an applicant passes your phone pre-screening, you can schedule a showing with them. Let any current tenants know about a showing at least 24 hours ahead of time. 1:1 showings allow you to give an applicant all of your attention. Group showings are, however, more time-efficient. It's a good practice to confirm a showing the day of, to have a good idea of whether they will show up to it. It is helpful to arrive early to a showing to make sure the unit looks rent-ready. (I also like using virtual showings where I make a video walkthrough of the unit and upload it to YouTube. I have applicants watch it before scheduling a physical tour. This helps limit physical showings to only the more serious applicants.)

The tour is your time to shine with showing applicants all the awesome things about the unit. However, you should keep your safety in mind when you do any showings. You must answer their questions openly and honestly. In their book, Brandon and Heather provide the answers to the most commonly asked questions from applicants. Keep these FAQs (frequently asked questions) handy. It would be best to give the interested applicants written info about the property along with a rental application (or a link to the online application).

The Application Process for Tenants

The application should obtain all the info you legally require for properly screening potential tenants. There is no need for a complicated application, as long as it is detailed and lists your minimum qualifying standards. You should ask for things like their name, date of birth, Social Security number, references, rental history, employment info, how many pets and cars they have, eviction and felony conviction history, names of people who will live in the unit, and finally an emergency contact. There should be a signature line that allows you to use the info for screening. You can find a sample application on BiggerPockets.

Require a separate application and nonrefundable fee for each applicant aged 18 and over. The fee should be enough to cover the cost of the screening, or whatever is allows in your local laws. Don't take your ad off the market until you have accepted a tenant and also received their security deposit.

You should take the time to do the screening right. You can verify their income by talking with their employer and/or get copies of their recent paychecks. A tenant might lie about their prior murder conviction or an eviction. You can run background and credit checks to find out what is accurate about their history. You can either check public records yourself or use a service like www.RentPrep.com. You must always call their prior landlords to learn the truth about what they are like as a tenant. You can start by asking the landlord if they have any vacancies. If the applicant has a friend pretend to be a landlord, this could throw you off. You can also consider Googling an applicant, looking at their social media, and driving by their current residence to see how well they maintain it.

If you deny someone's application, you must give them written notification of the denial along with the logical and legal reason for why they were denied. This helps protect against potential Fair Housing complaints. One way around having to deny someone who can't qualify for a unit by themselves is to have them get a cosigner. The cosigner is someone who doesn't live in the unit but also agrees to be financially responsible for it.

After you decide to accept an applicant, you should agree on a move-in date to be within the next two weeks, collect the "deposit to hold" with 24 hours which reserves the unit for them and then tell them the next steps such as them needing to transfer the utilities to their name. If they back out, you keep the deposit to hold. If they move in, the deposit to hold is then applied toward their security deposit. You must require the full security deposit and the first month of rent before the tenant moves into the property.

Signing the Rental Contract

A good lease is needed to protect both the tenant and the landlord. Everyone should know their part of the agreement. Whenever possible, you should have leases end during the summer when most people move. The legal things to include in a lease will vary between cities and states. A local attorney will know for sure what's allowed and what's not allowed. However, every lease should include legal language that describes the names of the tenants, dates, lease term, address, policies/rules/regulations, price, where they can pay rent when rent is due. It should also include late fees and other fees, security deposit info, who pays which utilities, the landlords right to access the property, move in and out condition checklists, any addendums, and signatures.

It is best to prepare the lease before the lease signing appointment. You should have two copies of it (one for you and one for them) if you are using paper copies. It is advisable to walk through the unit with the tenant and fill out the move-in condition checklist. Take pictures and videos of the unit as necessary for proof of the unit's condition.

It's helpful to do a short orientation for new tenants. This way, they will learn the responsibilities of both the landlord and tenants, how maintenance works, when rent is due, consequences of late rent, and general rules of the property.

Managing Tenants

Your tenants will need to receive ongoing training on your rules and policies. For example, you should tell them what your office hours are, and then only respond to non-emergency calls during those hours. They will still need to know who to contact for emergencies outside of your business hours.

There are a few ways to collect rent. One option for rent is to have tenants mail it to your PO Box. If you do this, you can have a specific date by which the rent is received and not just mailed. If you have an apartment building, you might have a dropbox (which needs to be secure). An automated clearing house (ACH) can transfer money from a tenant's bank account directly to yours for a fee. PayNearMe is a service that allows tenants to pay cash rent at a 7-Eleven, and it then gets transferred to you for a fee. Online rent payments, however, are likely how all rent will be paid in the future. There are many options for online payments. It is NEVER a good idea to collect rent in cash in person. That puts you at risk of getting robbed. Cash rents that are mailed or put in a dropbox are also a bad idea due to the risk involved therein. Also, do not let tenants drop off rent at your house (unless you live in the same apartment building as your tenants).

Some states require grace periods for rent payments. This is when rent is due on the first of the month, but the tenant can pay it a certain number of days later without incurring any fees or penalties. You must keep in mind that people who live off Social

Security receive their money on the third of the month. If you give people a grace period until the fifth day to pay rent, you should then absolutely charge a late fee starting on the sixth day, so they know that rent is an important priority. This is part of training tenants to pay rent on time.

Since rents generally go up over time, you'll need to get used to raising rents for your tenants. Tenants understand this, although they probably aren't huge fans of it. As long as your rent rates remain competitive with the market, rent increases probably won't cause tenants to move out. Even a $25 "nuisance raise" per year is better than a $200 increase every four years. Usually, a 30-60 day written notice before the end of a lease is needed to raise rents but always check with your local laws for specifics.

You can't count on every tenant to keep you updated about every maintenance issue. You must conduct periodic inspections (at least every six months) to see what repairs need to be done. You can then bill the tenant for the repairs of any damages that they had caused.

If you have a property with enough units, you may consider hiring one of the residents to be an on-site manager. That could be either for a fee or reduced rent. You can have them take care of things like lawn care, snow removal, answering calls, and doing minor maintenance. Whether you hire a resident to be the manager or hire a professional property manager, you will still need to manage the manager too. It's still your business, and they will never care about its success as much as you do, of course.

As with any relationship, communication is key when dealing with your tenants. You need to be responsive to their concerns and requests. Also, it's helpful to document your communications with them because you never know when you need that, such as for a lawsuit. To reduce your risk from lawsuits, make sure your property is habitable and safe, repairs and maintenance get done promptly, you handle and disclose any environmental concerns, and you follow the terms of the lease.

To increase your profits, you need to either increase income or decrease expenses. Income can be increased by doing things such as raising rent, charging various fees, charge for extra amenities like a garage space or storage, or have coin-operated laundry in a multifamily property. You can decrease your expenses by doing things like having tenants pay for their utilities, fix running toilets, and dripping faucets to reduce the water bill. You can also use cheap advertising like Craigslist, challenge your county's tax bill if you think it is too high, and make the property energy efficient with better lightbulbs and low flow toilets.

Dealing with Problems

When you are a landlord, you will encounter problems that need to be solved. While each problem has a unique situation, the solutions can be broken down into themes. Brandon and Heather cover the most common problems, along with their solutions.

If a tenant doesn't pay rent by the due date or if their check bounced, you should address it immediately because it's a form of theft. Since eviction can be a long and expensive process, there are other things you can do first. Start by calling the tenant that rent and the late fee are now due. You can also email or text them if they don't answer your call. If they aren't able to work it out with you to get caught up, then they will need to move out. Housing costs are usually people's biggest expense. If someone starts to get behind on that, it becomes only harder to catch up with it as more time goes by. You will only regret it if you don't hold tenants accountable for the rent rules. Your real estate is a business, so you must treat it that way.

Handling maintenance issues is part and parcel of being a landlord. You should line up handymen and contractors beforehand, so you know who to call when there are issues. It's helpful to use a system for documenting and keeping track of maintenance requests and their resolutions. You can offer your tenants options for making maintenance requests, such as online, phone, text, etc. You should get to know your local laws for doing maintenance.

If you believe that a tenant may have abandoned (moved out of) the property without informing you, then you can try to contact them. Find out your local laws about what you are permitted to do when a unit was abandoned by a tenant. If they left any items, you might be able to sell them after a certain period to pay for any damages or unpaid rent.

If a tenant dies in the property, you need to contact the police first. If there were any other tenants in the unit, they take care of the deceased tenant's items and continue with the lease. If the deceased tenant had no housemates, then you need to contact who was in charge of their estate to handle things. If there isn't anyone to do that, then you handle it the same way as you would do so with an abandoned unit.

It's very important to understand that illegal drugs are bad news for both you and the tenant. They increase the chances of late rent, maintenance issues, as well as criminal activity. However, proving illegal drug use can be difficult. You will wish to consider an option from the next section.

If a tenant is not complying with the rules of the lease, then you can send them written notification (as described in your local laws) to start complying within a certain number of days or face possible eviction. If they leave junk outside on the property or have other cleanliness issues, then you can ask them to clean it up. If they have an unapproved roommate staying for more than two weeks, then you can inform them that the roommate needs to go through the standard application process to become a tenant and pass, or everyone could be evicted.

If a tenant smokes in a non-smoking property, then you can send them the letter explaining how they can be liable for the expense of cleaning up after any smoke damage. If they have an unapproved pet, you could either have them sign a pet addendum and pay the pet rent/deposit or demand that the pet is removed from the property. If the tenant causes a bug or rodent infestation, then you can educate them on how keeping the place clean helps to prevent pests. If they caused and/or did not report a mold infestation, get it cleaned up right away, charge them for it, and then educate them on how to prevent future mold.

If you ever get any noise complaints from one tenant about another tenant, ask the first tenant to talk with their noisy neighbor to create some resolution. If that's not possible, you can request the noisy tenant to keep the noise down. If the noise persists, then you can send a lease compliance letter.

If a tenant tells you they want to break the lease to leave early, you can explain that they are responsible for paying the rent through the term of the lease. One option is to tell them that you will work on getting the unit re-rented, but they then have to pay the rent until it is rented out again.

Getting Rid of Bad Tenants

For various reasons, you will sometimes need to "fire" a tenant in case things aren't working out with them. This could mean not renewing their lease, offering them "cash for keys," or even doing an eviction. If you don't fire a bad tenant, it will only cost you more time, money, as well as a fair amount of hassle. The 80/20 rule states that 80% of your problems will come from 20% of your tenants.

If someone violates their lease, you could just go through the eviction process. An easier and cheaper approach is to simply give the tenant the required amount of notice that you are not going to renew their lease when their current lease expires. That would be in place as long as the local laws allow this.

Cash for keys means offering a bad tenant money in exchange for them moving out early. To do it, you can tell the tenant that things are not working out, and you would like to give them some money (perhaps $300-500) to help them find a new place and be all moved out within the next one to two weeks. Explain that the money will be given to them if the unit is clean and free of their personal items. Once they are moved out, and the place is clean, you can have them sign the paperwork to relinquish their tenancy before handing over the money. Even though it might pain you to give money to a bad tenant, it is still a win-win situation. You get your unit back in hopefully good condition. You and the tenant both avoid having to go through the eviction process. The tenant avoids having an eviction on their record.

Sooner or later, you will need to do an eviction, and the rules about them vary between different states. DO NOT try taking things into your own hands by doing things such as turning off the utilities or changing the locks. There is a legal process in place for eviction, so you should follow it. Even though it costs money, hiring an attorney will help ensure things are done in a way that can handle any possible lawsuits. When you have to do an eviction, the following are the steps involved, but may vary based upon local regulations:

1. Give or use certified mail to get a Pay-or-Vacate/Quit Notice to the tenant. This describes that they have X number of days (per state law) to pay rent or face eviction. If their violation

was something other than nonpayment of rent, then use a Notice to Comply form.

2. Go to the courts to officially file the eviction after those X number of days has passed. You should also include the tenant's lease, a copy of the notice you gave to the tenant, and a short description of the situation.

3. The lawsuit then gets served directly to the tenant, usually by a third party.

4. At the scheduled court date, you need to bring the tenant's lease, any written communication that occurred between you and the tenant, the notice that was given to the tenant, written documentation of everything you've done regarding the situation, and finally a copy of the lawsuit that you filed. The judge will then hear both sides. The better documentation you have, the better chances you have of winning and receiving a Writ of Restitution.

5. Once you've won the lawsuit, you can then bring the Writ of Restitution to the county sheriff to schedule a removal date.

6. If the tenant is still in the property when the sheriff comes, the sheriff will remove them if needed. However, you would be in charge of changing the locks as well as removing any of the tenant's remaining items. Use a camera to video record the tenant's items before placing them by the street. If you are still owed money from the tenant, it is unlikely you will ever collect it from them.

Only when the other options are not possible, should you focus on evicting a tenant. An eviction could cost you one or more months of your time, around $5000 between court fees and lost rent, and the need to clean up after the evicted tenant leaves. When you go into a unit after its tenant was evicted, you will often find that it has been trashed.

Dealing with Contractors

Contractors can be a pain to deal with. However, the more you know about how contractors work, the better off you will be at dealing with them. A general contractor (GC) is like a project manager who oversees entire projects and would hire subcontractors like plumbers and electricians to do smaller tasks. A specialist is a licensed electrician or plumber who is highly skilled in their field. A handyman is usually an unlicensed jack-of-all-trades who can do a wide variety of tasks quite well.

A licensed contractor is good because they are more skilled, committed to doing good work, better insured, and can diagnose problems a lot faster. An unlicensed contractor is good because they are less expensive as opposed to licensed ones. Decide for yourself which type of contractor is better for each project.

Just because a contractor has a license, it doesn't mean they are any good. You can find good contractors through personal referrals from other homeowners and contractors. You can also search online through Craigslist (or Angie's List), and you can ask the employees at construction supply stores who they think is good. Once you find a contractor whom you think is good, it's time to screen them. Talk with them on the phone or in-person to get the feel if they would be right for your project. Search online to see any reviews, if they are licensed/insured, and if there are any criminal issues. Ask them for references from their previous projects and call up those references. You can always hire them to do a small project and see how it goes before giving them larger ones.

It's usually better to pay contractors by the hour for smaller jobs that are less than $500 and use bids for projects larger than that amount. You should always get a signed contract that outlines a few key things. These will include what the contractor will be doing when it will be done, and how the compensation works. You should be specific and clear with contractors, so they know exactly what you want. With large projects, you can make the payments at specific benchmarks instead of all of them upfront because that keeps the contractor focused on completing the project. You should get invoices for their work, so you have a good record of it. When the project is done, you should have a contractor sign a lien-release so they can't put a lien against your property. It is recommended to always confirm that the work is all done before you make the final payment. When you have a good contractor, you should reward them with compliments, good reviews, and perhaps even a bonus.

What to Do When Your Tenant Is Moving Out

When a tenant informs you that they plan to move out, you need to get it in writing in a Notice to Vacate form to avoid any potential misunderstandings. This gives you protection if they, for example, decide not to move after you already have a replacement tenant scheduled to move into the unit after they are expected to move out. Your lease should have information about things like the amount of time in advance to give written notice, that security deposits are not a replacement for the last month of rent, and how long they need to pay rent to remain compliant with the mutually agreed lease term. Military tenants are allowed to break a lease early without repercussions when they get deployed for duty.

You should give the departing tenant a move-out packet that includes things like an acknowledgment of notice to vacate, an itemized list of common deposit deductions, cleaning instructions, and a forwarding address form. Hence, you know where to send the deposit refund or bill for repairs/rent/cleaning, a copy of the Move-In Condition Report of pre-existing damages, and possibly a copy of the lease and a move-out survey. You can find examples of these on the website www.BiggerPockets.com/LandlordBookBonus.

After the tenant has moved out, you should do a final walk-through, and complete a Move-Out Condition Report to document the condition of the entire property. Take pictures of any damage or issues. You can either do this alone or with the tenant, depending on the local laws. You should complete any needed cleaning or repairs to prepare the unit for the next tenant.

Ideally, you will be able to give the tenant back their entire deposit because the unit is clean, in good condition, and already ready for the next tenant to move into the unit. Otherwise, you can use the deposit to cover any damages, cleaning, fees, or any missing rent. The Disposition of Deposit Form lists the charges of things that the deposit was needed to cover. It is best to use certified mail to send it, along with pictures of damages and documentation of repairs, to the tenant within the timeframe required by your state.

If the tenant disputes the charges, your documentation will help you win a potential lawsuit. If they owe more than what the deposit covered, you can decide to eat the cost, bill the tenant repeatedly until they pay, negotiate with them for a smaller payment, send their bill to collections, or take them to small claims court to get your money back.

Keeping Organized

Whether you have one unit or 100+, being organized saves you time, which allows you the freedom to not be tied to your desk and stress. It helps ensure that you stay on the right side of the Law, and it helps your real estate become more profitable. To keep things organized, you require the right tools. These include several things, so please take notes. You would need an organized file cabinet to store the mountain of paperwork and receipts, a good quality printer/scanner/copier, either a fax machine or an online fax service, a physical inbox for mail and paperwork that needs to be processed. You will also require a key box or other systems for storing and labeling keys, a bill payment system to keep up with all of your bills, a log or notebook to keep track of your mileage (which is tax-deductible). Furthermore, you will require a directory of all your tenants, a business phone number that is separate from your personal number (Google Voice is free and allows people to call a business number that forwards to your phone), a system for keeping track of maintenance requests, a list of contractors whom you like. Finally, you will need a business website that can do things like advertise your openings and accept rent payments. (There are more and more online property management software companies that can do many of these functions for cheap or even free if you look hard enough.)

Good bookkeeping is a vital part of your business success. You can decide to either do it yourself or hire a bookkeeper instead. You should keep your business and personal expenses separated from each other.it is important to track every receipt and label them clearly in case you get audited by the IRS. You should itemize all of the income as well as the expenses into the classifications listed in the IRS Schedule E Form. This needs to be done at least every month to save yourself a big headache during the tax season. You should reconcile your income and expenses with your bank account to ensure that everything is accounted for accurately. This reconciliation will save you from things such as a double charge from your insurance company. Using an electronic bookkeeping method is better because it makes it easy to create reports such as a profits-loss statement.

13 Principles for Being an Awesome Landlord

1. Commit to taking your role as a landlord seriously. Hard work and creative thinking are needed to be successful.
2. Run your real estate like a business, because that's exactly what it is. Create good systems, constantly improve things, be both firm and fair with tenants, follow the laws, and ask for help whenever you need it.
3. Create a solid foundation for your business before you sign the first lease. This includes things like good insurance as well as a policy binder.
4. Follow the Fair Housing Laws to avoid fines and potential jail time. Keep good documentation that shows that you are following the law.
5. Use smart marketing to find great tenants.
6. Pre-screen tenants to keep potential people who won't meet the minimum requirements from applying, or even from contacting you for a tour.
7. Utilize an effective application process to keep from having bad tenants in the first place. Taking the time to do this is better as opposed to dealing with bad tenants after the fact.
8. Sign an awesome lease that protects the business relationship between both you and your tenants.

9. Train your tenants on how to be good tenants starting from day one until the day they move out.
10. When problems do occur, handle them respectfully and effectively.
11. Have a good system for managing your contractors.
12. Keep organized to gain freedom, remain legal, and also increase your profits.
13. Be prepared to handle tenant turnover well.

Conclusion

Don't let your education stop here, as you can always learn how to become a more effective landlord. My advice would be to listen to podcasts, network with other landlords, join the BiggerPockets Forums, and read other books related to this topic. The Appendix has various templates for forms that you will need as a landlord, as well as resources for all 50 states in the USA. (I'm not able to give you the forms due to the copywriting, so you would need to either buy the book or go to www.BiggerPockets.com to get those.)

Additional Reading

How to Manage Residential Property for Maximum Cash Flow by John Reed

Landlording on Autopilot by Mike Butler

Chapter 12: Long-Distance Investing

Long-Distance Real Estate Investing by David Greene

Introduction

You don't have to limit yourself to only buying real estate that is close to where you reside. If you keep doing things the way you have, you'll keep on getting the same results. This book shows how to use today's technology to feel equally comfortable with investing both near and far from you.

Why You Should Consider Investing Out-of-State

Andrew Carnegie, who became incredibly wealthy in his day, said that 90% of millionaires did so through investing in real estate. Furthermore, he stated that more money had been made in real estate than all of the other industrial investments combined. If you're wise, then you will invest your money in real estate.

Many investors seek out reasons to avoid doing something, and that includes out-of-state investing. They might not think of it as safe or stable. This, in turn, causes them to miss out on many opportunities to become wealthier faster than they could by only investing locally. David describes and answers the main concerns that you might have and show how long-distance investing is quite similar to investing in your neighborhood. People fear the unknown, so it's very common for people to be afraid or uncertain when it comes to investing in properties that aren't within easy driving distance from your home. However, to truly be successful in real estate investing, you need to take your emotions out of it.

When David was starting, he worked 90 hours per week on his real estate business. While you don't have to necessarily do that, you do need to be hungry for success and willing to do whatever it takes to achieve that. By focusing on your goals and dominating your competition, you will be able to make your goals become your reality. You will also need to bring value to others by creating win-win scenarios for everyone.

It is true that long-distance real estate investing used to be more difficult as you could only go through a broker to find deals. However, the internet has empowered you to easily obtain information about opportunities far away from you with the click of a button. Now, from the comfort of your own home, you can find out which neighborhoods in which cities are up and coming. For example, www.Zillow.com gives lots of great, although not perfect, information about properties and neighborhoods all over the USA.

Investing in properties near you can be easy since you are likely very familiar with the area. However, you don't necessarily have to live in an area to be able to get to know it all that well. What matters most is that you have a complete understanding of an area. (See chapter 20 about the *Best Ever Real Estate Syndication Book* to see some resources on how to hone in on areas that would be right for your investing strategy.)

Think of different parts of the country as different fields where you could grow crops. Similarly, you could think of each area in terms of different soil, access to water, levels of sunlight, etc. Each field will be better for one type of crop or another. If your neighborhood is best suited for growing soybeans, but the soybean price isn't the best right now, then you would look at other places that can grow a more profitable crop. The concept of growing a crop is the same wherever you are located. By making the appropriate adjustments to your approach, you can yield a cash crop in many places. A wise farmer grows more than one type of crop. Similarly, a wise real estate investor invests in more than one area to cushion themselves from any hiccups that may occur in one area.

David started investing out-of-state because his area was not very profitable. He says that his advice will help you to buy, manage rentals, update, and flip out-of-state properties. He became a millionaire by doing so and wants to teach you the secrets of his success.

The Power of the Internet

You can find a treasure trove of knowledge just by searching on Google. Granted, you need to sort through the garbage info on the internet. However, once you know where to look, you can obtain all the info you need about out-of-state investing opportunities. The internet allows you to obtain data, see pictures of properties, as well as contact people who can help you.

The most common way to look for properties has been the multiple listing service (MLS). Before the internet, you would have had to go to a real estate agent's office and then looked through a large printed book of all the listings. Your access to info now is much easier and quicker. (My real estate agent created an MLS search for me with the specific criteria I'm looking for in a property. I also get an email every few days with updates to my list of potential properties. However, I have to search elsewhere for off-market deals.) Other popular websites include Zillow, Trulia, and Movoto, which get their info from the MLS. (You can even find mobile apps for these websites on your respective app store such as Google Play Store for Android devices and the App Store for Apple iOS devices.)

If you go to the website of the county tax assessor of the area where you are looking, you can usually find out the property tax information for a specific property. Zillow often has this info too. Property taxes vary greatly, so it's very important to know what you'd need to pay as part of a potential investment.

You'll also need to know what your property insurance costs might end up being. You can get an initial estimate by emailing a few homeowner's insurance companies for quotes. (You get what you pay for. If you buy the cheapest insurance, you will only get the minimal coverage on your property.)

When considering an area's desirability, look at the local school rankings. You should also look at the "walk score" to see if tenants can walk to local restaurants and stores, crime statistics, sex offender map, as well as rental rates. This info can be found through a simple online search. www.Rentometer.com, www.Zillow.com, and www.Craigslist.com are good resources for getting a good idea about local rent rates. The most accurate way to tell is by talking with a local property management company that knows the area well.

Many counties offer you the ability to see what repairs have been done on a specific property. They can do this by showing you the permits that have been done for it. This makes it easy to find out things like how old the roof and HVAC are, for example.

Believe it or not, David does not personally look at most of the properties he buys. He confirms that they pretty much exist because of the documentation, pictures, and videos about them. He also gets confirmation from his team members that the properties are real. Videos that his team members make on their smartphones allow David to see what needs to be upgraded and then document the progress.

The smartphone apps David uses include a calculator, Mortgage Calculator Plus to see potential mortgage payments, JotNot Pro to scan documents with his phone, DocuSign to electronically sign documents, a spreadsheet app like Numbers or Excel to calculate returns and keep track of properties, Rev for the creation and the playback of audio recordings, and a home search app such as Keller Williams.

Rules and Relationships

Finding deals is very essential to real estate investing. To be truly successful with that, you need to find deals that are less than the market rate, and allow you to get the most bang for your buck by adding value. Also, to be successful with that, you need a competitive edge in your business, such as by having an efficient system with great people working in it. Your people are your biggest and most important asset.

Depending on your investment strategy, you will want to invest in a different market area. If you are flipping houses, you want an area with properties that can sell for more than the cost of the purchase and repairs at the least. If you want to buy and hold, you want an area where rents are more than the cost of owning the property. You will need to do your homework and due diligence to decide which investment strategy to pursue.

A common rule for estimating the profitability of a rental property is the one percent rule. If the rent the property brings in is at least one percent of the purchase price, it's generally a keeper. For example, a $100,000 house should bring in at least $1000 in rent each month. If it brings in more than that in rent, it's probably a better than average deal. If the property is in poor condition or a dangerous area, then you may apply the two percent rule instead to have enough cushion to handle any potential problems. There are, of course, many other factors to consider, such as management costs, taxes, vacancy rates, etc. If a $100,000 property is bringing in $2000 per month in rent, you should be cautious about the additional problems you might have to face with owning it.

If you are doing flips, the 70 percent rule is a better one. Take the after-repair value (ARV) times 0.7 and then subtract the repair cost. That then equals how much you should be willing to pay for a distressed property to flip. For example, if the property will be worth $100,000 after you do $15,000 in repairs, then $100,000 x 0.7 = $70,000. $70,000 - $15,000 = $55,000 is what you could potentially offer.

The 50 percent rule is where you conservatively plan on spending 50% of the rental income on repairs and hold costs that don't include the mortgage costs. If you end up needing to spend less than that, it's all the better.

There are many different ways to invest in real estate. David mainly flips houses and owns rental properties. An example of another approach is something called the "slow flip." That is where you buy a property for less than market value, fix it up, maybe live in it, own it for a year or two, and then sell it for a profit. Vacation rentals are another example of a way to invest in real estate. You might be able to get a higher return by renting out your properties for short terms through places such as Airbnb, Craigslist, or VRBO. (Look into the local laws first before jumping head first into doing vacation rentals.)

The First People to Include on Your Team

Whether you're investing across the street or the country, you need to partner up with other people to maximize your success. (I've heard it said that your network is your net worth.) You don't have to know everything right now to be successful as long as you start working with people who already know what you want to learn. You can start by making a list of the people you already know who invest in real estate or are connected to real estate in some way or another. They are your first connections into the world of real estate and can also put you in touch with their networks as well.

Even if you think that no one can do things better than you, you only have so much time each day. It's time to start leveraging other people's knowledge and skills to help you in achieving your goals. If you had a restaurant business and you were the only one working there, how many customers could you serve by yourself? Probably not very many. However, if you automate it and have a team of people working at it, your customers will be served properly, and profits will go way up. The same is true with real estate where it's essential to work together with others. www.BiggerPockets.com is a website for investors at every level. It's a community that allows you to instantly grow your network and quickly build your knowledge base.

When you are building your team, you will require a deal finder who could be a real estate agent, broker, wholesaler, and property manager, etc. You could then train them on the specific criteria you want in an investment property, and pay them well for finding deals that match your criteria. Go to Zillow or make some calls to an area where you want to invest. This way, you can get referrals for the top real estate agents and brokers in that area. Those are the people you want on your team.

Once you narrow it down to an agent that you like, you can start by emailing them. In your email, you should mention that you are an investor and you understand real estate. Then, you should describe what you are looking to invest in, talk about how you will purchase the investment(s), and mention how you heard about them. In the book, David gives some examples of emails to send to real estate agents as well as lenders. The agents who respond will probably have some questions for you. It's best to get to know those agents to see which of them align closely with your investment plan. If they own any real estate investments and they used a system for finding those investments, that's all the better. Once they trust that you're dead serious about investing, they can close quickly, and aren't a total pain in the butt. Hence, they will start sending the best deals your way.

Unless you have an unlimited supply of cash, you will need to work with a lender at some point. A lender could be a bank, credit union, savings and loan institution, hard money lender, or even someone you know who is willing to lend you money. The options you will find with mortgage lenders will vary widely. Therefore, it's worth your time to shop around for one that matches your investment plan.

By knowing what banks want to see will help make your lending smoother. The main thing lenders look at when considering to loan cash to you is your debt to income (DTI) ratio. Your income needs to cover the cost of the mortgage payments. Paying off your credit cards is the quickest way to improve your DTI. Lenders also look at the loan-to-value (LTV), which determines whether the bank can recover their money through foreclosure if you stop making payments at some point. A bigger down payment results in a more favorable LTV. Another key thing that lenders look at is your credit score. That describes your credit trustworthiness. The better score you have, the better rates and terms you will get with your loans. Once you have five or more loans out, the rules about them start to become stricter. If you have ten or more mortgages, you may have to get a portfolio lender who gives you one mortgage that covers multiple properties.

It helps to find a lender who is willing to work for you. You can build a better relationship with them by offering a larger down payment, sending them referrals for new business opportunities, or offering to open an account at their institution to keep your earnings from the property. Credit unions tend to have more flexibility with these kinds of things. An internet search for investor-friendly lenders in the area will help you in narrowing down your search for a lender. You could also ask for referrals from other investors that you know.

The Next People for Your Team

The next person you'll need is a good property manager who manages the day-to-day operations of your property. This is especially true when you have a property that is far away from where you reside. Like most things in life, you get what you pay for. To get a good property manager, you need to pay a good rate, and that will vary based on the size of your property. On average, David pays his property managers 7% of the rental income he earns each month as their commission. For example, if a house brings in $1000 in rent, he pays the property manager $70 of that. (Often with smaller properties, you will have to pay upwards of 10%. Sometimes, places with 100+ units can pay their property managers as little as 3-4%. You are better off paying more for a great manager than paying pennies for a terrible one.) Your property manager takes midnight calls from your tenants, deals with angry tenants, and oversees repairs and upgrades. It is recommended to treat them well, so you don't have to handle all of these things by yourself.

Before you hire a property manager, ask them the following questions:

1. What is your experience in property management?
2. What monthly percentage of rental income will you be taking as a commission?
3. What are the other fees that you would charge?
4. How often will my property get inspected throughout the year?

5. How do you handle maintenance requests that come your way?
6. How well do you handle evictions?
7. What is the average amount of time you spend turning a vacant unit?
8. (I also like to ask them for some referrals of the other property owners they are working for currently.)

You will also need good contractors who can do the repairs/upgrades that your property manager cannot and will not do. These will include roofers, plumbers, painters, flooring installers, etc. You should Get multiple bids for each project, and ask for itemized lists of any repairs. This way, you know what your money is getting you.

David goes into good detail on how to work with property managers, so you can get the best value for your money. You can get referrals for good property managers, handymen/women, lenders, and real estate agents through other investors, real estate investment associations (REIAs), or just by going on good real estate websites such as www.BiggerPockets.com. Word-of-mouth from other investors, BiggerPockets, (and www.AngiesList.com) are also great resources to find contractors.

How to Understand Your Market

With each market, various factors impact how many people are moving there and what the rental rates will be. These are things such as jobs, wages, local economy, taxes, weather, etc. When these things change, so does the housing demand. You will want to choose a market that works well with your specific investment strategy.

The value of real estate is cyclical in nature, where it goes up and down. Over the long term, it does go up in value. Do not wait to invest in real estate. It's better to invest in real estate and then wait instead. Real estate is not a get rich quick scheme. However, it a solid way to get rich slowly. It's impossible to guess where property values will be in the next couple of years. If the values do go down, you only lose money if you sell. When the prices of properties are going down, that's a great time to be buying them at a discount. When you know why prices are going down, that helps clue you in as to what to expect for the future. For example, if jobs are leaving the market for good, then you might just want to sell right away and accept the loss.

It's helpful to know the ins and outs of the area. A local property management company can help you learn them well. If there's a changing shift in a neighborhood that you can use to your advantage, they can then clue you into it.

Don't spend all of your time looking for deals. Instead, you should look for people who can find the deals and then help you with them. A local realtor or property manager can keep you updated on changing rent rates, what amenities tenants expect, local laws, market trends, and market conditions, etc. It sets you up for success if you buy in an area where the demand is increasing for rental space. Counting on appreciation is tricky business, so you should focus instead on the supply and demand.

How to Work with the Market

"Look at market fluctuations as your friend rather than your enemy; profit from folly rather than participate in it." -Warren Buffett

When David looks at a property and a market, the main formula he uses is known as the return on investment (ROI). This is calculated by taking one year of cash flow and dividing it by your initial down payment. The ROI can change from one year to the next as it is based on the rates of rents and expenses. You can use ROI to quickly compare properties and markets. However, ROI does not show the whole picture.

There is another formula you can use as well. It's called return on equity (ROE). It is calculated by taking the annual cash flow and dividing it by the equity in the property. The equity is how much value is in the property that isn't covered by a mortgage or any other lien. If your ROE is lower than your ROI, it is better to consider cashing out the equity to invest in another property.

When you are considering a property to buy or market to invest in, you should think about how much a headache it will give you and if the money you will get is worth it. You need to see if it is a needy property or market that you're willing to deal with due to the awesome cash flow from it. Do you prefer a lower cash flowing property or market that is very much hands-off? Or do you want something in between? Are you buying a job, or creating an investment? Find what works best for you.

One way you can decrease your headaches is by improving your ROI. That can be achieved by decreasing expenses and/or increasing income. If you have a good tenant in a unit, you may wish to think about whether it is worth it to raise their rent and risk losing them or to keep their rent the same and miss out on the potential increased income instead. An efficient system and an awesome property manager will help take away many of your headaches before you even have them. You will still need to supervise the property manager, though. If you do find yourself getting into problems, consider them to be learning opportunities that will help you become a better investor and landlord.

David likes to set up leases so that they expire in the beginning or middle of the summer. This is because it puts him in a much better position to raise rents. After all, people don't want to try to find a place at the same time when everyone else is looking. If a tenant decides not to renew their lease, it's easier for David to find a new tenant or just sell the property. Rents tend to go hand-in-hand with home prices, and prices are higher in the summer because the market then is hot.

If you find yourself in a situation where you need a tenant to leave (such as you selling the property or needing to do an eviction), one option is called "cash for keys." This is where you offer a tenant some money to give you the keys and break the lease, and you can maybe even help them find a new place to live.

How to Manage Your Out-of-State Properties

The main question of this book is: How is it even possible to find, rehab, and manage out-of-state properties? Real estate investing takes a lot of work, whether it's across the street or the country. The long-distance approach just requires some variations or extra steps to make it work. If you buy a property that doesn't need any or much work done on it, it's called a "turnkey" property. While turnkey properties are easier, they also have a lower profit margin than properties that you can just rehab to add more value to them (value-add). If you want to build wealth faster, you may wish to go with value-add properties. If you prefer to maintain the wealth you already have, then turnkey properties might be better for you.

If you invest in any value-add properties, you will need to work with contractors. Make sure you get an itemized bid from each contractor that lists the full scope of their work, the price for each thing, and the timeline for completion. (Consult an attorney for the full details on contract law.) The two main things that can go wrong is the rehab cost goes up, and secondly, the timeline gets extended past the deadline. Both of these will cost you money. David likes to offer contractors a bonus if they finish up a project on time (he even gives them an extra week past what the contractor requested), but also charge a penalty if they finish after the deadline. In the contract, he'll write something like "Contractor will be paid a 5% bonus if the project is finished by X number of days. Contractor will be assessed a 5% penalty after the deadline for each additional week they take to complete the project. Owner retains the right to approve the quality of the completed work."

This accountability clause helps motivate the contractor to do good work within the expected timeframe, both through positive and negative reinforcements. David also tells the contractor that he will have professional pictures take on the work when it's complete. He will then put those with the contractor's name all over social media. This further motivates the contractor so they can keep a good reputation.

When getting started, you may wish to choose and buy the building materials yourself instead of having the contractor take care of that end. This helps prevent an overcharge, you know what you will be getting, you have more control over the project, and it also teaches you about the materials and construction. (Some stores, such as Home Depot, will give you great discounts, do a free analysis of what materials you need, and ship the materials to your property for free when you sign up to be a contractor with them, which is also free to do.) Some contractors might allow you to use their contractor accounts to purchase the materials too. The more you are involved, the more of your time and energy will be required. However, keep in mind that while contractors care about their work, they don't care about your project nearly as much as you do.

David creates an atmosphere for his contractors to keep them motivated to do good work. He also makes them aware that if they do slow or bad work, it will hurt their business. He helps them see how his goals and their goals are aligned. David, however, avoids harassing, threatening, or micromanaging his contractors.

You will, of course, need to pay your contractors for their work. It is not a good idea to pay contracts the full price before they do the work. David prefers to pay them after the work is done and possibly break it down by paying the contractor portions of the payment per the steps of the project as they are completed on time along with good quality. You may need to pay some money upfront so the contractor can buy the materials if you want them to be in charge of doing that. You should ALWAYS verify that your contractors have completed their work adequately. This is, so you know that what you agreed upon is what you are getting in the end. Asking for pictures and videos is another great way to do this.

Think of the people working with you as your partners. These include contractors, lenders, real estate agents/brokers, property managers, etc. You should show them that their opinions and insights do matter and that they are an important part of the project. This proactive approach will show them a level of respect and inclusion that will, in turn, increase the chances of them reciprocating the same. This is especially important when you are not going to physically be at the property regularly. You should ask your team members what you can do to add value to them. This might include things like giving them referrals, praising them on your social media, or introducing them to other people who can help them.

How to Find Materials

Finding the materials might be intimidating, or it might be exciting if you love the house flipping shows you see on HGTV. After you go through the process of finding and buying the materials once, it gets a lot easier after that. You should collaborate with the contractor, so you are on the same page with the type of materials to be used. If you need ideas, go to websites like Pinterest, Houzz, or Tumblr. There's no need to reinvent the wheel when it's much easier to just copy the approaches and systems that other successful people are already using effectively.

Other people have already done similar projects to yours, and you can simply duplicate what they have already done. You can even use social media, BiggerPockets, a personal blog, or emails to get advice from other people on which designs they think are the best considering your budget and the property's location. You can use services like MailChimp to send a mass email to multiple people without them knowing that it's a mass email. David credits BiggerPockets for giving him the confidence to stick with real estate investing and also become successful with it. It's an online forum that you can join for free and share knowledge with and ask for advice from other real estate investors.

Malcolm Forbes said, "Never hire someone who knows less than you do about what he's hired to do." If you are more knowledgeable than a contractor about their work, then you should find a better contractor. They should be able to give you some samples and design ideas of what they can do for you. Contractors probably think about becoming an investor like you. They should have some great design ideas because they know the variety of designs that are being used in the field.

Once you know the colors and style you want, it's then time to start shopping around for good prices. The design specialists at supply stores, such as Home Depot or Lowes, can assist you in this regard. If David is having a kitchen updated, he will call a store, talk to the kitchen design specialist, and email or text them pictures of what he is looking for. Then the specialist can send David pictures of what is available in the store that matches his requirements. David then makes a note of the model numbers and prices so he can see if another store can offer a better value. You might even be able to negotiate for better prices. At the very least, it doesn't hurt to ask even if there is no negotiation in the end.

When deciding what upgrades to do, it's best to keep your emotions out of it. This is an investment and not a remodel on your residence. Look at the surrounding neighborhood and do upgrades that make your property on par with the properties in the surrounding area. If you do too little, you won't maximize your profits. Similarly, if you overdo it with the rehab, then you won't be able to increase the rent enough to account for the extra rehab expense. Your goal is to spend the minimum amount of money necessary to get the most bang for your buck. Part of knowing the right amount of upgrades comes from good experience, whether it be your experience or that of someone you're working with on a project. Part of it is math because you are aiming for a certain after repair value (ARV), and you want a certain return on your rehab money.

Some repairs/upgrades might be necessary, such as a working roof, windows, appliances, flooring, doors, and even toilets. Some are unnecessary perks that may not pay off. These could include stone accents, built-in bookshelves, upgraded baseboards, fancy landscaping, a security system, heated floors, or skylights. The kinds of things from the second list may or may not impress buyers or renters enough to get you higher prices. However, that depends on what things are considered standard for the area. If an upgrade isn't going to increase the value of your property, then it's recommended to not do it!

One investment strategy is called "house hacking," which is when you buy a house, live in a part of it, and rent out the rest of the portions. The rents then make it, so you live for free or very cheaply. Many people (including myself) find this to be a good way to start in real estate investing. David says that you can "hack" your contractors by using their strengths while minimizing their weaknesses. Ask them what work they do themselves and what work they hire subcontractors to do. Furthermore, ask your contractors where they can bring you the most value and who they know that can do the same with things your contractors aren't necessarily the best at doing.

David has coined the idea of hacking upgrades as well. This is when you already have to replace something, such as a kitchen countertop. Instead of replacing it with similar materials, he considers whether paying more to get better materials will, in turn, essentially create a better return. Essentially, if you were already going to pay for a replacement, why not pay a little more for an upgrade when it makes more sense? An easy version of this is replacing old white appliances with new stainless-steel appliances that are cheap. This is because they are last year's models. This then allows you to charge more rent when renting and also a higher price when selling. David likes to focus on hacking the upgrades with paint, flooring (especially in bathrooms), showers, rainfall showerheads, cabinets, countertops, and adding extra bedrooms.

The main factors that determine value include the location, square feet, number of bedrooms, as well as upgrades in the property. While it's rather difficult to change a property's location, the other factors are much easier to control. Before you start adding bedrooms to a property, you can ask your team whether that will add enough value to make it worth doing so. It is probably worth it except in a very cheap market. Focus on turning a two or three-bedroom property into a three- or four-bedroom property to maximize your profits.

You'll need to also consider whether a property has space for additional legal bedrooms. You'll need to see if the property has space such as a large storage area, a den, a bonus room with no door, a playroom, extra family room or living room, an unfinished attic, an unfinished basement, a large mudroom, a covered patio, or a sunroom. If that is the case, you are in good shape. (If you have a duplex with an unfinished basement, you could just rehab it and add it as additional space to one of the two units instead of going through the hassle of getting the property rezoned into a triplex.)

You can certainly build an addition to the house when it makes good sense to do so. However, it's much more cost-effective to simply convert a pre-existing space into a bedroom. When looking at potential investment properties, you should consider if there are such spaces that you can convert into bedrooms and/or bathrooms. Raised foundations and big backyards also make it easier to add additions to a property.

To sum it up, you can build long-term wealth by increasing both your equity and cash flow. When you create equity through upgrades, you can just refinance to pull out some of that equity. Then, you can reinvest that money into buying your next property. (See my chapter on the BRRRR method for details on how to do this.)

How to Maximize Your Return on Investment

If you are willing to do some extra work, you can get larger profits with value-add properties relative to turnkey properties that are already in perfect shape. One thing that many people overlook is to add value by adding or removing walls. For example, removing a wall between the kitchen and dining room can create a modern open look that will appeal to both renters and buyers. Just be sure not to knock down a wall that is also bearing weight. If you have a large storage space or an extra living room, you could add a wall in the middle to turn it into two bedrooms.

David recommends buying bad homes in good areas as opposed to good homes in bad areas. You can improve the home, but can't improve the location. If you buy the best house in the neighborhood, there's no room for improvement. If you buy the worst house in a good area, then there is potentially a lot of profit that can be made. There are good opportunities when there are a lot of houses on the market, when a property is in poor condition, or when the owner is motivated to sell quickly.

Houses in good condition can be bought with bank loans for top dollar. David finds houses in poor condition that won't qualify for bank loans. Then he's only in competition with the smaller number of cash buyers. As mentioned earlier, DO NOT over upgrade the properties that you rehab to make them nicer than the other houses in the neighborhood. If you do so, you are pretty much throwing your money down the toilet. Over upgrading a property is like putting $5000 rims on a $3000 car. To prevent yourself from over upgrading, look at pictures of other local homes, or have your local partners tour local homes.

Tips and Tricks

You can set up electronic rent payments, so you don't have to wait for checks to arrive in the mail. Automatic direct deposits scheduled for the beginning of each month work the best. However, you can also accept credit card payments, Venmo, PayPal, or any other money transfer apps.

Leveraging other people's money to make you money is a beautiful thing. As long as you are bringing more money in than what is going out for loan payments and other costs, you are golden. Using long term low-interest loans on your rental properties, you are pretty much maximizing your returns on your investment. If you only use other people's money on a deal, and you still make an income from it. Therefore, you are getting an infinite return on your $0.

When interest rates are low, you might consider doing a cash-out refinance. You can also get a home equity line of credit (HELOC) on your property. This is a line of credit that you can use to invest in other things, such as investing in another property, or performing upgrades to your existing property. As long as your tenants are paying enough to cover the mortgage and/or HELOC payments, long-term debt is a great way to leverage your property value.

Some states have friendlier landlord laws than others. Some areas have a greater "pride in ownership" where tenants take very good care of properties. Some markets have employers who retain their employees for longer and also give good pay. Many cities have limitations on the number of new houses that can be built, thus increasing the demand for rentals. Rougher neighborhoods tend to have older properties. The newer the property, the fewer repairs and upgrades you'll need to worry about. A better market will have better property managers, contractors, lenders, and agents.

If you spend your energy micromanaging your investments, you will fall into the trap of busywork and start to hate real estate. What you need to do is instead of focusing on the day-to-day operations of your real estate portfolio is to focus on the bigger picture things such as finding and acquiring new properties or building relationships with lenders, brokers, as well as other investors.

While you can certainly find good deals on the multiple listing service (MLS), David likes to find the best deals through REO, short sale, NOD, and other unfinished projects. A good realtor or broker can help you find a shortlist of these kinds of deals. Then, you can send letters or make calls to the homeowners to offer them solutions.

Real estate owned (REO) are properties that have been foreclosed on by the bank. The bank doesn't want to own property because they are not in the real estate business. This is why they are often willing to sell at a discount. Double-check that there aren't any hidden liens on the property that will eat into the profit margin. You should ask if there are other offers on the property because a bidding war will result in a much higher purchase price. You can check out www.HomePath.com to see a list of foreclosures that Fanny Mae wants to sell directly to investors.

Short sales are when the seller sells their property for less than what they owe on the mortgage, and the bank agrees to it. This way, they get some of their money back at least. These pose more challenges than regular home purchases. This is because they are contingent on the bank's approval of the discount sale. It can take many months to hear back from the bank about their final decision. If the property decreases too much in value while you are waiting, you can always cancel the deal before the bank gets back to you with their decision. If the property increases in value while you wait, then that's just some extra icing on the cake for you.

A notice of default (NOD) is issued when a homeowner is behind on their mortgage and is in danger of foreclosure. When you buy a NOD property, you save the owner from having a foreclosure on their credit report. It is helpful to build rapport with them and find what their motivations are. Also offer them solutions that match those motivations.

Unfinished projects are when someone else was doing a rehab but didn't finish for one reason or another. These tend not to qualify for conventional loans and, therefore, making the purchase only available to cash buyers. These homes can be purchased for a discount. Plus, it's nice that the construction is already partially completed. If you don't have enough money yourself to make a cash offer, you can just do a joint venture with other investors to make it happen.

You should always get an inspection before things are finalized. If possible, you should put an inspection clause in your offer. That way, you can renegotiate the price, have the owner get some repairs done, or just back out of the deal if needed. You need to make sure you are aware of potential issues for the local market, such as mold, termites, dry rot, frozen pipes in northern climates, or roofs needing to be replaced often in rainy Florida.

When you have a real estate agent/broker, they get paid a commission to find the deals, and they then help you negotiate them. Once you're more experienced, you could consider an approach of not having a real estate agent of your own. You would need to then search for, analyze, and then make offers directly to the owner or their agent. If you ask the seller's agent to be your agent as well, their commission will increase if you decide to make the purchase. That is a huge incentive for the seller's agent to help you become the buyer, even if it means that the price has to drop for you to make the purchase.

On page 276 of his book, David shows you the script that he uses for the initial communication to a seller's agent for this method. Since David doesn't want to get endless emails in an email drip campaign, he asks the agents to just keep him in mind about specific property criteria instead of setting him up on a general search. David also likes to offer agents a bonus of around $1000 for finding him deals that he then purchases. This motivates the agents to use all of their resources and connections to bring David awesome deals.

The methods to use for long-distance investing are no different from what you would use locally. The main difference is in your head. If you think long-distance investing is hard or risky, then you will find it to be so. Instead, you can use resources on the internet as well as your team to make it as smooth as investing in your neighborhood. There are countless more investment opportunities when you stop limiting yourself to your local market. Find the hard-working agents, contractors, and property managers willing to do the hardest work, leaving you with the fun parts of investing in real estate.

Conclusion

This is an excellent book at teaching you the skills and inside tips to be more efficient and effective as a real estate investor. Long-distance investing forces you to give up things that would be relatively easier to do at close-by properties. However, you can apply all of the things from the book regardless of where you decide to invest. This means that you are delegating every task that can. This allows you to work on growing your business instead of doing the day-to-day tasks in your business.

Additional Reading

Long-Distance Real Estate Investing: Find Properties with Real Potential and Achieve Wealth and Cash Flow by Robert Smith

Out of State: A Practical Guide to Long-Distance Real Estate Investing by R.M. Andrews

Chapter 13: Short-Term Rentals

The Airbnb Expert's Playbook: Secrets to Making Six-Figures as a Rentalpreneur by Scott Shatford

Introduction

Written in 2014, this book stands the test of time in describing how to be successful with Airbnb. Scott talks about the story of how he got into renting his apartment on Airbnb and how nervous he was to do it. He had experience in the field of corporate analytics while working in corporate America. He then put it to use in the analysis of his Airbnb business. He improved pricing, cut utilities, automated the check-in process, and successfully increased his monthly income while decreasing his work time to less than four hours per week.

Then, he expanded and rented out a second apartment that he got specifically to have as another Airbnb, which he turned a profit on. He then started adding a new rental on Airbnb about every four months. Without actually owning any properties, he made a profit of about $180K per year in 2014. He focuses on renting high-end apartments in touristy areas, and then Airbnbs them out year-round. Each apartment provides approximately $25K in profit the first year, which then increases to around $35K each year after that.

A shared economy occurs when you use your assets by renting them out when you're not using them. If you have tools or a car and you're not using them all the time, why not rent them out the rest of the time to pay for their cost? Airbnb allows you to rent out your couch, room, apartment, home, yard, boat, RV, yurt, cabin, treehouse, castle, or experience to create an additional stream of revenue for yourself.

History of Airbnb

Here's how Airbnb started, or rather how three guys went from nothing to a $35 billion company as of 2018. Joe and Brian were two guys living in San Francisco. They decided to rent out three air mattresses on their floor for $80 each so that they could afford to live in their apartment. In the year 2007, they made a basic website with simple maps. Joe and Brian thought that this could be a big idea. They built up their website some more with the help of their other roommate, Nathan, and then launched at South By South West for some funding and got some bookings. They made $200 per week for months. They then uploaded better pictures of their rental spaces and doubled their weekly income to $400. They raised $200K, then $7.2M, then $112M, and blew up from there.

Airbnb has disrupted the hotel industry by making every person into a micro-entrepreneur who now has available space to rent. There are millions of people in this world who would be interested in renting your space or just the experience. As of 2019, there were over six million Airbnb listings worldwide. On average, there are over two million people who stay in an Airbnb rental every night. It is truly a monster machine. By participating in being a host, you can also get a piece of this gigantic pie.

Rental Arbitrage

Scott created an Airbnb analytics tool called AirDNA. This lets you know how many listings are in your city (only applicable in the United States) and how much they are charging for those listings. He rents out high-end apartments and then re-rents them through Airbnb. This is what is known as an arbitrage opportunity. You need to just make sure that there is a significant enough difference between what you're paying for rent and what you're charging for Airbnb rentals.

Airbnb has a guest screening and reservation process. That takes care of many of the administrative duties so that you don't have to bother with those. This brings your operation costs down so much that it makes it easier for you to run the rentals at a profit.

Scott gets questioned by his friends how he could have replaced his corporate six-figure salary just by simply re-renting out local apartments. They question if it is legal, whether he let his landlord(s) know, and if he is worried about regulations.

Scott's website www.RentingYourPlace.com will let you see your area and the current prices for comparable places, occupancy rates, as well as estimated income. AirDNA can even help you find existing successful properties and then replicate them to capitalize on the need that is already existing in that area. You can copy the general location, amenities, pricing, decorations, style of photos you use, and the content you put in your listing.

You may first wish to approach your landlord about subleasing your space. Approximately 75% of Airbnb hosts are breaking the terms of their lease because most rental leases have a "no subleasing" clause. (That can cause legal issues if the landlord or apartment management finds out you're subleasing without approvals and breaking terms of your lease. You may lose the right to lease that property, and that would leave you with legal issues. It might be just that many property managers don't want strangers wandering around or hurting themselves and then filing a lawsuit. When it comes down to it, property managers and owners just want to know whether they are going to get paid each month.

Scott has some tips, listed below, about finding property managers who are open to you renting out space with Airbnb:

1. Bigger is not always better. Approach smaller property managers who have smaller and fewer buildings. They have the authority to be more flexible.

2. Get your landlord involved. You could give them some extra income by having them do the guest check-ins for a fee that you pay directly to them.

3. Act like a professional. You should show the property manager that you are a professional by talking about your previous experience with using Airbnb and how well you have been taking care of the apartment.

4. White lies don't hurt. If you are telling them you are going to be re-renting the place to strangers from the internet, they may be less likely to be open to working with you.

However, if you tell some white lies about it just being occasional to have people over, then they might be more willing to allow it.

Airbnb's Competitors

There are many competitors of Airbnb who provide similar services. These include www.FlipKey.com, www.VRBO.com www.HomeAway.com, and www.VacationRentals.com. Some people even list their space on multiple sites and then coordinate to make sure their space doesn't get double-booked. (I've seen a lot of people who drive for both Uber and Lyft and toggle their picks between the two apps so that they can maximize their profits.)

The other sites often charge you an upfront fee as the host, and then try to upcharge you for a "premium package" to make your listing more visible than others. Airbnb, on the other hand, only charges you when a booking has been confirmed. Airbnb is different than the other sites. This is because it has fewer restrictions and a more dynamic marketplace. It handles the transactions for you, allows for their bookings to be done instantly, and streamlines the reservation process, so you have to do very less legwork. All these things together allow for a higher volume of bookings at your place.

Airbnb may not necessarily be the right option for everyone. If you have a higher value place, such as over $500 per night, or are looking for mainly longer-term tenants who last for more than a month at a time, then you should consider one of Airbnb's competitors.

There are ten reasons why Airbnb ranks on the top of the short-term rental market.

1. Airbnb appreciates and rewards those hosts who are responsive to guests and receive great reviews by improving the searchability of their listings.

2. The transactions are hassle-free for both you and your guests.

3. Airbnb provides one-click reservation options with its "Instant Book" feature.

4. Airbnb has a great review process in place for the guest to review the host and vice versa.

5. It is popular internationally, so you will have potential guests from all over the world.

6. It is pretty much one-stop shopping for vacation rentals.

7. Airbnb has a better interface that is user friendly for both the renters and the hosts than their competitors.

8. There is a ton of flexibility with everything, including the space you rent as well as the scheduling.

9. Airbnb manages the calendar for you. You set your availability, and it takes care of the rest of the scheduling. (You then wait for an email or notification on your Airbnb app about a rental request from a prospective guest.)

10. The bottom line is that Airbnb just gives you excellent results.

What Kind of Airbnb Person Are You?

Instead of a micro-preneur, Scott sees himself as rental-preneur. Also, there are five different types of Airbnb entrepreneurs.

1. The Couch Surfer: www.CouchSurfer.com is like a free version of Airbnb, where you can lend your couch out to travelers and borrow other people's couches when you travel. The couch surfer approach to Airbnb works by looking for other budget-minded travelers by selling themselves as much as their Airbnb space. Their potential guests are more interested in learning about the host as opposed to the shape and size of the room.

2. The Savvy Opportunist: When there is a big festival or sporting event in your town, you can take advantage and capitalize on it. (The Super Bowl was in my city just a few years ago, and I knew of a lot of people who didn't want to deal with the craziness and traffic that weekend. They then left town but rented out their home or apartment to make TOP DOLLAR during that time.) It could be other things like film festivals, art festivals, marathons, car shows, the Olympics, business conferences, and tourist events. Instead of thinking about the best season for you to visit a destination, you need to think about the best time that someone else would want to visit your city. If you do this right, then you can finance your entire next vacation by just renting out that peak time for tourists to come to your area.

3. The Jet Setter: These are people who live quite a spontaneous lifestyle. They are occasionally at home but are often traveling. Whenever they happen to be away is the time they rent out their space on Airbnb. This is a great approach for people who have flexible schedules or jobs that cause them to travel a lot and be away from their primary residence. This is also a great approach to make extra cash if you have a significant other, friend, or family member whom you can stay with for a few days. If you do this, you will want to make sure you have very clear house rules including what is off-limits to your guests so that you protect your items. You should be sure to keep the common areas clean so that your guests can feel at home as much as possible.

4. The Traditional Vacation Home Owner: These are people who are perhaps accustomed to the old-style vacation rental model and then apply it to Airbnb. What happens is that by listing their rental space on multiple websites, spending a lot more time managing their calendars, extra screening, requiring a higher security deposit and longer stays, and by not allowing instant booking, this group potentially keeps away good renters as well as rental income. This group needs to learn how to trust more in the Airbnb approach.

5. The Full-Time Rental-preneur: These people have one or more properties they rent all the time and focus on maximizing their revenue by getting to 100% occupancy. The best way to make this approach is to test the waters by

renting out your primary residence during your time off, very much like the jet setter, or the savvy opportunist. If you do well with that, you can then expand to your next rental location(s).

Creating and Marketing Your Listing

The goal from your listing is to get as many bookings at your place to maximize your profits. Your listing should include the following:

1. An eye-catching headline that makes people think that your place is a once-in-a-lifetime must-have experience in four or five words. Things like "Charming Cottage in the Mountains," "Chic Apartment Overlooking Downtown," or "Ski to the Hot Tub" are fine examples.

2. An exciting description that is both punchy and precise. Talk about what makes your place stand out, such as how your amenities create a great experience. You should finish with a call to action, such as "Act fast to guarantee your booking!"

3. Beautiful pictures are the most important part. It is recommended to use a wide-angle lens and lighting to make the place look bright and airy. Take shots from the corner of rooms from a high angle to accentuate the size. You should Include some close-up shots of details like flowers or artwork. Also, you can include pictures of the surrounding area, such as the views of nearby attractions. Airbnb is willing to visit your place once to take pictures as well.

4. A quality personal profile shows that you are personable and trustworthy. That is the first impression the prospective renter gets from you.

Airbnb has an algorithm that you can hack to make your listing be shown to more people. You can do so by doing things like responding quickly when someone inquires, keeping your booking calendar up-to-date, allowing reservations to be instantly booked by guests, linking your Airbnb account to your social media.

Determining Pricing

Around 60% of your income comes from your property's quality, location, and amenities. The other 40% comes from using an effective strategy for pricing. You can start by looking at what other similar places in the area are charging during the next three to six months broken down by the days of the week. Your daily rate will need to vary depending on the supply and demand.

When starting, rent your place for around 25% below market value before slowing raising the rates. As a general rule, if at least 25% of the dates are reserved three months in advance, it's time to raise your rates. When you have vacancies in the next week, you should drop your rates down. By reducing your rates by about 5% per day during the final seven to ten days, Airbnb seems to increase the visibility of your listing.

You could charge security deposits and fees for additional guests, but Scott does not recommend doing so. Airbnb allows you to charge an extra cleaning fee per stay. That encourages guests to stay for longer to get their money's worth. You can also consider requiring a minimum number of days guests have to stay, which is especially helpful when you have three to four days open in your upcoming calendar.

When there are special events like a big sporting game or festival, you might be able to charge up to five times your normal rates. There are often more last-minute bookings during big events. You should pay attention to the upcoming local event calendar and use it to your advantage.

Furnishing Your Airbnb

You need to understand who the guests are who will rent your place and what their expectations are. Business travelers will want different furniture than budget-minded travelers. Things like a printer vs. a piano will attract a different crowd. Technology is an important part of a smooth-running property. Wireless locks, wi-fi, smart TVs with streaming services, and wireless thermostats are good additions.

You should decide on a theme to the furniture and design to make it appear authentic and local. For example, if your Airbnb is on the beach, you can use a beach theme with seashells. Similarly, a place near a major stadium could have a sporting theme. Pretend like you are staging the property for sale.

It is recommended to use neutral colors for walls and color to accent the place through the furniture, artwork, and accessories. You should limit the number of expensive and breakable items, though.

You want the place to be as welcome to everyone as possible. You should, hence, avoid excess clutter, personal items, and religious/political things.

To maximize your income at a property, you should find a way to have as many beds as possible. For example, the couch in the living room could be a futon or a sleeper sofa. You are better off buying better quality furniture that will last as opposed to using cheap stuff that always breaks. Craigslist, Ikea, Urban Home, Cort, and Facebook Marketplace are good places to find affordable and possibly good yet slightly used furniture.

How to Run Your Airbnb Business

The fewer vacancies you have, the better it is for your Airbnb business. People who book long stays are best. It's okay to decline requests of people wanting to only stay a few nights if the days they booked create awkward calendar gaps before and after their stay. Scott has also declined to rent to people asking to use the space for events, such as a party or for filming.

You might sometimes come across a guest who will trash your place or steal things, but this is a very rare occurrence. Airbnb allows you to screen potential guests by looking at their member profile, connected social media, Airbnb's ID verification process, and also reviews from previous hosts.

Closing the Deal

If you handle the reservation requests yourself, you will get requests at every time of day and night and need to respond to them quickly, so that you don't miss the potential income. You need to respond with a sense of urgency that your place is available for now but that someone else is also interested. Some people will try to wheel and deal with the price, but don't give too much away as it will very likely eat into your profits. Using the instant booking feature allows you to confirm requests automatically, but then you have less control over the scheduling calendar.

You should exercise caution when accepting payments outside of Airbnb. Be warned that doing so can get you banned since it cuts into their profits. Airbnb is also against the sharing of personal contact info. You might be able to get through Airbnb's message filters if you direct guests on how to search for your website where they would be able to find your contact info. You can also then add a link on your website to connect people to your Airbnb listing. Once someone stays with you, you can then exchange contact info to discretely rent to them again outside of Airbnb if you so wish.

Cancellations, Refunds, and Reviews

Airbnb has three types of cancellation policies: flexible, moderate, and strict. Flexible means that a full refund, minus service fees, will be provided if the guest cancels at least one day before arrival. Moderate is similar. However, it requires a five-day advance cancellation. Finally, strict provides a 50% refund after fees with a cancellation at least one week in advance. Scott recommends using the strict policy to protect you from having to scramble to fill an opening at the last minute. Decide for yourself how flexible to be when people give you reasons why they have to cancel. The Airbnb Resolution Center can help mediate cancellations, refunds, and other issues if needed. You should contact them early to make sure your side of the story is heard.

It's important to have great reviews of your space to get lots of bookings. Your guests can review you on the accuracy of your listing, how good the communication was with you, how well the check-in went, and the cleanliness, location, and the value were for your rental space.

The ratings go both ways so you can rate your guests as well. You and a guest won't be able to see one another's review of each other until you both have written and posted them. Not everyone will leave you a five-star review, or even a review at all. To get more five-star reviews, you should make sure your listing accurately represents your space to manage expectations, keep your place clean, have an easy check-in system, send a welcome email after a guest checks in to ask them how things are. Furthermore, if you can help them, you should send them a personal thank you note after they check out where you ask for their feedback and a positive review. If you suspect that a guest will leave less than a five-star review, delay or skip giving them a review and hope they forget to give you one.

Automating Your System

Scott spends less than two hours weekly on each of his Airbnb properties. You should sync your Airbnb reservation calendar with a Google calendar to improve your efficiency. You should get to know the whole process well for cleaning, buying household goods, check-ins, communicating with guests, and accepting reservations, so you know what it takes to do them all well. You should then start outsourcing the parts you don't want to do yourself. Otherwise, it can be easy to get burnt out on those tasks.

There are lots of websites that can help you with outsourcing your Airbnb tasks for fees between 3-13% of your revenue. For example, www.Guesty.com will quickly respond to guests for you. www.KeyCafe.com covers the house key exchanges. Various local providers can take care of cleaning and restocking supplies. www.RentingYourPlace.com provides consulting on how to improve your Airbnb knowledge. www.BeyondPricing.com uses an algorithm to automatically adjust your prices. All of these are handy for you as you run your Airbnb business.

You should automate your check-in process as much as possible, so anyone can easily do it. When you have fewer problems, it means that guests contact you fewer times to solve issues. You should include a house guide that describes things like how to work the TV, thermostat, use the wi-fi, and how to checkout. You should replace your regular locks with either keypads or smart locks that guests can open with their smartphones. You should make sure guests have everything they need by checking the inventory of things at your space monthly to see when you need more shampoo, trash bags, towels, etc.

Handling Taxes and Insurance

Airbnb has a "$1,000,000 Host Guarantee" insurance policy to protect you from property damage and theft that your insurance didn't cover already. You need your very own insurance first to be covered by Airbnb too. You should consider getting landlord insurance, which protects you from lawsuits and property damage. Rental insurance covers you for lost income if something like a fire or hurricane interrupts your income.

Taxes vary depending upon where your rental space is located. If you live in it less than 10% of the days it's rented out, then you can write off all of the overhead costs in your taxes. This means the money that you spent on utilities, cleaning, supplies, furnishings, your home office, travel expenses, interest on credit cards, depreciation, repairs, insurance, legal and professional services, and renting the space are all tax-deductible. You can also reduce your taxes by being a "material participant" in the business by just being the main person who runs the business.

Airbnb will send you an IRS 1099 form each year, which reports your revenue. Keeping good track of your income and expenses makes it easier for you during the tax season. Use a sperate business checking account and credit card to help keep things organized. Scott likes to use www.LegalZoom.com to have his Airbnb business set up as an S-corporation. This allows him to limit his tax responsibilities and allow the profits to pass through to him. When you are just getting started, you may want to use a sole-proprietorship for the first year and then an LLC after that.

Conclusion

Airbnb and other similar vacation rental companies allow an average person to become an investor in their very own place of residence. However, to do it successfully, this book gives you all of the best insight that Scott has learned. In my mind, learning from other people's mistakes is way better than suffering through all the rookie mistakes by yourself. If you want to maximize your Airbnb profits, I recommend reading Scott's full book.

Additional Reading

Optimize YOUR Bnb: The Definitive Guide to Ranking #1 in Airbnb Search by Daniel Rusteen

AIRBNB, SHORT & TOURIST RENTALS: More Strategy To Earn Your Property And Make Money With Airbnb, Short And Tourist Rentals: A Fast And Simple Business In Real Estate by Mark Auklund

Chapter 14: Real Estate Investment Trusts

The Intelligent REIT Investor by Stephanie Krewson-Kelly and Brad Thomas

Introduction

Investing in a real estate investment trust (REIT) isn't like other forms of real estate investing. It's more akin to owning stock in a company that invests in real estate. As a REIT investor, you follow the usual laws as you do with other stock investments. REITs don't give you the tax benefits of owning real estate directly. However, the hands-off approach and liquidity of REIT ownership can be quite attractive to many investors. The tenants of a REIT property will never know that you are a part-owner of that property. If you want to make good money through REITs, this book will help you go in the right direction. However, the laws surrounding REITs have changed a lot in recent years.

The Intelligent REIT Investor is in the process of being retired and now replaced with a newer book, *Educated REIT Investing* by Stephanie Krewson-Kelly. This newer book was not yet released at the time I wrote my book. If you want to invest in REITs, I recommend you to buy Stephanie's new book and read it, so you understand the updated laws.

What is a REIT?

A REIT, which is pronounced "reet," is a trust that invests in real estate. You can be a shareholder in that trust, which is run just like a corporation. However, the taxes are paid by the shareholders in direct proportion to their stake of ownership. The same is true of the dividends that get paid out to the shareholders. A REIT can be either privately owned or publicly traded. Public REITs are traded similarly to stocks. Most REITs have some privately-owned units called operation partnership (OP) units. REITs must pay a dividend to its shareholders of at least 90% of what would be considered taxable income. They then pay income on whatever else it keeps from the net profits. A REIT that pays 100% or more of its taxable income is therefore exempt from paying taxes.

Between 2000-2015, REITs had an annual return rate of 11.1% at a time when the stock market only did about 5% in that period. As of 2015, $939 billion was invested in publicly-traded REITs. The National Association of REITs (NAREIT) has various educational resources and information on its website www.REIT.com. (As of 2020, there were 219 publicly-traded REITs on the NAREIT worth an approximate combined value of a whopping $2 trillion.)

The two main types of REITs are equity and mortgage. There were previously REITs that were a hybrid between the two but were then reclassified as mortgage REITs in 2010. Equity REITs get their main income from rents that are paid by tenants. Mortgage REITs (mREITs) get their income by lending money to owners, who then make mortgage payments to the mREITs. REITs can also be described based on their types of investment property, such as retail space or apartments.

REITs usually own a portfolio of properties either in a specific region or are spread across the country. The rates of return vary widely between types of REITs, regions they cover, what they invest in, and also what type of real estate is hot at the time. The things that can be controlled for improving the return include improving the management of properties already owned, acquiring or developing new properties, and either getting better financing terms or selling properties. In general, developing properties is riskier as compared to acquiring properties. Acquiring properties is riskier than focusing on managing the properties already owned. The more debt a REIT has, the higher the risk of it going bankrupt. REITs with more equity are better equipped to handle it when the economy downturns.

You can search the list of publicly traded REITS on the Financial Times of London and also the London Stock Exchange (FTSE). The Dow Jones Equity All REIT Index (REI) also has info about the status of publicly-traded REITs. Once you find the one you like, that REIT's website will have more info about it, including financial reports and press releases.

You are also able to buy an index/bundle of REITs similar to a mutual fund if you wish. This is called an exchange-traded fund (ETF). The top three are the Vanguard Group (VNQ), iShares U.S. Real Estate (IYR), and iShares Cohen & Steers (ICF).

Why Should You Invest in REITs?

REITs give a better cash dividend yield (average of around 4.3% as of 2015) as opposed to government bonds or several other investments, which gives you some passive income. If a REIT's dividend yield is much higher than that of its competitors, then it just might be too good to be true. REITs usually provide an average return of 10-12% per year over time. About 75% of the time, REITs tend to grow faster than inflation. They also allow you to diversify your investment portfolio of stocks and bonds. Some studies recommend investing up to 20% of your portfolio in REITs to help diversify your other stocks and bonds investments.

REITs also give you some risk protection that you wouldn't have if you had owned the real estate directly. You can also buy and sell ownership in a public REIT much faster than you could with real estate. Private REITs tend not to have this same level of liquidity. REITs are scrutinized daily by analyst groups, which helps provide reassurance that they will endure.

Dividends from REITs

The dividend yields are the main thing that appeals to REIT investors. The basis for a REIT's distribution is the taxable income, as identified by the IRS (Internal Revenue Service). REITs have to pay at least 90% of their taxable income to their investors through dividends. This means that REIT dividends tend to be higher than those from other stocks and bonds.

To figure out the yield that a REIT has, you take the current annual dividends for a share and divide it by how much each share costs. Some REITs pay dividends monthly, but quarterly dividends are more standard. The REIT dividends need to be sustainable for them to make sense. Some REITs offer a "sucker yield" that is high, but too unpredictable. The dividends will vary regardless based on a REIT's profitability and the need to keep a cash reserve at any given time. The less debt a REIT has, the more likely that it will be able to pay its dividends.

You can measure the safety of a REIT's dividends by looking at the near-term expected earnings growth as well as the REIT's balance sheet leverage. The expected payout ratio is determined by taking the current annualized dividend and then dividing it by the expected amount of next year's funds from operation (FFO). This is how REITs examine their profitability. An FFO of less than 1.0 is good. An FFO above 1.0 means that it poses a higher level of risk.

The more the REIT pays in dividends, the less tax is due overall. REITs will sometimes pay more than 100% of their taxable income in the form of dividends. That extra money returned to investors is considered a return on capital and is not taxed. That's the icing on the cake.

REITs don't pay all of their income out in the form of dividends because they first deduct operating expenses and depreciation as permitted by the IRS. REITs usually disclose their tax and dividend information in a press release at the beginning of each year. You can see these on the website of each REIT if you wish.

As of 2015, REIT investors owe a tax rate of 25% of the dividend income they make from the REIT. This is lower than the tax rate that the REIT would have to pay on any taxable income it keeps. If the REIT sells any property for a profit and you get cashback for that sale, then that income is taxed at capital gains rates. However, capital losses do not get passed onto the investors. REIT dividends are not labeled as "qualified dividends" and are exempt from paying the "double tax" that other C-Corporations end up having to pay.

If you buy preferred stock in a REIT, it could have a bigger dividend as compared to the regular common stock. However, the common stock's dividends could increase above that of the preferred stock, making it difficult to sell your preferred stocks.

Leases

The REIT acts as the landlord of the property and issues leases to tenants where the tenants pay rent, which is usually monthly. There are four main types of leases that REITs use.

1. Gross leases are used with lower priced and lower quality properties for the short term. Tenants pay the landlord a fixed rate, and the landlord then takes care of all of the insurance, taxes, and even the operating expenses. The landlord pays for any increase in the cost of the expenses.

2. Net leases are used with retail, industrial, and single-tenant properties. Tenants pay the landlord a fixed rate and also take care of some of the maintenance and operating expenses. A double net lease is where the tenant pays the

rent, taxes, as well as insurance. A triple net lease is where the tenant pays the rent, taxes, insurance, and maintenance costs.

3. Modified gross leases are used with industrial and office properties. These are double net leases where the tenant pays a maintenance fee as well as any increases in the taxes and insurance.

4. Full-service leases are used with offices. This is like a gross lease where the rent increases to cover any increase in costs.

If the tenant goes bankrupt when they are leasing from a REIT, that tenant still has to pay rent until a judge permits them to stop paying. The tenant's rent holds a senior position over the tenant's responsibilities to other lenders. This then helps protect REITs from themselves going bankrupt.

Property Types

A specialty REIT only invests in one type of property. A diversified REIT invests in two or more types of properties. The following are the types of properties where REITs invest.

1. Triple net REITs tend to rent a property to one tenant for ten or more years, such as to a fast food restaurant or an auto parts store. These tend to have less profit as compared to other properties but are more predictable in the long term.

2. Healthcare REITs rent space to healthcare providers, usually on either triple net or modified gross leases. As the baby boomer population increases, so will the need for healthcare facilities as well as medical offices.

3. Industrial REITs rent to warehouse, manufacturing, and research and development businesses. This is a very stable asset class that does not appreciate quickly. (When marijuana becomes legal in each state, the demand for warehouses for it will likely increase, especially in the colder northern states.)

4. Lodging and resort REITs own hotels that are usually popular brands and are located in urban areas. These perform better than other REITs when the economy is going up, and also worse than other REITs when the economy is declining.

5. Mortgage REITs lend money directly to real estate owners through mortgages. It is very much like a bank would do. They tend to focus on either commercial or residential loans. They perform the best when interest rates are stabilized.

6. Office REITs invest in a wide variety of office buildings and normally use full-service leases with tenants. The returns go in cycles and do relatively better when the demand for office space exceeds the supply of it.

7. Residential REITs invest in multifamily apartments, single-family homes, as well as mobile homes.

8. Retail REITs invest in places like malls, grocery stores, movie theaters, restaurants, auto parts stores, etc. Tenants usually sign net or modified gross leases. These are normally pretty stable, but many retail businesses have been negatively impacted by the growth of online sales. (However, grocery stores have actually been minimally impacted by online sales due to their nature.)

9. Self-storage REITs have month-to-month leases, which mean profits can vary. (These tend to be stable though regardless of how the economy is performing.)

Technical Details

Before 1992, REITs only owned real estate through joint ventures between investors. After that, the Operating Partnership Unit (OP unit) and the Umbrella Partnership REIT (UPREIT) structure began to be permitted with REITs. In UPREIT structures, investors own stocks in the REIT. The REIT then owns OP units in an operating partnership (OP), which is a type of limited partnership, and the OP runs the real estate properties. When the OP earns money from the properties, it then pays dividends to the UPREIT, which in turn pays dividends to the investors.

The OP can buy new real estate properties and pay for them in OP units or cash. OP units are similar to shares of stock but are not publicly traded, however. OP units can usually be traded one-for-one for common stocks or cash; however, that would then be a taxable event. When you get paid in OP units instead of stock or dividends, you are deferring your tax liability, similar to a 1031 exchange. Most REITs are UPREITs. Some older REITs use the DownREIT structure instead. This is where they own some properties directly and some that the OP buys a specific portfolio of properties.

REITs can be publicly traded, public but non-listed on the stock exchange, or even privately held. The main differences between publicly listed vs. non-listed and private REITs are that public REITs are more transparent and easily bought and sold, but also have more daily fluctuations in their prices. Private REITs are the only REITs that aren't governed by the rules of the Securities and Exchange Commission (SEC). The costs and fee structures will vary widely based on the type of REIT it is and also by the specific REIT company. (Read the fine print and any public financials before you purchase.)

In addition to paying 90% of their taxable income through dividends, REITs must also fulfill certain requirements. These include: be a USA corporation, have a board of directors or trustee, have shares, get at least 75% of its gross income from rents (or mortgage interest for mREITs), invest at least 75% of its assets in real estate or mortgage loans, and not own more than 10% of a different company or REIT.

How REITs Perform

Different factors impact a REIT's performance and the worth of its stock. When the market is on an upswing, REITs tend to perform better as compared to other stocks. However, when the market is going down, REITs tend to perform even worse than other stocks.

Like most things, a great demand with a small supply will increase the price of a REIT stock. If multiple REITs issue too many new shares at the same time, then that can flood the market with too much of a supply.

During the savings and loan crisis of the 1980s, REITs were able to buy real estate holdings from savings and loans for deep discounts. This then resulted in significant growth for REITs, as well as a lot more investment in them. The 1986 *Tax Reform Act*, the 1994 *REIT Simplification Act*, the 1999 *REIT Modernization Act*, and the 2015 *Protecting Americans from Tax Hikes Act* also updated the structure of REITs in a way that further aided their growth.

REIT fluctuations appear more due to market forces but not real estate fundamentals. For example, in 1998 and 1999, during the dot-com bubble, people pulled their money out of REITs and then put it in technology stocks. REITs did poorly then but quickly rebounded once the bubble had burst. During the credit crisis of 2007 and 2008, REITs provided a negative return before moving on to have a seven-year rally upward. An upswing followed a downswing, as seen in these cases.

All REITs are impacted by the fundamentals of real estate, the structure and duration of the leases they use, and also the cost of the financing that is used. Different types of properties will have different levels of demand during the various stages of the economic cycle. A REIT's performance can differ from the market performance, especially when the market is in a transitional stage.

This is because the real estate market tends to lag behind that of the stock market.

The property cycle and the economic cycle interact with each other. Knowing where we are in a cycle helps you know what the best time is to invest in REITs. When the economy is recovering after a recession, and the demand for rental space increases. Furthermore, there isn't much new construction going on, the existing rental spaces are cheaper to buy and give a great return, and REITs can perform really well. When the market is in the expansion phase, there are still many opportunities. Though there are not as many as in the recovery phase. The market will then have some equilibrium before going into a phase of oversupply or lack of demand for rental space. Then a recession hits to reset the process.

Retail space often has triple net leases that go for a good ten years. The onset of a recession has a less immediate impact on triple net spaces than it does on hotels, which don't have leases with their tenants. Health care, self-storage, apartment (especially in the B class), shopping center, and industrial REITs are also better suited to weather the challenges of a recession as and when it happens. Office REITs do well in the first year or two of a recession before declining in performance due to the length of their leases.

The shorter the lease term that a REIT uses, the more volatile it will become. However, a REIT with short term leases can earn the most profits when the market is rising as compared to the other REITs. This is because it can adjust its rental rates to the new market rate. A REIT with longer-term leases will be more stable, but it won't adjust to an improving market as quickly. You should choose your style of REIT based on your risk tolerance.

A REIT's weighted average cost of capital (WACC) can be found by adding up its debt, preferred stock, and also common equity. You then compare each part of the capital with the average cost of each of those pieces. A REIT's WACC is essentially its cost of doing business. Lowering its debt is a solid approach to improve a REIT's performance. The interest rate a REIT pays on its debt will also impact its profit margin.

REIT Analysis

Even though publicly-traded REITs report their financials per the SEC rules and Generally Accepted Accounting Principles (GAAP), each REIT does so slightly differently. This creates a challenge when comparing them. You will want to look at a REIT's Forms 8-K and 10-K to see it's financials.

There are a few base metrics to know when you analyze a REIT. The net operating income (NOI) is calculated as the total income the REIT brings in after the property operating expenses have been paid. The same-store earnings are the revenues from the assets the REIT has owned for at least 12 months. The same-store earnings let you know how well the REIT manages investments after they have been stabilized. Funds from operation (FFO) is calculated as the net income, not including the depreciation, gains/losses/write-offs on previously depreciated properties. FFO growth is how much of a percentage change that a REIT has achieved in the current reporting period as compared to the previous reporting period. The cash available for distribution (CAD) is a great indicator of a REIT's ability to safely pay out dividends without breaking the bank.

As mentioned earlier, the more debt a REIT has leveraged out, the higher its risk and the higher returns it will have. REITs tend to play it safer and more conservative with their level of debt. As of 2006, REITs owned their real estate through a 57% debt-to-gross ratio, which is quite safe and conservative.

The weighted average cost of capital (WACC) is determined by comparing a REIT's total market capitalization against the total cost of its debt, preferred shares, as well as common shares. If a REIT's WACC is higher than that of its competitors, then it is either riskier, newer to the public market, or both.

A good way to see if a REIT offers good value is by calculating the price/earnings (P/E). This is done by dividing the current stock price by the FFO per share. If a REIT's P/E is lower than its competitor, it might be a better deal than them.

In addition to analyzing the REIT itself, you should also look at how the managers of the REIT are handling things. You need to see if they are improving the cost-effectiveness of operating the properties and selling off the low-performance properties when needed. You next need to see if they are buying new properties to grow the portfolio when it makes sense to do so. Then, you can see how much debt they are leveraging when taking market conditions into consideration. Finally, you need to see what their historical track record is for managing the REIT.

Perhaps, the main decision-making criteria investors consider is a REIT's net asset value (NAV). This is an estimation of a REIT's current market value minus the non-real estate assets as well as any liabilities. The authors describe the complicated method required to calculate the NAV. By dividing the NAV by the number of shares and OP units, you can get the NAV per share.

Conclusion

The end of the book has some appendices that list out the various REITs and also some information about them. There is also a glossary section that describes the main terms that you will need to know as a REIT investor.

REIT returns are relatively more difficult to predict than many other investments but also have been a solid producer during the long term. You should educate yourself on the different types of REITs and the different companies within the REIT type that you like. Since there are so many REIT investment options, shopping around is a smart approach to find a REIT that's right for you. If you are interested in REITs, you should read *The Intelligent REIT Investor*, or the newer version titled *Educated REIT Investing*, to acquire all the knowledge and tools you need to be successful.

Additional Reading

Educated REIT Investing by Stephanie Krewson-Kelly

The Complete Guide to Investing in REITs -- Real Estate Investment Trusts: How to Earn High Rates of Returns Safely by Mark Gordon

Chapter 15: Mortgage Notes

Paper Profits by Joshua Andrews

Introduction

What could be better than owning real estate directly? Joshua would say owning the mortgage note that is secured by that real estate is a lot better. Note investing does not provide all of the same tax benefits as property ownership does. However, it also has many other benefits, such as not having to repair toilets. This book goes through the step-by-step method that Joshua has used to buy several mortgage notes over the years. If you follow it, then you, too, can make passive income through mortgage notes.

Benefits of Buying Notes

Our hunter-gatherer ancestors had to forage each day just to survive. Most people today are still in a similar state of such day-to-day survival. However, with enough financial knowledge and persistence, you can become financially independent. Financial independence means that you have enough cash flow to cover your expenses, whether you work or not.

Joshua has explored investing in multifamily apartment buildings, single-family rentals, stocks, as well as owning a business. However, his favorite form of passive income is buying and holding notes. Investing in notes and mortgages has apparently been around for centuries. In Joshua's book, he shows you the fundamentals of how you can achieve financial independence by investing in them with as little as $10K. Furthermore, you can even do so with your retirement money or a self-directed IRA. The reason to buy notes is to get a return on your investment through monthly payments.

Notes and mortgages are secure because they have the collateral of actual real estate. If the owner doesn't pay you, then you can legally sell the property to still get all your money. Note investing gives you the income that is predictable down to the penny. You can buy a note from someone else for less than it's worth. This then guarantees that you will make a profit. If you have a fund manager, then you get to just sit back and watch the mortgage payments get deposited into your account each month. It doesn't get better than this!

Notes and mortgages are a great form of real estate investing because you don't have to take care of the property. The owner simply takes care of all of the repairs, tenants, taxes, etc. You can easily own and take care of notes anywhere nationwide. You can even do so through a self-directed IRA to very steadily grow your retirement fund. This also means that compound interest will be working in your favor!

How Notes and Mortgages Work

Notes and mortgages are two separate documents that work together to secure a real estate loan. They outline the loan terms, make things official, as well as add the transaction to the public record. They protect the lender if the borrower defaults on the loan.

When someone says that they are buying a note, this means they are buying both the note and the mortgage for a property.

Mortgages are also known as a "Deed of Trust" (DOT). They have existed since the year 1190 in England. Mortgages are loans that are secured by real estate. They allow people to buy a property when they don't have the cash to purchase it outright. They act as a lien against the property until it is paid for in full. The promissory note is a separate document that defines the terms of the loan. This includes the due date, interest rate, repayment schedule, prepayment penalties, and also when the loan has to be paid in full. Essentially, the note is the borrower's promise to pay the lender.

The note owner has the right to be paid by the borrower, sell or transfer its ownership to whoever they choose, and enforce the terms of the loan. The note owner does not have the right to enter the property, own the property, take any actions beyond the terms of the note, or even change the terms of the note without approval from the borrower. When you own a note, you can have a servicer who collects the payments for you and also makes sure the various laws are followed. Joshua uses www.MadisonManagement.net and www.TrustFCI.com.

Joshua focuses on buying notes for single-family homes. However, you can also buy them for commercial properties, mobile homes, raw land, cars, as well as defaulted credit card debt. He prefers single-family homes. This is because the owners tend to want to do what it takes to make mortgage payments so they can keep their homes.

Get to know these basic terms:

- Performing means that the borrower is making their payments on time.
- Non-performing means that the borrower stopped making payments and then goes into default.
- Re-performing means that the borrower stopped making payments, but has started paying again. That is, perhaps, due to a modification of the loan to help them get back on track.
- Secured means that the loan has collateral that the lender can repossess if the loan defaults.
- Unsecured means that there is no collateral for the loan, such as credit card debt.
- An unpaid balance (UPB) is the amount left for the loan to be paid off.
- Origination means creating a new loan. Loans can originate from banks, individuals (seller-financing), or even private lenders (hard money).
- Yield is the interest rate you receive annually on your money.
- A discount is when you buy a note for less than it's worth. You can buy discounted notes to ensure you make money on them. They are easy to find!
- An amortization schedule is the schedule of the payments for the loan to show how much interest is paid over a designated time.

Notes vs. Other Investments

Buying notes is like being the bank. You can earn principal and interest on your investment. When you own a note that is secured against real estate, you know you will get your money. With discounted notes, you will make money whether the borrower pays in full today, makes their regular payments for the full loan term, or defaults, so you have to foreclose. Since foreclosing is a hassle, it's better to receive the mortgage payments without any effort on your part at all.

By saving up the payments made to you, you can then turn around and buy more notes. If you owe a debt for anything, you can buy discounted notes for less than your debt. Then the payments from your notes can pay off your debt and then some. Joshua gives the example that if you have $110K in student loans and buy $40K on discounted notes, you will pay off your student loans, get your $40K back, and even pocket an additional $22K!

While stocks can be a good passive investment, they don't allow you to control the rate of the return on your investment. To make money with stock, you need to pick ones that will increase in value before you sell them. There are dividend stocks, but they only provide a small yield. Notes are more secure and predictable than stocks.

Mutual funds are a mixture of stocks, bonds, as well as other securities. They depend on the marking going up to make you money. The mutual fund manager decides how your money is invested. They are paid by fees and not based on how well the mutual fund performs. Notes give you more control and reliability as opposed to mutual funds.

Bonds are securities and are much akin to a loan to a government or institution. While they are considered safe, they produce a very small yield that may not even keep up with inflation. Notes tend to give yields of 8-12%, which is a lot better.

A tax lien is put on a property when a homeowner doesn't pay their property taxes. Tax liens are prioritized above all other liens, including the first mortgages. This means the tax lien gets paid off first before any other liens during a foreclosure. You can buy a tax lien and be confident that you will make a profit. On a rare occasion, you can buy a house for pennies on the dollar with a tax lien. Tax liens, unlike notes, do not provide cash flow. They do require you to wait sometime before getting paid.

Investing in rental properties can create a lot of wealth. However, you will be responsible for the physical structure, taxes, insurance, tenants, repairs, property management, and even mortgage. Real estate generally appreciates over time, provides good cash flow, and gives you awesome tax deductions. Owning notes involves much less effort on your part, and you're not even required to visit any properties.

Investing in notes does have some downsides. Unlike real estate, you can only get tax deductions for your business and not the properties themselves. Notes never appreciate in value, and will eventually get paid off.

Inflation

The concept of the time value of money (TVM) is that money today is worth more than the same amount will ever be in the future. The price of goods and services goes up over time by about 3-5% annually, which then decreases your purchasing power. Money kept in a savings account or under your mattress is also losing value.

Inflation occurs when governments print too much money, hence increasing prices. Since savers turn into losers, you should make sure your money is doing better than the rate of inflation. Notes are a great way to stay ahead. (When I analyzed how much my 401K and Social Security would be worth when I'm 65 compared to today, I realized that I was on the path to poverty if I didn't take control of my investment plan.)

Doing Due Diligence

Due diligence (DD) is when you research and evaluate a potential purchase. Joshua recommends learning DD from an experienced note investor. When you are doing DD, you should focus on buying notes where the property is worth more than the loan and other liens. This means the property has equity, which acts as a cushion to ensure you will make money. Aim for properties with at least 15-20% equity.

Investigate what the probability is that the lender will make their payments and what the risk is if the borrower defaults on their loan. Owning the first mortgage is safer than a second mortgage if there is a foreclosure. This is because the first will get paid before the second if there's even enough money left over for the second mortgage. (However, it's easier to buy second mortgages at a discount.)

Before Joshua buys a note, he reviews the entire copies of the note and mortgage documents. He looks online to get an estimate of the fair market value of the property. You can do this on www.Realtor.com, www.Zillow.com, or www.RealtyTrac.com. He looks at the property online using Google Street View to make sure it's not a total dump. He asks the note seller for the borrower's payment history and credit report. This is to obtain proof that the payments are getting paid on time and that the borrower has a credit score above 500. He checks the public records to see the borrower's bankruptcy history. That all is part of the due diligence process, and it is very important.

If all of the above looks good, then you can order an ownership and encumbrances title report (O&E report) to verify that title is clean and your information about the mortgage is accurate. Joshua uses www.ProTitleUSA.com for this. From there, you can have a broker pricing option (BPO) done to do an appraisal without having someone need to enter the property. The O&E report and BPO together will cost around $150-350 but are money worth spent to know what you are buying.

Using a Self-Directed IRA

If you have a self-directed IRA or convert your retirement account(s) into one, you can use that retirement money to purchase notes and other investments. This gives you a level of control over your retirement money that you don't normally have. Your gains go into the self-directed IRA and are usually tax-free.

You will need to use a company called a "provider" to ensure that the IRS tax laws are followed properly with your self-directed IRA. Your provider can also help you transfer money from other retirement accounts into your self-directed IRA, provide you with education (but not advice), help you buy/sell assets, and report any distributions appropriately to the IRS.

Once you find a note to buy, you should make a purchase agreement where your self-directed IRA is the purchaser and not yourself. Your provider will help you with the needed forms. Setting up a self-directed IRA is pretty easy. Joshua recommends using the website www.QuestIRA.com.

Foreclosure and Bankruptcy

What happens in case one of your borrowers goes into foreclosure or bankruptcy? Foreclosure laws vary from state to state. You can find state-specific information at www.RealtyTrac.com/real-estate-guides/foreclosure-laws. Most people don't decide to go into foreclosure. It usually happens because there was a death, divorce, loss of employment, or usually medical issues. Normally, 1/200 properties require a foreclosure (but will vary based upon market conditions).

If you have to do a judicial foreclosure through the courts, it could cost you between $3-7K and take at least 12-14 months. Non-judicial foreclosure is when there is specific language in the deed of trust, which permits a foreclosure when certain milestones are met. That will only cost you $2500-5000 and about 3-12 months. Whichever type of foreclosure you do, the borrower or the property will reimburse you of the foreclosure costs.

Once you take ownership of a home through foreclosure, you can then sell it, rent it, or live in it. If you sell it, you can do seller financing to continue your income stream. When it comes to bankruptcy, that does not wipe out someone's mortgage that they owe you most of the time unless there is a special court order.

If someone goes into Chapter 7 bankruptcy, then their assets are sold to pay off their debts. Secured loans, such as a mortgage, are much safer than unsecured loans, such as credit card debt. The borrower can potentially keep their house if they recommit to continue making their mortgage payments. However, you can foreclose if they don't.

If someone does Chapter 13 bankruptcy, then they go onto a payment plan to pay off all of their debts as long as they have enough income to do so. This could extend their mortgage payment schedule if they recommit to making their mortgage payments. Chapter 13 can delay, but not stop, a foreclosure from happening.

During a bankruptcy, junior liens could become unsecured debt if the property doesn't have enough equity to cover it. When a borrower falls behind on their mortgage payments, it works best to have your servicer communicate with them so they can understand their situation. You should verify what they say, and find out if there is a way that they can work things out with you. Foreclosure is more of a last resort. Solutions could include a repayment plan, lowered interest rate, lowered payment, or even forgiving a payment.

Diversification

When you buy multiple notes, you spread out your risk. If you have $100K, you could buy one $100K note or even five $20K notes from five different borrowers. The second option is safer as it provides diversification. You could even buy notes in different asset classes, such as residential, commercial, raw land, or trailer parks.

You can buy performing notes, which are "turnkey" investments that are low risk. Re-performing notes can also be purchased as great deals where the borrower fell behind but eventually got back on track. Non-performing notes are in default and can be purchased for deep discounts. Joshua often buys non-performing notes because the high-profit margin makes the risk worth taking.

If you do buy non-performing notes, then it's best to have an exit plan. The hardest part is getting in contact with the borrower. Once you do, you can reinstate the loan and then have them make payments as planned, create a new payment play, modify the loan, reduce the payoff amount, sell the house, short sale the house, foreclose, do a deed in lieu of foreclosure, or just foreclose and rent the house. Since this type of note is bought so cheaply, you have more wiggle room with potential options. Buying both performing and non-performing notes is a good way to diversify your note investing, depending upon your risk tolerance.

Calculating Yields

The yield is the best metric to determine whether a note is a good one to buy. The yield is even more important than the discount you get on a note. To determine the yield, you need a financial calculator, such as the Hewlett-Packard HP12C. You can also download a financial calculator app from your favorite app store.

Once you have your calculator or app, you will notice that there are lots of strange-looking buttons, but you can ignore most of them. The keys you need to know are N=number of payments, I=interest/yield, PV=present value, PMT=payment, and FV=future value. Create a table that looks like this:

N	I	PV	PMT	FV

In the N spot on your table, you should put the months (not years) remaining in the mortgage. Save the I spot for last. For now, you should just know that the interest you will see in the I spot is per month, so you will need to multiple it by 12 to get the annual yield. You should put the purchase price in the PV spot as a negative number. If you bought the note for $10K, then enter -10,000. The PMT is the monthly mortgage payment, including both the principal and interest portions. FV is 0 unless there will be a balloon payment paid as a lump sum to pay off the loan. If there is a balloon payment, you can put that final amount as the FV.

To put the numbers into your calculator, you enter the number and then the corresponding key. If you make any mistakes, you can just press the yellow F key then the CLX key to start over. Suppose you want a 10% yield and are trying to figure out how much to pay for a note. Enter in the number of months remaining, the monthly yield you need (10÷12=0.83333), the monthly payment amount, and the balance remaining once the amortization table is done (0 if there is no balloon payment). Then, click the PV key to show how many dollars you can pay for that note and get your 10% yield. From there, you can start negotiating with the note seller. You can also use these keys to calculate the modification of a loan to reduce a borrower's payments, increase the number of months in the amortization table, and still get the yield you need for things work.

Getting Started

The first step from here is to determine what your financial goals are. Start with the end in mind and avoid becoming distracted by the various shiny objects upon the way. The more specific you are with your goals, the better. Simply wanting more money isn't a good enough goal. You need to break down your goals into actionable and measurable steps that you take daily.

Once you know your "why," ask yourself what sort of investor you are and what skills do you need to gain to be successful. Are you a passive or active investor? If you are an accredited or sophisticated investor, then you can invest in a note fund. To be accredited, you need either $1M in assets, not including your residence, an annual income of at least $200K, or a combined annual income with your spouse of at least $300K. To be considered a sophisticated investor, you need to be financially savvy with investments.

Next, it's time to start buying notes and collecting the income from them. Since you can't do this on your own, you must build good relationships with others who can help you. A key relationship to build is with a mentor. Start by adding value to them before asking for anything in return. Find someone whom you can trust, is an expert, and has excellent experience.

Conclusion

This book does not and cannot cover all aspects of note investing. You can think of it as a start to your note buying education. It's up to you to take ownership of your education from here. Finding a mentor is a great way to help you progress faster than you could do so by yourself.

Additional Reading

Invest in Debt by Jimmy Napier

The Banker's Code by George Antone

Chapter 16: Tax Liens and Tax Deeds

Profit by Investing in Real Estate Tax Liens: Earn Safe, Secured, and Fixed Returns Every Time by Larry Loftis, Esq.

Introduction

Tax liens are a relatively safe and stable form of real estate investment. Essentially, what happens is that you buy the right to have the property owner pay you their property taxes in full, plus any interest or fees. (The taxes and fees are paid to the county and then forwarded to you.) Christopher Bullock said, "Tis impossible to be sure of anything but death and taxes." If a property owner doesn't pay their real estate taxes, they then risk losing their property. If you own a tax lien, you can be confident that you will get paid sooner or later. There's at least that guarantee.

There are gurus out there who say that they can guarantee that you will make great profits by investing in tax liens. The bad news is that so many of them have done little to not tax lien investing themselves. Larry has the benefit of having done tax lien investing in ten different states and can also give you the inside information from his personal experience. He's heard enough misinformation at real estate seminars that he had to write this book to set the record straight.

Tax Lien Investing

With a few exceptions, almost every property is taxed. This includes houses, office buildings, apartments, retail stores, and even empty lots. These taxes are used to pay for community services. The local jurisdiction, usually the county, will assess the worth of each property and the taxes that are owed for each of them. Counties often assess properties at 85% of their worth but are sometimes way off. The county assessor doesn't always even physically look at properties before assessing them! Each property owner gets a tax bill following the tax assessment. If they don't pay by a certain date, additional fees are charged, and then a lien is put against the property.

When there is a tax lien against a property, it stays there until the lien is paid off. After the county gets tired of unsuccessfully trying to collect the unpaid property taxes, the tax liens are then sold to investors. When a property owner eventually pays the property taxes to the county within the "redemption period," the county then passes the money onto the person who had previously bought the tax lien.

Interest incurred on the tax lien during the redemption period will normally range from 0.25-18%. Redemption periods range by state from six months to four years but are generally one or two years. If a tax lien is not paid off within the redemption period, then the tax lien investor can foreclose on the property. It is, however, possible to get a house for pennies on the dollar this way, but it is extremely rare due to other liens such as a mortgage.

It's better to invest in tax liens than the stock market because you can get better returns, have more control, and enjoy much lower risk. After all, they have a property as collateral. Granted, stocks are more liquid than tax liens. However, tax liens have a fixed value, so you know what your return will be. At the same time, you never have to pay a commission on a tax lien purchase.

Tax liens generally give a 10-25% return and usually pay you in the first year or two. If the property owner doesn't pay off the tax lien, then you can take possession of the property for a cheap price. However, there may be other liens that need to be paid too for you to own the property. A tax lien almost always has the first position before any mortgage or other liens can get paid off. The only exception, in this case, is a "weed lien," where the city had to mow the lawn of an abandoned house.

Tax liens are sold at a government auction. When more investors are bidding at an auction, the returns will be a bit worse. The county may put a notice in the newspaper about an auction but doesn't advertise beyond that. Brokers aren't involved with tax liens. And tax lien investors don't normally spread the word around about tax liens. Therefore, many people haven't ever heard about tax lien investing.

Around half of the states in the USA use tax liens, and about half use tax deeds. Tax deed states then auction off the property itself to pay for the tax bill. Tax deeds will be covered more later. A few states are hybrids where the investor gets the property's title, but the previous owner can redeem ownership by paying back the taxes and fees. Furthermore, some states have both lien and deed sales separately.

Properties with Tax Liens

A common misconception is that only rundown houses have tax liens. Tax liens happen on every kind and quality of the properties. They also happen with well-known companies like Walt Disney World, Citibank, or McDonald's. Well-known athletes and actors forget to pay their property taxes on time and get tax liens on their properties as well. Larry even once bought a tax lien on a building where the sheriff's office was. The sheriff was responsible for enforcing the lien on their own building!

Real estate developers have been known to delay paying their property tax bill until their development sells. One such developer in Orlando told the newspaper that he saw that delay as a sort of short-term loan that he didn't require a bank to obtain. Liens can go on banks themselves when they don't pay the tax bills on their foreclosed properties. Like the developers, the banks are also waiting to pay the taxes until the time the property sells.

When Larry was living in a small gated community of 16 homes valued between $750K-$1M, he had noticed that 25% of them had tax liens on them. These were for different reasons, including foreclosure, divorce, and one owner living abroad, for example. The annual property tax bill is usually between 1-2% of the property's value. If a property has a lot of equity, the owner is unlikely to give up the entire property for so little money. (If someone owns a $1M house free of any mortgage, would they do whatever they could to find the $10K to pay the tax bill and also keep it?)

Returns of up to 300%

Between the years 1926 and 2000, the stock market saw an annual average gain of 11%. Then a recession hit, and fortunes were lost. (After this book was written, the Great Recession in 2008 and COVID-19 crash in 2020 have also wreaked havoc on the stock market.) Even the best planning with stock market investing cannot prepare for the eventual big drops that inevitably do occur. Each crash requires years for investors to merely recoup what they lost.

Tax liens, on the other hand, provide predictable returns regardless of the state the economy is in. The minimum and maximum returns on tax liens vary widely between the states. States with a statutory rate use that as the start of the auction bidding. For example, a state may start bidding at an 18% rate but could go as low as 0.25%. That all depends upon the lowest rate an investor at the auction is willing to accept. The better a property is, the lower the rate will usually end up during the bidding process.

Why would an investor buy something that has a 0.25% rate? The answer requires you to know the difference between an interest rate, penalty rate, and a rate of return. If Larry bought a lien on a great property in Florida at a 0.25% rate, then he would just get an 8-10% average return on his investment. This is because Florida has a minimum 5% penalty fee. If the tax lien was paid off in a month, then the annual return would be 60% (5% times 12 months). A penalty rate is a fee that is charged upfront on a tax lien. The penalty rate of 20% on a Georgia lien of $10K will make you $2K regardless of when it gets paid.

The rate of return from tax liens doesn't work the same way as cash-flowing properties. (A cash flowing property give you profits each month that exceed the benefits, tax write-offs, appreciate, and depreciation that adds up to annual returns year after year.) A tax lien investment gives you a one-time payout, which could occur days or years after you had bought it. If a $10K lien has a $2K penalty that pays out after one year, this equals a 20% return on investment that year. If it pays out after one month, then that return gives you a pace of a 240% annual return ($2K x 12 months ÷ $10K investment). The longer it takes for this sort of lien to be paid, the lower the annual return on investment will turn out to be.

When the payoff occurs, then you can reinvest that money into more tax liens. Just keep in mind that it takes different property owners varying amounts of time to redeem their tax liens. You may sometimes want a lien to be paid off later. That's the case as in Iowa, where the fees stack up monthly. Texas has the highest potential annual rate of return at 300% if a lien there is paid off within a month. You know how much money you will make on a lien you buy. You just don't know exactly when you will get paid, though, but will most likely be paid in the first year or two. Larry has even won a tax lien at auction, and then the lien was paid off by the property owner before Larry even had a chance to pay for it!

It sometimes happens where a property owner gets tax liens on their property two years in a row, and the first one had not yet been paid off. If you want to buy the second one, then you may want to at the same time pay off the first one, which is owned by another investor. You will then later get paid for the new larger lien.

Where will you decide to invest? Each state has different rules for tax liens. Do you want a tax lien, deed, or hybrid state? Do you want to invest where you live or do some traveling? Online bidding is available in some states. However, you should only do online bidding if you are familiar with the area. You should choose a place where either you live, you travel to often, or you can get the best deals. The list of states and their rules in Larry's book is tremendously helpful in narrowing things down to the states that are right for you.

Auctions

Lien states normally have annual auctions. Deed and hybrid states normally have their auctions more often than that. Some counties in Pennsylvania even have weekly auctions, for example. Some counties charge you a fee or deposit to participate at an auction. A county may allow you to bid online or even require you to be there physically, and some require certified funds to be used. You should contact a county to learn its specific rules and auction schedule.

Auctions across the country are held throughout the year. It helps to plan with your schedule. This way, you can attend the auctions in the states and counties that interest you the most. You can even time it out to attend one auction in the morning and a nearby county's auction later in the afternoon. If you use your security number along with your corporate tax ID number and the social security numbers of family members, you can also get multiple bidding cards at an auction. This can help in winning you more liens.

Online auctions allow you to participate in multiple auctions simultaneously. However, with online auctions, you should place your best bid ahead of time and can't get the feel for an auction's progress. Online auctions will then award a lien to the best bid. If two bids tie for first, then a winner is randomly chosen. If you bid at the lowest at 0.25% and the next lowest bid was 8.25%, you would win with 8%. Big institutions have been known to regularly bid at the lowest 0.25%.

Every county requires you to register in advance before you can participate in a lien auction so that they can report your lien income to the IRS. You can usually do this by completing a W-9 form for each Social Security number or tax ID number along with the county's registration form.

How to Bid at Lien Sales

There are five main types of bidding systems that counties use.

1. The "bid down the interest" system is where a county has a maximum rate, and then investors bid it down to whoever

is willing to accept the lowest rate. Bidders simply yell out the rate they offer until the auctioneer hears the lowest one. Bidders who work for large institutions will often yell "quarter," and that means they will buy a lien at 0.25%.

2. Premium bidding is when where investors bid to see who offers the highest premium over the lien amount. You might buy a $1K lien for $2K. The extra $1K is known as the "premium" amount. The lien and premium may both receive interest or penalty, only one receives interest or penalty, or just that the investor cannot recoup the principal from their premium. It's ideal when you can make money on both an interest rate as well as a penalty.

3. Random selection counties randomly select a bidder to ask if they want the tax lien. If that bidder decides to decline, the process then repeats until someone is found who wants it. It's not unusual for a county to switch to a random selection toward the end of an auction day to catch up on lien sales when they are behind.

4. Rotational bidding is where bidders are given an order. Bidder #1 is the first one to be offered the first lien. If they decline it, then the option goes to #2 and so on. Bidder #2 then gets the first shot at the second lien. The auction continues this way, giving all bidders fair and equal opportunities to buy liens.

5. "Bid down the ownership" is the worst of the bidding systems. Bidders bid down on how much a lien will

encumber a property. It starts at 100% encumbrance and then goes down from there. It's more difficult to get paid out on these liens, especially when they are bid down to low encumbrance.

If a lien's rate drops too low for you during the bidding, then you can certainly just stop bidding on it. You should keep good track of your bidding card. Larry tells a story of a clueless newcomer who accidentally took someone else's bidding card and was unsure if she had bought any liens with it.

It sometimes happens that not all of the liens were purchased at an auction, or a bidder didn't end up paying for the liens they won. You can then go to the county afterward to buy them "over-the-counter." This is great because you will then get the maximum rate on them.

It helps to go to auctions at smaller counties that have populations under 500K since there will be less competition, especially from the large institutions. Smaller liens usually have higher profit margins but with smaller total profit as opposed to larger ones. Larry focuses on buying liens of at least $450, or at least $750 if there aren't any institutional bidders at the auction.

At in-person auctions, you should not hesitate because bidding occurs so quickly. A great time to bid is during lunchtime or after 5 pm because there will be fewer bidders will be in the room. Auctions sometimes continue into the evening if the auctioneer needs to catch up on lien sales. Stay through the last day of the auction since many bidders will have left. Furthermore, there are sometimes extra liens being sold that weren't on the official roster.

Foreclosing

Since property taxes are vital to keeping the government running, they are almost always put in the first position ahead of any other liens against a property. If a property may go into foreclosure because the mortgage defaults, the tax lien is what gets paid first. If the tax lien's redemption period expires and it was left unpaid, the bank of the first mortgage will usually redeem the lien to protect the mortgage. Mortgages can get wiped out in a foreclosure, but never tax liens.

Some states do tax lien forecloses through an administrative filing, whereas others do it through tax deed sales. In an administrative filing state, you need to tell the county and the property owner of your plan to foreclose when the redemption period ends. You may also need to pay a fee and pay off other tax or weed liens. Tax deed sales are where the property itself gets sold to pay off the different liens in order.

You can usually get a better deal on buying a house at the tax deed sale than you could otherwise at a mortgage foreclosure sale. It's pretty common to be able to buy properties for 10-65% of their value at a tax deed sale. Vacant lots are especially cheap to buy this way.

Low Risk with Tax Liens

It is usually true that bigger risks benefit you with bigger rewards. Tax liens are perhaps the best exception to this rule as they give you great returns for minimal risk. The biggest tax lien investment is on worthless empty lots that could just be a drainage ditch or next to a transformer. There are other minor risks to be aware of, as well.

Sometimes, a property may have an IRS lien. By law, the IRS has 120 days after a tax auction. That is the time in which it can buy out your position if the IRS also had a lien on the property. Otherwise, its lien gets eliminated. To do this, the IRS has to pay for the lien amounts in full plus 6% annual interest and also cover the expenses from the sale. Larry recommends that you avoid buying these liens since they can be more trouble than they are worth.

Less than 1% of liens involve a property owner who files for bankruptcy during the lien's redemption period. If this happens, the bankruptcy judge will then usually keep your lien in first place secured against the property. This process is a pain and accounts for delays but does not prevent your payout.

Buying larger liens helps in preventing you from many issues. It's also beneficial to physically look at the properties before you buy their liens or to at least look them up online. Homesteaded homes are people's primary residences. The tax liens on them are more likely to be redeemed. The more you know an area where you are investing in liens, the better success you will most likely have.

Tax Deeds

At a tax deed sale, investors are actually buying properties. They can sell the properties, live in them, or even rent them to tenants. The previous owner knew that this was coming because they had years of warnings from the county about it. They also don't have a chance to redeem it in a normal deed state.

Hybrid states allow a previous owner to redeem their property back sometime between 6-24 months after its sale. To redeem it, the previous owner needs to pay you the back taxes, the premium paid at the sale, as well as the penalty incurred. For example, if you buy a property at the deed sale for $60K and $6K of that was the back taxes, the previous owner would then have to pay you $60K plus whatever penalty fees the state allows. This is unlikely to happen. However, don't do too much rehabbing during the redemption period just in case the property does eventually get redeemed. Tax deed investing involves more risk as opposed to tax liens. However, this extra risk comes with the potential for greater profits.

Low-Cost Deed Investing

Tax deed auctions mainly sell houses in poor condition, empty lots, as well as worthless land. Counties are more than happy to sell you drainage ditches all day long. Properties usually sell for around 50% of their value at deed auctions. You might be able to get a property at a tax deed sale for mere pennies on the dollar. However, it is unlikely. If you do manage to get one, you should plan to fix it up or sell to a flipper to get the most profit.

You will have more luck buying a house for pennies on the dollar at a tax lien sale and then later foreclosing on it if the lien isn't redeemed. That is also a rare event since there will most likely be other liens on the property. The bank with the first mortgage will probably buy out your position. Also, a property owner won't want to lose a property that has a ton of equity.

Empty lots always give the best deals at tax deed sales. Larry has bought empty lots for as little as $75. He's also flipped lots to other investors for big profits without doing anything to the lots.

Avoiding Risks with Deeds

Commonly, bidding will start at what is owed in back taxes. However, some counties allow opening bids less than that, sometimes for as little as $0.50! You should be warned that some properties are simply not worth buying regardless of the price. Some empty lots might be too small to allow buildings, some properties are underwater, and others still could be contaminated with industrial waste. Larry once tried to look at a condo before an auction and discovered that it didn't actually exist. It's well worth your time to look at properties before you buy them at a deed sale.

How to Bid at Deed Sales

The vast majority of mistakes at auctions can be avoided by doing your homework in advance. Review the county's file on each property to find out details like if it is homesteaded or an empty lot, and what the assessed value is. Ask the county assessor's office for comparable sales (comps) to know what the property is likely worth. You should find out the street address if the property is an empty lot. You can physically visit each property you are considering buying to get a better feel for it.

These steps help you know which properties you want to bid on and how much you are willing to pay for them. It is highly recommended to not exceed the maximum bids that you planned so that you don't get caught up in the moment while bidding. Since deed auctions move along quickly, you should be assertive with jumping in to place your bids. Some seasoned investors will jump in to place a high bid at the last moment to surprise the last bidder and get the property for what they wanted.

Selling a Property

Whether you obtain a property through a tax deed or lien sale, it will be different than buying a property through a "normal" method. It's important to clean up the property's title because you won't get any guarantees from the county that everything is in good order. The county's only goal was to simply collect the back taxes.

Your next step is to pay an attorney $1-3K to submit a "quiet title action" to the courts. Anyone who might have a claim against the property has to respond to this action, or they will just lose their rights to the property. If the redemption period has passed, it's unlikely that this action will be challenged. You can then sell it at its full market price yourself or via a real estate broker. You could also consider selling it quickly at a discount to a flipper or wholesaler.

When you sell, you can consider offering seller financing. This is where you act like the bank, and the buyer pays a down payment and mortgage payments to you. If you don't want to wait 30 years to get all your money, you can require a balloon payment. It would be such that the balance has to be paid in full after a few years. Another similar method is a lease option (also called rent-to-own). With seller financing, you have the option to sell the mortgage note to a bank or even another investor. Whatever you decide to do, don't sit on the property without doing anything with it. This is because it will deteriorate and unnecessarily rob you of profits.

Conclusion

The appendices in Larry's book are very helpful, so you should go through them. The first appendix gives you several sample walkthroughs of how auctions work in actual counties. The second appendix lays out all of the action steps to do well in tax lien and/or deed investing.

Tax liens and tax deeds are a great way to make profits in real estate. They don't provide cash flow but do bring you predictable profits. They are the kind of investment where you need to do many of them so you can make a good living. With today's technology, you can do so comfortably from your own home in some counties. Larry's book helps set you on the path for success.

Additional Reading

Zero Risk Real Estate: Creating Wealth Through Tax Liens and Tax Deeds by Chip Cummings

The Complete Guide to Investing in Real Estate Tax Liens & Deeds How to Earn High Rates of Return – Safely by Alan Northcott

Chapter 17: Commercial Real Estate

Crushing It in Apartments and Commercial Real Estate: How a Small Investor Can Make It Big by Brian Murray

Introduction

Brian decided to invest in real estate while he was a teacher. He bought his first commercial property in 2007. A mere seven years later, he received an award for having the national real estate company of the year. That's quite a journey, and his book will tell how he got there in the first place. His approach to commercial properties was not complex, but it did differ vastly from how other companies ran their businesses. There are certainly other ways of investing in commercial properties, although Brian's method is quite successful, as you will read in his book. In his book, he provides you with insight on how you can also make the jump from small properties to larger ones. It is just like any form of real estate investing in that it is not a get-rich-quick scheme. It will require effort on your part.

Commercial Basics

When Brian began, he thought that he could only invest in smaller properties and never thought about commercial ones. However, he had trouble finding the "right" property. This is because the single-family houses and duplexes he looked at did not provide the returns he was looking to achieve. He then widened his search criteria and started to become curious about commercial properties.

There is a wide variety of commercial real estate. This includes things like small and large apartment buildings, office buildings, industrial, warehouses, self-storage, hospitality, laboratories, agricultural, parking lots/garages, mobile home parks, retirement communities, and retail space. You will need to decide the type of commercial real estate in which you want to invest. (I'll go more in-depth on some of these types in subsequent chapters.)

For example, apartment buildings and mobile home parks are great investments because people always need a place to live. Multifamily properties with 75+ units are more efficient to operate, although 100+ units are even better for that matter. Self-storage properties are popular as well. The ones in large metropolitan areas with a lot of drive-by traffic and a shortage of storage space especially do well. Retail space is attractive because they allow for triple net leases. This is where the tenants pay the rent, taxes, insurance, and maintenance costs.

Brian discovered that someone could buy commercial real estate even if they didn't have enough cash to do so. Brian's first commercial property was a 50K square foot office building listed for $1.2M. He negotiated the price down to $836,500, took over the seller's mortgage, and got $50K in credits. This way, he only had to put down around $34K of his own money.

There is value to learning real estate by starting small; however, you can just jump in and go big from the beginning. After all, fortune favors the bold. Perhaps surprisingly, investing in commercial real estate really isn't much more complicated than the small stuff. There is an economy of scale where larger properties are cheaper to maintain per square foot as compared to the smaller ones. Furthermore, commercial properties offer significantly better returns than smaller properties do.

There are a lot of big players who dominate the world of commercial investing. You, as a new person, can still compete and win. You should find a down to earth broker who can help you with the process. You would need to explore creative financing options if you can't put 25% down plus the closing costs to buy properties. Commercial investing can make you wealthy, but that's not always a guarantee.

Commercial financing can be as complicated as you want to make it. It's better to just focus on keeping it simple. You don't have to know how a car is built to be able to drive it. Start by adding up all of the annual expenses and income. If you subtract the expenses (except any loan payments) from the gross income, you will get the net operating income (NOI). The NOI is the single most important number for you to know about any commercial property.

Other concepts that show the true power in real estate include cash, leveraging, and compounding. Cash flow is king. It is the lifeblood of your real estate because it pays the bills and also helps you grow. The amount of annual cash flow divided by your initial investment in a commercial property equals the cash-on-cash (CoC) return. Leveraging happens when you use other people's money to make yourself money. This could be money from a bank loan/mortgage or other investors. However, you need to be careful about over-leveraging yourself by taking on too much debt because that can put you at much greater risk. (A lot of investors lost everything during the Great Recession of 2008 due to being over-leveraged.) Compounding happens when you reinvest your earnings, which then exponentially accelerates the growth of your income stream.

Let's break this down with an example. Suppose you buy a 30-unit apartment building for $1M. The income is $200K per year from rent, parking, and laundry, etc. The annual expenses, excluding loan payments, are $100K. This means the leftover $100K is now your NOI. The bank loan covered $750K, and the seller gave you a second mortgage of $150K for a combined annual loan cost of $63K. You only had to pay a down payment of $100k to buy this property. $100K NOI minus $63K for loan payments equals $37K annual cash flow. $37K divided by your $100K down payment equals a 37% CoC return.

But wait, there's more! The loan payoff is what creates equity. If you decrease expenses and/or increase the income, you end up getting a better return. There also are many tax benefits as icing on the cake. Each type of commercial real estate has its perks for you to enjoy.

To know how much any commercial property is worth, you need to be able to understand capitalization (cap) rates. A property's cap rate equals the purchase price divided by the NOI. Therefore, your

30-unit property's cap rate would be $100K/$1M=10\%$. The higher the purchase price, the lower the cap rate. A higher cap rate means that you're getting more bang for your buck, but that there may also be more risk involved. It's a bit of a 'high-risk, high- reward' approach if you play your cards the right way.

Sweat Equity

Are you willing and determined to do whatever it takes to achieve your goals? You need to put in the sweat equity to make things happen for you. Just don't jump into things blindly as that can cost you greatly. When first getting started, you should leverage your current resources to get things done without spending all your cash. There's no need to buy a new car, computer, or office space for your business before it's time to do so. With each expense, you need to ask yourself it is really necessary. Your cash is better used to buy deals instead of unnecessary things.

Brian's first office building brought in enough income to support his entire family. However, he still kept his day job for a while so that he could reinvest his real estate earnings into growing his real estate business. If you have a day job now, you'll have to decide if and when to quit based on your progress towards your goals. You have to put in the hard work while learning from your failures, and you can achieve success. It's okay to make mistakes along the way, as long as they don't destroy you completely.

Investing Locally vs. Long-Distance

In which city do you want to invest? You should choose a place that is well suited for your goals and the type of commercial properties you want to buy. Regardless of where you invest, you need to understand the local market there.

Investing in your own backyard is attractive because you already have some understanding of the local history, neighborhoods, population, businesses, and school districts, etc. It's a lot easier to build relationships with local real estate brokers, lenders, contractors, government officials, potential partners, and your tenants. And you are more likely to be in tune with shifts in the market.

Even if your local market isn't favorable for investing, you'll still have an advantage over long-distance investors. Don't just limit yourself to looking in your local market as there are good deals to be found in any market for that matter. You just need to take into account the extra risks from investing from a distance. It's essential to get a local team you trust when you do any kind of long-distance investing. You should keep close tabs on your distant properties so that you know things are in good order.

Choosing Your Battleground

Whenever Walmart has moved into communities, various mom and pop stores were pushed out of business. The ones who still flourished focused on selling goods and services that Walmart didn't offer, or they catered to customers who didn't shop at Walmart.

When it comes to commercial real estate, you should avoid going into direct competition with the bigtime investment firms. You can make a lot of money investing in niche types of properties that other people miss.

Some types of commercial properties are owner-operated and require specialized knowledge. These include properties such as farmland, resorts, and hotels. The "easier" types of commercial properties include multifamily apartments, retail, office space, and mobile home parks. They can also be mixed-use such as when a multistory building has retail stores on the first floor and apartments above them.

Brian recommends that when you are first starting, don't develop a property from scratch. Instead, you should buy a pre-existing property that already has a strong cash flow that can carry you through any challenges. A property with more units is safer than one with a single-tenant because the rental income is more spread out.

All commercial properties (and even neighborhoods and tenants) are divided into class A, B, C, or D. Properties in each class are classified based upon their age, condition, and general quality. The difference between the classes is rather ambiguous as the different criteria for them will vary between markets as well as investors.

Properties can also have pluses and minuses, such as B+ or C-. For example, A+ properties are the newest with the best quality and amenities. B properties are mid-range and are older than A, but still have a stable tenant base. C properties are usually older and outdated with blue-collar workers. Finally, D properties tend to be very old, in rough shape, and have a lot of crime. A's are expensive with low cap rates, while D's are cheap with high cap rates. A's tend to be easier to oversee. This is because they are in great shape with good tenants. B, C, and D properties all have opportunities for big profits by fixing them up and then improving the tenant base. (I especially like C+ and B properties. This is because I can add a lot of value to them without being overwhelmed by the amount of work involved.)

If you want to buy large commercial properties but don't have the money to do so, you may have to raise money from other investors. This is what large real estate firms also do. If you do it, you should underwrite your properties very conservatively so you can be confident that you will be able to pay out the expected returns to your investors. Large investors will often pass up properties that are smaller or less stable than what their investors want. You can then come in and reap the rewards from properties that other people didn't realize could be good deals.

Choosing a Property

After you have decided on the market, type of property, and specific class you want, it's time to start hunting for a commercial property. Your goal here is to find as many properties as possible that match your criteria as close as possible. This is a numbers game. It involves a lot of work. For about every ten properties you look at, one will be worth analyzing. About one in ten properties you analyze will be good enough for you to put an offer on them. About one out of 20 of those properties will then lead to a purchase. This means that you may have to look at 2000 properties to find one that you actually buy. You should not expect to find a property that is 100% perfect. Patience and perseverance are necessary to find those few deals that go through.

Commercial real estate brokers will be your lifeline to finding commercial properties. Their knowledge, experience, and listings will be very valuable to you as you look for the properties that fit your criteria. Many properties are listed online through the multiple listing service (MLS), CoStar, and LoopNet. Good brokers want to spend their time working with investors who can close deals. Therefore, it is best to build and maintain good relationships with them, and they will then bring you the deals you want.

You can also find deals by networking with people such as property managers, lenders, contractors, other investors, or by reaching out directly to owners. If you reach out directly to owners, you should be respectful to them and about their property. You need to tell them that you like the property and its location and that you would be interested if they were open to selling it. You should offer them your contact info. They could very well say no as they might change their mind down the road.

Auctions are another great place to find deals at bargain prices. However, auctions come with extra risk. They involve short closing windows, properties that are often distressed. Furthermore, you might not get to inspect the property before purchasing it. You should do as much advanced research as possible on a property up for auction. Check the tax records, neighborhood and look at the property from the outside. If you end up buying a lemon of a property, it's okay to just sell it and cut your losses.

Analyzing Deals

Most markets have so many commercial properties that you can't reasonably look at all of them. It would take you a very long time and effort to do so. Hence, you should narrow down your search criteria so that you have a much more focused search. After you find a property that you think is worth considering, do both a qualitative and quantitative analysis of it. Due diligence would be absolutely necessary here. Having said that, a quick overview is all that is needed now. You will do more in-depth underwriting after you have a property under contract as part of your due diligence.

Your initial screening can include a few things such as looking at satellite images and Google Street View, driving by it, considering its location and condition, seeing if there might be ways to profit by improving it, and then finally deciding if it matches your investment criteria.

The next thing you have to do is to run the numbers. If the property is listed through a broker, they will have prepared a pro forma document with all the relevant info about the property. With that info, you can calculate the NOI. If you know the going cap rate for that type of property in the market, then you can estimate what the sales price should be. You should be aware that the pro forma tends to look at a property's performance through rose-colored glasses. Your analysis needs to only look at the property's actual performance as opposed to its potential performance under perfect conditions.

A proper analysis means that you will need to ask for data on all of a property's income and expenses for at least the past year. This is also called the trailing 12 months, aka T12. The main part of the income is shown in the rent roll. That is a list of the tenants and how much they pay in rent. The income can also include pet fees, laundry/vending income, parking, security deposits, storage fees, and utility rebilling, etc. The expenses can vary throughout the year and can include utilities, snow removal, landscaping, property management, taxes, insurance, repairs, maintenance, legal fees, and advertising, etc.

Use the seller's pro forma as a starting point to then create your own pro forma. In this, you need to examine how you plan to operate the property. You need to know very well how you conservatively expect it to perform based upon the improvements and other changes you will make on it. You have to know what the value of the NOI and property will be once you have executed your business plan. You have to be aware that your property taxes may increase if you buy the property for more than what the last county tax appraisal calculated it as its worth. The various expenses tend to increase over time as well.

If you are getting a bank loan to buy a commercial property, then the bank will have expectations regarding the debt service coverage ratio abbreviated as DSCR. The DSCR equals the NOI divided by the mortgage payments. This just means that the property's income can cover the expenses and mortgage payments with some leftover. Lenders usually look for DSCRs of at least 1.25. If the mortgage payments are $10K per month, then the monthly NOI needs to be at least $12,500, but it should be preferably higher. Low DSCRs are higher risk because there is only a narrow margin of error if anything goes wrong.

After you get a commercial property under a sales contract, it is then that you will begin your due diligence period. Due diligence is also known as underwriting. This is where you take a deep dive into a property's books, and its other records. The point here is to see that if you can confirm whether your initial analysis and assumptions were accurate.

Since the T12 doesn't always tell the whole story, you need to look at the actual leases for every tenant. You have to see if the owner cut down on expenses leaving some deferred maintenance. That makes it look like the expenses were lower than they should be. If at all possible, look at the actual expenses and income for the past two years to get a more accurate picture. You should tour every unit with a contractor and look at things like the landscaping, the windows, and whether the tags are expired on the fire extinguisher tags or the HVAC.

If there are major red flags during your due diligence, then you can renegotiate the purchase price or terms if so needed. If you do that for no good reason, it's considered bad form and is called "retrading." Retrading can hurt your reputation and also make it harder to get future deals. It is very important to trust your instincts about what to decide about a property.

Underwriting Considerations

Since every type of commercial real estate investment is unique. Therefore, there are different things you will need to consider while underwriting. Office buildings will range from class A-C. A's are brand new or newly remodeled. C's are dated but quite functional. And B's are in between. You need to think about a property's design, quality of materials used, parking, access to major roads and public transit, and how close it is to hotels and restaurants. The tenant would pay for their utilities and custodial work, and you would then pay the other expenses. Office leases usually last three to seven years. Medical office buildings will need more plumbing and electrical wiring as compared to regular offices.

Retail properties could range from a small shop up to a giant mall. The surrounding traffic should be appropriate for the specific retail location so the businesses within that location can get enough customers. There needs to be adequate signage to attract customers. Leases usually last from five to ten years, and major companies may even sign 25-year leases, for example. Leases are on a (single, double, or triple) net basis where it will vary in which expenses are paid for by the tenant vs. the landlord. Some leases may have the tenant pay a flat fee in addition to a portion of their profits.

Industrial real estate includes light or heavy manufacturing, warehouses, and distribution facilities. It's okay if they are older areas as long as they have good access to major roads. About 10-20% of industrial space is made up of offices. Properties normally need to have high ceilings, think floors, truck bays, and ample electrical capacity. Leases are on a net basis and usually last between three and five years. The landlord is usually only responsible for maintaining the outer walls and the roof.

Multifamily apartments are needed in any market. Their profits can be stable, although multifamily requires a lot of work. Good property management is essential to their success. They normally have one-year leases and higher turnover as compared to other asset classes. Ongoing marketing is necessary to keep occupancy rates high. You should give strong consideration to the demographics of the local tenant base, economic factors such as rent and employment rates, proximity to schools and shopping, and the local laws and taxes.

Hospitality is both very lucrative and very sensitive to market trends. These include hotels, resorts, theme parks, golf courses, and restaurants, etc. Such properties can raise rates quickly when the market is going up but can feel it first during an economic downturn. They are even more labor-intensive than multifamily and may have franchise fees for you to pay as well.

With hotels, you are buying both the real estate and the business that comes within it. They are analyzed through their average daily rate (ADR) and also their revenue per available room (RevPAR). To find the ADR, take the total room revenue during a period divided by the number of occupied rooms. ADR times the occupancy rate equals to the RevPAR. The franchise fees and management fees run around 5% of gross revenue, respectively.

Residential healthcare facilities such as nursing homes, independent living, and assisted living all provide varying levels of care to their tenants. Independent living facilities don't receive government funding and are thus not regulated by it as such. Nursing homes and assisted living facilities are eligible for government funding and the regulations that come with it. The local demographic will determine the demand for these facilities.

Creative Deal Structures

You make money in real estate when you buy and not when you sell. It's essential to buy properties at the right price. The structure of a deal is just as important. The structure involves the down payment, closing costs, interest rate of the loan, amortization schedule, concessions, etc. It often takes creative structuring to make deals work for you. There are various options for this.

Seller financing is when the seller owns their property without debt or be able to pay off the debt. They then act as the bank where you make the mortgage payments to them. This gives the seller continued cash flow while avoiding a big capital gains tax bill from the sale. There is often a lot more flexibility on the terms for a seller financing transaction as opposed to an actual bank.

A seller may be willing to give you 100% financing if they are motivated enough. You can even combine seller financing with a bank loan. For example, you might get a bank loan for 75% of the purchase price and then seller financing for some or all of the rest. You need to know that not all sellers are open to doing seller financing. It can help to start by offering them a lower price without seller financing, but then to make a higher second offer with it.

A master lease agreement is another great option if you find yourself short on cash. This is like doing rent-to-own, except with a commercial property. You won't own it yet but can still rent it out for any cash flow as well as tax benefits. With the master lease agreement, you put down a smaller down payment and make rent payments to the seller. You should just make sure that your rent payments to the seller are getting paid to their mortgage in case they have one. You and the seller agree to a sales price that is good for a specific period. During that time, you can raise money for a full down payment and arrange traditional bank financing. The property may even appreciate enough so that you can get 100% financing for the previously agreed price.

It's possible to assume a seller's mortgage loan. In such a case, you would be taking on the preexisting interest rate as well as loan terms. The seller's lender has to be on board for this to happen. This is a great way to save cash at the closing if that mortgage exceeds 75% of the purchase price.

A rarely used option is called a wraparound mortgage (wrap). This is when the seller keeps their mortgage in place, and in their name after the sale is completed. The seller then gives the buyer owner financing for an amount greater than the mortgage. Wraps are not usually possible because many mortgages do not permit them.

Syndication allows you to buy bigger properties if you have little to no money of your own. (It is my favorite option of the bunch.) This works because you can pool together the money of other investors to be able to buy those properties. These investors would be partial owners. However, you would still have some equity and also be in control of the property. You can make money with syndication by charging fees, splitting the cash flow with the investors, and/or getting part of the sales profits when you later sell the property. Syndication is complicated and requires you to follow MANY rules. Do not attempt this without assistance from a real estate attorney.

Grants, tax credits, and other government programs can also help you buy commercial properties. You will have various hoops to jump through if you accept these government subsidies. It can take you a lot of time as well as effort to get them. They can certainly be of good help if you are passionate about restoring historic buildings. (I've also seen them help people invest in affordable housing.)

You can also get creative with the closing of a sale. Maintenance credits can help cover your cost of taking care of deferred maintenance. You should always have an inspection done, so you are aware of any such issues. If the seller is motivated, you can potentially negotiate to get a credit equal to the amount of their escrow or reserve accounts. When you schedule a closing to occur early in the month, you can get the prorated rent for the rest of that month at closing. At closing, you will also gain stewardship of any security deposits of the tenants. Negotiating for a lower interest rate and down payment are both fair game as well.

There are many approaches to negotiation. The more you know about a seller will help you determine which approach to use and also what the seller wants most out of the transaction. If you can give the seller's most important concessions and terms to them, it will be easier for you to get the concessions and terms that are also important to you. For example, if the seller mainly wants a specific purchase price, you can also show them how you can make that happen with a creative financing option.

Before you get into a legal commitment with a property, you should always consult with a qualified professional first. It is well worth your money to hire a good commercial real estate attorney. There's nothing wrong with walking away from a deal if so needed. Sometimes, your best deals will be the ones you walk away from.

Using Banks

The easiest time to get a bank loan is when you don't need it. It's very interesting that banks also make it very hard to get loans when you do, however, need them. However, a bank loan can certainly allow you to buy real estate that you couldn't have been able to otherwise. Don't just look at big banks. Smaller local banks can also offer you great deals on commercial loans. Start building good relationships with lenders so that they will understand your investment plan and then be willing to give you loans when you need them.

Different lenders require various amounts of information as part of your application for a commercial loan. You should expect that you will have to provide the property's financials, the purchase agreement, the proformas, your personal financial statement, recent federal and state tax returns, and your business plan and project summary. Since you usually won't get to make an in-person sales pitch, you should ensure that your application documents are in good order.

It's really helpful to get to know the bank's approval process by reading the Office of the Comptroller of the Currency Comptroller's Handbook. The more you understand things from the bank's perspectives, the better prepared you can be with your loan application. Essentially, banks want to make sure that a commercial property, your creditworthiness, and your business plan for it are all very solid. The DSCR and loan-to-value (LTV) are vital to the bank's underwriting process. The LTV is equal to the loan amount divided by the property's value. Banks usually want the LTV to be a maximum of 75% on a commercial property.

When a bank accepts your application, you will then receive a commitment letter. It will contain any contingencies that the bank will require, including but not limited to, the following: An appraisal may be required to confirm the property's value. An environmental report determines the potential environmental impact of a property. A property conditions assessment does just as its name describes.

Title insurance may be required to protect against potential issues with the title transfer. Tenant estoppel agreements can confirm the terms of any leases. An insurance binder proves that the property will be covered by insurance.

When you have some seller financing on top of a bank loan, this is called "mezzanine debt," and that is second to the bank loan. For this type of situation to work out, you will need to prove to the bank that the property will have enough income to have a DSCR that covers both mortgages.

A mortgage broker is an independent consultant who can aid you with the loan application process and then even knowing which banks would be good for you to approach. They charge you a fee of 1-3% of the loan amount you receive. (They are costly, but can be worth it if they get you better terms on your loan.) A mortgage banker, on the other hand, can help you through the loan application without charging you any fee.

You should always check the references of a mortgage broker or mortgage banker before you bring them onto your team. Having a professional on your side can help you through the complexity of bank loans. For example, a loan can be recourse or non-recourse. With a recourse loan, you would be held personally liable for it. Whereas, you cannot be held personally liable with a non-recourse loan.

Treat Your Real Estate Business Like a Business

Once you've bought a good commercial property that fits your investment goals, you are already ahead of the majority of people that only dream about investing. However, you still have a lot of work to do. Most real estate investments are not 100% passive, like owning stocks or bonds. This means that you also have a lot more control over the success of your real estate investments. Luck is not a factor, but hard work and determination are.

Part of that control means making decisions about how to operate your real estate business. Will you hire a professional property manager or manage things yourself? Brian recommends to self-manage when you are first starting in the field of real estate. Good property management companies are hard to find, and will usually charge you 3-7% of the gross income. You can save money and gain experience/knowledge by self-managing. You should just know that you will have to delegate things like property management to scale your business to grow.

There's no real good way to do everything yourself in your commercial real estate business. You need to build a good team to help you as your business grows. You should think about which parts of your business you enjoy, are good at, or could learn how to do. You should hire people to do the tasks that you can't do or aren't interested in doing. Don't hire out before you need it. You should be slow to hire people, yet quick to fire them when things aren't working out. Brian includes an extensive list of potential team members in his appendix.

As your business grows, you will need to adapt and change. You should consider your options before making decisions. When will you hire a property manager instead of self-managing? Will you hire various people as part-time or fulltime, as contractors or full employees, as temporary or permanent? Will you manage the employees, or hire a manager for that? If you outsource the property management and/or employee management, you will still need to manage the managers. You need to communicate regularly with them and maintain high standards for success.

Value-Add

Unlike with residential real estate or your stock portfolio, you have more control over the value of your commercial real estate. As mentioned previously, a commercial property's value is determined by the cap rate and the NOI. You can't control the going cap rate, but you can improve the NOI by increasing income and/or decreasing expenses. Improving the NOI by some means is called a "value-add."

Let's suppose you spend $10K to fix up a distressed unit. That renovated unit could perhaps bring in an additional $500 per month in rent, which then comes out to $6K per year. That's a 60% return on your $10K investment! And if the going cap rate was 9%, $6K divided by 0.09 means that your property increased its value by $66,667. There should be some dollar signs appearing in your eyes right about now.

In addition to renovating units to get higher rents, you can discover other value-add opportunities for your properties. Repurpose storage space into office space or renovate a three-bedroom apartment into two one-bedrooms. Improve energy efficiency by installing low-flow toilets, faucet aerators, LED lighting, motion detector lighting, or better insulation. Cleaning up the landscaping and repainting are easy ways to upgrade a property's appearance. Create new income streams with things like paid parking or vending machines. Improve the advertising to boost your occupancy rate. Raise or lower rents to be in line with the market rate. You could change out your staff and/or vendors to get better value from new ones. Improve the property management so that it becomes a well-oiled machine.

The renovations you do on a property to increase the NOI are defined as capital improvements. The dollars you spend on doing those are your capital expenditures (CapEx). Effective capital improvements will get you better tenants who pay more and lower your cost of operating the property. They cost you extra in the short term but are gifts that keep on giving over time.

One great thing that comes with CapEx is the tax benefits that come with it. Hire a skilled tax accountant to ensure that you can minimize your tax liability. They will depreciate the cost of your CapEx as fast as legally possible. You can reinvest that extra money back into your business instead of it going to the IRS.

Brian's first office building was losing $40K annually before he purchased it. It had a high vacancy, a ton of deferred maintenance, and out of control expenses. Many people tried to talk him out of it. However, he had the foresight to see all of its problems as value-add opportunities. He systematically improved the efficiency of the heating/cooling, reduced the property tax bill, fired the terrible property manager, cleaned up the place, and built positive relationships with commercial brokers who helped rent out the vacant office units. His changes made the property start having positive cash flow from the very first day.

Renting to Tenants

It is normal to want to have a zero percent vacancy while receiving top dollar for rent. You will have to decide for yourself how to balance wanting higher rents while minimizing vacancy. If you overcharge, you may end up with vacant units, high turnover, and needy tenants. You should focus instead on offering good value to tenants. And if you slightly undercharge rent, you'll have high occupancy, low turnover, and a wider pool from which to find awesome tenants.

You should think about who you want your tenant base to be. You will want to do things differently if you are catering to senior citizens as opposed to college students. With commercial properties, it is especially important to have the right mix of tenants. For example, you may not want a liquor store put in a strip mall next to a daycare. However, it would probably be fine to put that liquor store next to a tattoo parlor or even a marijuana dispensary. Having two competing businesses next to each other is something that would create an unhappy situation. Your goal is to create an atmosphere of harmony with and among your tenants.

You should always screen your tenants. You don't want to be locked into a legal agreement with someone whom you will regret. Commercial leases tend to be for longer periods than residential leases. Your screening should include a potential tenant's credit score, criminal history, references, income verification, as well as eviction record. Local laws will vary on what is permitted with tenant screening. Many online screening companies can help with the process. You will have to gauge the risk of accepting a retail tenant who is starting a new business because so many of them fail.

Inevitably, your operating costs will increase over time. It's normal to increase the rent as well to keep your profit margins stable. Hiking up prices quickly will run the risk of upsetting your tenants. It is better to be patient and raise rents more gradually. And you should be considerate if you have elderly tenants who are on a fixed income. Open communication helps to alleviate tenants' concerns about potential rent increases or other changes.

You will have many tenants who are great with good communication, keeping things clean, and always pay rent on time. At the same time, you will likely have some tenants who are less than perfect. Perhaps they are drug dealers, skip out on rent, or maybe they are just plain crazy. Brian has plenty of horror stories, such as the surgeon who left animal blood smeared all over his apartment when he moved out without notice. In addition to good screening, you can keep an eye on things and address issues when they occur.

There are various methods for advertising your open units. You can hang signs out, advertise through word-of-mouth, run open houses, offer bonuses for referrals from current tenants, use commercial brokers, submit press releases, or post ads in places like online classifieds, Facebook, Craigslist, or numerous other websites. You should find the methods that work best for you and your units.

When you buy a property with tenants, you inherit their leases as well. When their leases expire, or you get new tenants, you can then start using your lease. You can then use a proper lease template created by a good real estate attorney. Creating your own could get you in legal trouble, unless of course, if you are a good real estate attorney yourself.

The lease is a legally binding document meant to protect both you and your tenants. If a tenant violates the terms of the lease, then you have to decide how to proceed. Suing and/or evicting them will cost you time and money. Therefore, it should be considered a last resort. Brian has only had a 50% success rate with suing tenants who owed him money. A quicker and cheaper way to get out a bad tenant is called "cash-for-keys." This is where you can pay the tenant some amount of money to move out of the space and turn over their keys to you.

Ethical Investing

Brian's high level of integrity sets him apart from other commercial investors. It helps motivate him and his employees to achieve high standards of quality. Whereas unethical approaches would surely come back to bite you. Real estate is pretty much all about relationships and reputation. Build your reputation through daily choices, which are guided by integrity, high standards, as well as professionalism.

Your tenants are your customers. You need to show them appreciation, empathy, and respect. Before you make any changes, you should consider how those changes could impact them. They will then treat your property well and stay longer. Keeping your tenants happy means fewer problems for you and lower turnover costs.

You need to think of commercial tenants as your business partners. Their businesses need to do well to be able to pay you rent. You want them to be successful so that the cash can flow. You can help them by keeping the property clean and in good shape. If a tenant's business starts to fail, it can become increasingly difficult for them to catch up on late rent due to the downward momentum.

One major stressor for many landlords is handling it when tenants don't pay rent on time. Sometimes a good tenant might fall on hard times and can't pay rent. Other tenants think that you're incredibly wealthy, and skipping rent won't hurt anybody. Some tenants will try to take advantage of your kindness.

If you do give anyone exceptions to paying rent or following other rules, word will spread, and you may then have to deal with additional problems. You are responsible for both your tenants and your real estate business. Hence, you have to decide what the right thing to do will be.

Growing Your Business

You want your business to be like a factory that works with high efficiency, whether or not you are in the office. To do this, you need refined processes. You need to document those processes well so that they can be taught to your employees. This isn't such a big deal if you do all the work yourself with a few units. However, if you plan to scale up to 100, 1K, or 10K+ units, you will need systems in place that are ready for it. Documented policies and procedures will help things run smoothly and efficiently without important things getting missed along the way.

At the beginning of Brian's real estate business, he found himself reactively putting out fires. He kept solving the same problems repeatedly until the point he got fed-up enough to create a process to prevent them from reoccurring. He recommends keeping paper and digital copies of your processes as they develop over time. There's no shame in copying procedures from others, such as from the *Housing Manager's Procedures Manual* that you can get for free online very easily.

Your business will need various structural components. The business development part will cover things like property acquisitions and leasing. Routine maintenance takes care of landscaping, snow removal, and furnace tune-ups, etc. Service requests give a workflow process to handle requests and complaints from tenants. Unit turns will allow unit upgrades to go smoothly in between tenants. Project management will then oversee contractors doing upgrades. Financial management oversees the bills. And finally, general management takes care of the day-to-day oversight of everything.

Know Your Why

With enough time, hard work, and focus, you can achieve great success with commercial real estate investing. If you think it will all be easy, then you are in for a surprise. Having a purpose and passion will carry you through all the difficult times and be the driving force behind your success. You should define specific values for your business as they will set the tone for the company culture. They will keep your employees on the right track to fulfill your vision.

You need to properly define your core reason for wanting to invest in real estate. You need to determine if you are passionate about creating jobs, improving people's lives and the community, achieving financial freedom to enjoy life fully with your family, building something amazing, or some other awesome goal. Whatever your reason is, it has to be more substantial than just earning money. You need to think of the big picture. (This is called your "Why.")

Holding vs. Selling

There are many strategies for how long to hold onto properties and also when to sell them. Flipping real estate can make you quick cash. However, holding onto it for longer gives you access to ongoing profits. Brian prefers the buy-and-hold strategy for the sake of maximizing the growth of his business. He recommends holding onto properties for at least two years to complete the value-add projects. One or two years of an increased NOI shows that the property is "seasoned" enough to account for a higher resale price as well. It's an effective long term strategy.

The transaction costs involved in a property's sale can be 5-10% of the sale price. When you buy and hold onto a property, you avoid having those costs eat into your profits. It is then possible to defer the capital gains tax from a sale by using a 1031 exchange. You should seek help from your commercial real estate attorney and tax accountant to make sure you follow all of the rules with it.

The longer you own the property, the more efficient and cost-effective your systems will then become. If you need to pull out cash to buy more real estate, you should consider refinancing instead of selling a property. Paying down the principal of the mortgage creates equity for you. And if you created value by increasing the NOI, then you have forced appreciation to occur. This is a great way to expand your real estate empire. David only sells a property if he never intended to hold onto it for a long time. When a great deal comes along, and he needs cash to buy, he will then sell that property.

Having Balance

It's an all too common occurrence that our work as real estate investors can swallow us up like a black hole. Endless tasks "need" to get done. As your business grows, this will only amplify. Too many people fail to prioritize and set limits when there is always urgent work to be done. If you are working 16-hour days, can't sleep, are responding to emails at 3 a.m., and find that your relationships are suffering, it may be then time to take a step back and rethink things.

Please don't get me wrong. Hard work is very necessary. And if you love everything you are doing, then it won't even seem like work at all. When every little thing feels like a chore, then you might be working too much in your business and not enough on your business to help it to grow at the pace you want. Brian Dyson, the former CEO of Coca-Cola, said that life is like juggling five balls named family, health, friends, and spirit. Having said that, you have to define your priorities.

Brian realized that the idea of sitting on a beach doing nothing did not excite him at all. He needed something more fulfilling. His driving factors include being productive, helping other people, feeling challenged, learning and growing, and then sharing with his loved ones. This is why he started teaching. The small salary brought him to real estate, where he was able to finally focus his inner passions.

You should create a plan of action for balance. Bringing work home can be positive if you share funny stories about it with your family or ask for their opinions about things. You can bring home to work by involving your family with small projects are showing what you are doing with the bigger ones. If you have a partner or close friend who is interested as well, teaming up with them can be awesome if you can manage this new dynamic in the relationship.

And make self-improvement as much of a priority as improving your properties.

Continue to Learn and Grow

You should think of Brian's book as a good start to your education in commercial real estate investing. Since there are so many types of commercial investments, one book couldn't possibly cover them all in-depth. You need to commit to continual learning and self-improvement so that your business can thrive.

You have to take ownership of your education in real estate, sales, and general business practices. You can do so through books, training courses, online videos, articles, blogs, podcasts, discussion forums, conferences, and various groups. You should be wary of the many gurus who charge high prices for training you even though they may not even have done any deals on their own.

One thing that can exponentially set your growth on fire is to get a mentor who is excelling at commercial real estate. A successful real estate investor's most valuable things to offer are their time and knowledge. These are priceless commodities, and for that very reason, they won't just give that to you for free, though. You need to first find a way to add value to them, which could range from doing volunteer work for them to paying them their consulting fees.

When it comes to learning new information, you should think of yourself as a starving person who goes to a buffet. You should just gorge yourself with as much training and education as possible. (If you listen to podcasts or audiobooks, see if you can still absorb the information at 1.5X speed or faster.) You have to soak it all up like a sponge while using your best judgment on what advice to accept.

You need to determine a few things for yourself. You have to know if you want to be the kind of person who makes excuses or makes things happen. Too many potential investors get sidetracked or just get engrossed and stuck in their education phase that they never actually take any action. If you are feeling overwhelmed, that's a very normal scenario. It helps to break large goals down into smaller and achievable steps. The hardest part of any big venture is to take the first step. After that, you should keep putting one foot in front of the other to make progress towards your goals.

Conclusion

Throughout Brian's book, he tells a quite interesting story about a mixed-use property he bought at an auction called the Solar Building. It was a historic building that was run down, infested with cockroaches, and had tenants dealing drugs as well as doing other nefarious things. He did such an amazing job turning around that building that it had the honor to be featured on the cover of the *Community Investor* magazine. Buying Brian's full book is well worth it because he speaks from the heart and provides invaluable real-world advice on commercial investing. This is one education that you won't ever regret investing in.

Additional Reading

The Due Diligence Handbook for Commercial Real Estate: A Proven System to Save Time, Money, Headaches and Create Value When Buying Commercial Real Estate by Brian Hennessey

Mastering the Art of Commercial Real Estate Investing: How to Successfully Build Wealth and Grow Passive Income from Your Rental Properties by Douglas Marshall

Chapter 18: Mobile Home Parks

How to Invest in a Mobile Home Park: For Business, Money and Profit by David Rousher

Introduction

David got started investing in mobile home parks (MHP) by learning from his father. Donald wrote the first book about investing in MHPs way back in 1974. Since then, the industry has grown leaps and bounds. There are around 50K MHPs today with an increasing demand for more. The quality of mobile homes has increased dramatically over time as well.

Mobile Home Parks

When Warren Buffet bought out Clayton Homes in 2003, people started realizing that MHPs could be a profitable business. If you have good business practices and make sure the numbers add up before purchasing an MHP, it can survive a recession and also give you great cash flow.

For many people who don't have a ton of money, purchasing a mobile home makes homeownership within reach. MHPs used to be called gypsy camps and then trailer parks. However, that all changed due to the prevalence of the derogatory term "trailer trash." Some MHPs can certainly be in bad shape if both the owners and residents don't take care of them. Modern MHPs are clean and can have great amenities like pools, tennis courts, playgrounds, clubhouses, and even golf courses.

New mobile homes usually cost between $35K-$65K to buy but can easily cost you over $100K. Their quality is regulated by the Department of Housing and Urban Development (HUD). When someone owns their mobile home, they pay rent of usually between $200-$800 for the land. Rent often covers trash removal but not any other utilities.

Some MHPs rent out both mobile homes and the land together. You can make more money renting out mobile homes, but it takes a lot more effort to handle the maintenance and other issues that happen. It's harder to refinance an MHP with a lot of rental homes, and you also have a higher turnover. Residents who own their homes will stay an average of five years. It costs around $5K to move their home somewhere else, so they are then more likely to sell their home instead of move it. As long as you don't raise the rent too much each year, then residents are unlikely to move out.

You will need on-site management to collect rents, do maintenance on rental homes, and rehab them in between tenants. Furthermore, they can take care of common areas and make sure that tenants follow the park rules. Managers stay an average of five to six years, which can be less if there are a lot of rental homes. David is not a fan of rental mobile homes due to the headaches they cause despite the extra cash flow they bring.

MHPs vs. Apartments

Affordable housing like MHPs and apartments are always needed. MHPs are a lot quieter than apartment buildings due to the lace of shared walls, have cheaper turnover costs, and tend to have a better sense of community among residents. When people own their mobile homes, they tend to take much better care of the space as compared to people who rent. Mobile homeowners take care of their property maintenance and repairs, whereas apartment renters would call you for that. Furthermore, apartment renters are much more likely to move out when there is a rent increase.

MHPs have great tax advantages. You can then depreciate apartment buildings over 27.5 years. The main parts of an MHP include roads and utility lines, which depreciate faster over only 15 years. MHPs use 30-40% of their income for operations costs. Apartments need 50-65% of their income for their operation costs.

Parks for Seniors

Florida has an ever-growing population of retired seniors who are on a budget. MHPs there tend to be focused on the needs of seniors. Seniors make wonderful tenants at MHPs because they pay on time, don't throw wild parties, tend to stay for a long time, and also take care of their space. You have to pay attention to local laws about rent as there may be restrictions on your ability to raise it at senior living MHPs. When a senior citizen passes away, it can be tricky to have to deal with their heirs regarding what to do with the mobile home.

Rating System

MHPs are ranked on a five-star system formalized by the Manufactured Housing Institute. More stars mean easier financing, better terms, and also at a higher sales price. David likes to focus on finding older mid-range MHPs with two or three stars. Insurance is cheaper for them, and it's also easier to add value to them.

The factors that impact stars include paved roads, amenities, the ratio of single vs. doublewide homes, condition of the utilities, occupancy rates, and also how the property looks. The five-star MHPs are in pristine condition, have pools and clubhouses, and are in beautiful locations. Avoid one-star MHPs as they are in a dilapidated state from which they can't recover.

Pricing Properties

The price of an MHP is impacted by local market conditions and the MHP's condition. However, the capitalization (cap) rate is the best way to then determine a property's worth. The cap rate is determined by dividing the net operating income (NOI) by the price of the property. The NOI is calculated from the total annual income minus all of the expenses, except for mortgage payments and depreciation.

You can determine the price of the property by dividing the NOI by the going cap rate for MHPs in the area. If a property has an annual NOI of $100K in a market where the going cap rate is 8%, then $100K÷0.08=$1.25M for the property's worth. You should aim to buy MHPs with cap rates between 5-10%.

Building Parks

The idea of having a shiny new MHP is appealing. However, government regulations on building one can make this difficult. An angry mob of neighbors once showed up to a city council meeting where David wanted to get approval for a new MHP. The neighbors were worried that the MHP would disrupt the town and also the water supply.

You need lots of time and money to build an MHP. This is because you need to plan it all out, get the proper permits, and build the infrastructure. From there, you then need to advertise the park, possibly with some model homes to show to people. The process from inception to fully rented takes several years.

Starting Out

If you are still interested in MHPs, then you need to first determine what return you want on your money, what type of MHPs you want to own, and what you are willing to do to add value to properties. You have to set your ultimate goals first and then work backward from there.

Senior living MHPs tend to have 5-6% cap rates with a 4-6% cash flow. Family orientated MHPs have 6.5-9% cap rates with 7-12% cash flow. The older MHPs that need a lot of work can be cash cows with 10-15% cap rates that cash flow at 12-20%.

If you limit yourself to only buying MHPs close to where you live for just the convenience, then you might miss out on better opportunities that are further from you. It's more profitable to expand your search nationwide to find hidden gems out there. It can also be nice to enjoy the boundaries you have when you don't live in the same town as your rental properties.

It's up to you how involved you want to be with your properties. David loves having a good property management company in place. That company can handle the rents, advertising, maintenance, repairs, and other issues that happen in the day-to-day operations. They can also save you money by being efficient at what they do.

Finding Properties

David recommends looking for MHPs on www.LinkedIn.com, www.LoopNet.com, www.MobileHomeParkStore.com, www.CraigsList.com, and just by searching on Google. David also stops by or makes cold calls to MHPs that he is interested in buying. You should search in towns that have at least 50K people to ensure that you can find enough quality tenants.

Look at the demographics for the areas within a town to find out where to concentrate based upon the type of MHP and tenants you want. You should also consider the area's unemployment rates, diversity of jobs, stability of the jobs at local employers, if there is bad weather that could destroy your MHP, and vacancy rates. If there is a nearby college, that is good because it means that you'll have a tenant base.

If an MHP's property manager doesn't like the current owner, they might then be willing to give you the info if you tell them that you want to buy the park and keep them as the property manager.

You can find out from banks which MHPs have been foreclosed. If you hire a real estate broker with an MHP specialty, they will do all the searching on your behalf.

Red Flags

You should avoid smaller towns, military towns, or places where the population is declining. You might struggle to keep your vacancy low there. If an MHP has a high vacancy rateand the seller is trying to sell it at top dollar as if it were full, purchasing it would then be like flushing money down the toilet. Only buy a run down MHP if you have the time, money, and business plan to turn it around.

If most of the homes in a park are owned by the park, be warned that you will be bogged down with maintenance oversight. If another landlord owns the homes and the MHP only rents out the spaces, then things could be catastrophic in case anything goes wrong between you and them. They might not maintain the homes or make sure tenants follow the park rules. Or they might decide to move all of their homes out, leaving your park empty!

Making Money

To succeed with MHPs, you need to work smarter instead of harder. David has done well buying distressed properties, fixing and cleaning them up, evicting the non-paying and/or lawbreaking tenants, and then putting in great tenants for excellent cash flow. While it wasn't easy, the rewards were worth it to him. You can make a lot of money by finding and buying mom and pop MHPs that have a lot of vacancies, rents below market value, and are also in a general state of disrepair. There is an opportunity here to add value as well as profits.

Properties with extra land allow you to expand as long as the city approves the planning and zoning to add additional mobile home spaces. If an open area is not right for homes, you could turn it into storage units or space for storing RVs and other vehicles. (I know a guy in Minnesota with a park next to a lake that rents out space for people's ice houses in the summer and then RVs in the winter.)

You should consider becoming a licensed mobile home dealer so you can buy homes at wholesale prices. You would the be able to resell them to your tenants for extra profit. Selling homes with payment plans creates even more cash flow for you.

Increasing income and decreasing expenses are the two main ways to improve the value of your property. It is best to raise rents each year, even if it's only by a little. You can charge for things like pets and long-term guests. You could get things set up, so each tenant pays for their own water, garbage, recycling, and sewer usage. If you are paying those bills, you can improve the energy efficiency by doing things like adding heat tape on the pipes or installing solar panels.

Conclusion

This book is an easy read and is packed with excellent tips. You can tell that David knows the MHP business very well. He invites you to contact him at 208-661-9799 or drousher@gmail.com for consultations and questions should you have any. When I talked to him on the phone, he said that he is always looking for new partners who want to do deals with him. His advice for new investors is to make sure the numbers add up before buying a deal. Buying at the right price is essential. You also need enough reserves to handle a recession since you will never know when it could happen. Even during a recession, he still looks for deals as they are still out there. You just need to look in the right places, and you'll find them.

Additional Reading

Mobile Home Wealth: How to Make Money Buying, Selling and Renting Mobile Homes by Zalman Velvel

The New Investor's Guide to Owning a Mobile Home Park: Why Mobile Home Park Ownership Is the Best Investment in This Economy and Step by Step Instructions How to Acquire and Manage a Profitable Park by Laura Cochran

Chapter 19: Self-Storage
Creating Wealth Through Self-Storage by Mark Helm

Introduction

Mark is a commercial real estate agent who got into buying self-storage properties through what would be considered a happy mistake. He was forced to create an effective system for analyzing self-storage properties that he has fine-tuned throughout the years. He now calls it the "greatest business on earth!" You can access his various self-storage resources on his website www.CreatingWealthThroughSelfStorage.com. This website can help you get started and expand your investments. The code "CWTSS" will give you $100 off his Valuator software.

Getting into Self-Storage

On a random day in May 1995, Mark happened to be in his office when a phone call came in from the acquisition director for a real estate investment trust (REIT). Mark wasn't the first person they called, but he was the first person who had answered their call. At this time, REITs were eager to invest in self-storage. The acquisition director asked Mark if he could help them buy some self-storage, which is something he had not yet done. However, if you ever ask a realtor if they can help you buy real estate, they will almost always say yes. Thus, began Mark's headfirst dive into the world of self-storage.

Mark previously focused on office buildings, which can cost a lot of money to operate. He had a preconceived notion that it was difficult to create wealth in real estate, mostly due to the operating costs. He saw self-storage as an asset type with great income potential with a minimal overhead cost. They are normally steel and concrete buildings that are inexpensive to build. During the 2008-2009 recession, self-storage lost only 6% of its occupancy, which was better compared to other forms of commercial real estate. Self-storage also has a lower rate of foreclosure than any other kind of real estate.

He started by gathering information from current self-storage owners and then analyzing that data. He used a financial analysis software program called Argus, and later developed his Valuator analysis software program. At that time, industrial warehouses generated $3.50 of income per square foot per year. However, basic self-storage space just generated $8.50-$9.00 of income per square foot per year. Self-storage that was climate controlled made even more money.

Self-storage requires very few capital improvements. There are generally no carpets to replace, no walls to paint, and no plumbing to update, etc. The only moving part is normally the door to each unit. The capital expenses are pretty predictable, such as the roof and paving. Rents can be raised systematically as the leases are all month-to-month. Raising rent by 3% annually doesn't normally cause people to move out.

The big secret for creating wealth in self-storage is to increase your income 1-2% more than your operating expenses increase each year. By doing this, you will then compound your profits year after year. Mark realized that to get into self-storage, he needed to raise the money for a down payment, qualify for a large loan, and make sure the purchase price allowed for him to get adequate returns higher than what the stock market produced.

There are two competing associations: The Self Storage Association (SSA) and Inside Self Storage (ISS). Mark is a member of both associations. The SSA makes updates for the industry in each state while the ISS has very good education and training material.

Self-Storage Data

The first self-storage facility was built in 1958 in Fort Lauderdale, Florida. Self-storage was originally pretty basic, but it then really developed in the 1970s. The rental rates per square foot per month went from $0.15 in the 1960s, to $0.60 in 1985, to $1.50-$4.00 today. Facilities today can now have all the bells and whistles. That includes cameras, top of the line fencing, truck rentals, box and lock sales, key-coded gates, and on-site managers.

As of the time of this book's publication, there were 48,500 self-storage facilities in the USA. They are more numerous in the USA than the McDonald's, Burger Kings, and Wendy's locations. They had an average size of around 51K square feet. The estimated gross revenue was around $24 billion back in 2013. REITs own 9-10% of self-storage facilities. 63% of facilities are mom-and-pop operations where the owners only have one location each. 8.96% of American households rent self-storage space, and each of those households averages 104 square feet of rented space. Most customers will provide a total of $3500+ in income to you, so you must treat them well.

While smaller units make more money per square foot, 10'x10' units are the most common ones to be rented. Mark can tell a lot about how well a facility is doing just based on the price of its 10'x10' units. All real estate that produces income is valued by taking the income (rent), minus the operating expenses, and then compare that to the going capitalization (cap) rate for the area.

Mark likes to purchase self-storage facilities with the plan of making them attractive for a REIT to purchase later. REITs focus on buying facilities that are at least 50K square feet, have 30% of the space be climate controlled, have at least a 50K population within three miles, and have around 1200 square feet of retail and counter space for things like selling boxes and renting trucks.

Households rent an average of 1.3 units, with an average unit size of 120 square feet. 80% of your customers will be residential and 20% commercial on average. Mark always hires independent third parties for conducting feasibility reports regarding the supply and demand in a market where he wants to invest. A feasibility report that he had made in Houston showed that within a five-mile radius of the facility, there were 34K households, and 9.6% of them were willing to rent an average of 120 square feet. This showed a market for about 500K square feet of residential and 125K square feet of commercial self-storage space. There was only a total of 127K square feet of rental space in the area. Therefore, he knew that there was a great opportunity to buy and expand.

Finding and Buying Properties

Most people find a self-storage facility just by driving by, the internet, and also through word-of-mouth. Mark offers a cash referral to anyone who refers a paying customer to his facilities. Mark also makes friends with other local facilities, as they might send him customers when they are at full capacity. You just won't get a very good return on your advertising dollars if you spend them on the yellow pages or other paper ads. It's best to invest in facilities that are visible from a major road and also have great signage. (I've heard of old department stores and Sam's Clubs being good locations to convert into self-storage.)

Mark recommends buying facilities that have the potential to expand to meet the market's needs, analyze and document the supply and demand, own properties that REITs would want to buy from you, consider if you can make your property the most expensive in the area, analyze the cash-on-cash return that you can get, and then ask yourself if you would be proud to own the property. If you are planning to do some expansion at your facility, the *Self Storage Almanac* has great information about what to expect when it comes to construction costs.

It's essential to be able to hire and keep good property management staff. You should pay more than your competitors in both salaries and benefits, provide great training, and give bonuses. It's not common to provide health insurance to self-storage employees. By doing so, you can attract many great people.

To purchase self-storage facilities, you must first find them. You can do so by going through a commercial realtor with this specialty, looking on www.LoopNet.com, networking at self-storage association events, or going through a commercial information exchange such as Catalyst. Once you have information about potential properties and their owners, you can mail them cards and letters letting them know you are interested in purchasing their property. Perhaps the best method is to build a reputation as the "go-to person" for purchasing self-storage. That itself takes time to accomplish.

Once you find someone willing to sell, the key is to be the quickest buyer to give them the best-perceived value. You need to be able to analyze quickly and negotiate well. This takes time and practice. REITs will be a major competition for you as they are eager to buy, can pay high prices, and will also close deals quickly.

In 2009, Mark wrote a letter of intent (LOI) to purchase a property that he wanted, but the owners never responded to it. In 2012, he met someone who knew one of the owners, who scheduled a lunch for Mark to meet them. This shows you that expanding your network gives you a lot of credibility and access to more opportunities.

The owners were willing to sell if Mark would assume their Wall Street loan and also pay what they would consider a "good price."

Mark informed them that he was interested but did not know how he would get the down payment money or approval to assume the loan. He wrote a new LOI with their asking price to get the property under contract. Then he had only 60 days to figure everything out to make the deal work for him.

Purchasing a Self-Storage Facility is Done in These Six Main Steps:

1. Find a property that the owner is willing to sell.
2. Do the preliminary analysis and due diligence to see if it can be a good deal.
3. Determine if you can afford to purchase it.
4. Write an LOI. If it is accepted, then get the property under contract with the assistance of an attorney.
5. Do in-depth due diligence with a feasibility report, physical inspections, financial analysis, and also apply for a loan. Your due diligence will require a title check to ensure there are no issues with ownership or pending legal problems against the property.
6. Once all of that is in order, you can close on the property and take it over.

Analyzing Deals

Once you find a property, it's time to analyze it (which both Mark and I find to actually be quite fun). It's easier to do this with financial analysis software, such as Mark's Valuator software. It allows you to quickly see how any property will likely cash flow, what occupancy rate you need to break even, and what the risk level is. Mark's Valuator software breaks things down by unit sizes, climate control, and even unit prices. This allows you to see if there is any variance in occupancy or rent rates by type and size of the units.

When analyzing a property, Mark considers a few things. He looks at why the owner wants to sell it, which helps with the negotiation. He also looks at how much of the facility is occupied, how many of the facility is producing rent, whether the facility has any problems, and if he can solve those problems. Good systems and property management can quickly solve any problems that occur. There may be an opportunity for you if there is deferred maintenance and the rents are below market rate. For example, you can then increase the occupancy rate and/or expand the property to have more square feet of rentable units.

You'll have to make some assumptions during your analysis. These include the final purchase price, the final interest rate, and terms of the loan. Furthermore, you will have to check if you will be able to raise the down payment and that you will be able to raise rents 3% per year. You need to realize that expenses will increase by 2.5% per year and assess the future occupancy rate and the construction costs if you plan to expand. The operating expenses you can expect to have will include advertising, personnel, repairs/maintenance, insurance, utilities, property taxes, office supplies, and a management fee. The latter only comes into play if you're going to use a third-party management company.

Once you have entered in all of your assumptions into the financial analysis software you're using, you can see how the cash flow looks from year one onward. If that isn't where you need it to be, you can adjust the purchase price until it does. While you can adjust the purchase price in your analysis to make the numbers work, do not reduce the expenses unless you are completely sure that you can do so. Mark wants to see a 12% cash-on-cash return during the first five years of his ownership.

Self-storage is different from many other forms of real estate. This is because you are not only buying the property, but also the business that is run on the property. It's vital to keep things in order with legal help. You should make very sure that your lawyer includes the following in the contract: names of the buyer and seller, what is being purchased, the price, the terms, and the amount of the good faith deposit. Furthermore, the lawyer should include a non-compete clause to keep the seller from buying self-storage in the same sub-market, an exit clause if the financing falls through, that you are buying the intellectual property such as the facility's name and website, how past due rent at the time of the closing will be handled, as well as any contingencies such as the inspection, business records, feasibility report, and the due diligence period.

While this is not a book about negotiation, Mark recognizes that he is not going to get what he wants in a deal unless he helps the seller get what they want first. He needs to know if the seller needs a specific price point, length of time to close, or other terms of sale.

You should find out what they need first, and then you can negotiate on the other points if so required.

Self-Storage Funding

Most banks expect a 25-35% down payment and a 20-year amortization period that will be due to be paid in three to seven years. Mark plans on having five years for the balloon payments of his loans, having a 35% down payment, then spending $35K to clean and refresh the property, and that the property will stabilize at 85% occupancy averaged over 12 months.

The loan that Mark needed to assume had a balance of $2M and a 5.5% interest rate. If he had paid the remaining balance of $4.5M in cash, then he would only have an 8% return. He either needed the seller to carry a second mortgage so he could get his needed returns or to pay a $286K deference fee to be able to pay off the other loan.

He wasn't excited about either option. Then he heard the seller complain that he was worried about capital gains taxes going up. He then fired up the Valuator software and saw that if the seller paid the deference fee, then he could get a new loan at a 4.5% interest rate and save $50K in annual interest fees. He convinced the seller that he would be better off paying the deference fee now as opposed to potentially paying larger capital gains taxes later. This was a win-win for both of them.

Once You Have a Property Under Contract, You Have Five Steps to Do Simultaneously:

1. Conduct a financial inspection of the books and other records. Look at the environmental study, rent roll, last three years of tax returns for the property, all service contracts, utility bills, architectural plans, capital expenditures, and the profit and loss (P&L) statements for the last three years.

2. Hire a builder and not a home inspector to inspect the physical property. They always find issues that Mark can use to renegotiate the deal in his favor.

3. Apply for a loan and do the underwriting. When you start, a local bank may be your best bet for a self-storage loan. Put together a binder for the bank that includes a summary of your plans, your financial analysis, the seller's marketing package, the feasibility report, the purchase contract, the property's financial history, the financial history of whoever is guaranteeing the loan, and finally a summary of your experience with self-storage and real estate. If you have no experience, it could be the experience of your partner or property management company.

4. Have a feasibility report done by a third-party. That shows the supply/demand for self-storage in the facility's market area.
5. Form your organization, such as an LLC or S Corporation. Mark prefers LLCs with a core group that puts the deal together and investors who then put money into the deal. The investors have "preferred" status, whereby they make back their investments first before the core group gets paid. Members of the core group can have different strengths, including accessing loans, raising capital, and even operational management.

Planning for the Future

Mark created a goal for himself to have a $60M self-storage portfolio. He just had the problem of needing the money and the means to make that happen. He believes that if you put all of your energy, focus, and belief into something, you can create that into reality. With real estate, you often have to find creative solutions to make deals work.

Mark needed a loan for 75% of the $6.5M but was only approved for a 65% loan. Time was running out, and Mark had to figure out how to make the deal still work. He asked, and the seller agreed to hold a short-term second mortgage. This way, he could raise additional capital.

The price to build a new facility is very similar throughout the USA. However, the cost for a customer to rent space can vary wildly due to the local supply and demand. Do not make the mistake of buying or building self-storage without first conducting local market research. Mark doesn't have a problem paying a high price for a property, as long as he can get the return he needs.

During the 2008-2009 recession, Mark didn't raise his prices. When times were good, he was able to raise prices as much as 8% in a year. That created an average annual increase of 3%. He breaks it down to raise the price of each unit size separately based on when they achieve certain occupancy thresholds.

To know what a self-storage facility will likely be worth in the future, you need to know what the property's net operating income will be and what the cap rate that buyers will expect. It will be hard to predict this perfectly, but you can have a good estimate based on the available data. The cap rate is only one metric to determine whether or not to buy a property. Mark prefers to focus more on whether he can create enough equity in the first five years to refinance and pay back the investors if there is enough cash flow to give the investors a 12% annual return.

Case Study

Mark ends his book with a case study about the property that he bought in 2008 to get back into the self-storage business after an unplanned hiatus. He was in his office in the summer of 2007 and received an alert that the property had just been listed for over $6M and only had 86K square feet. He almost decided to pass on it but called the listing agent anyway.

The property looked nice and was 85% occupied. He determined that it was worth a maximum of $5M. Then, based on what the projected future income would likely be, he was able to write an LOI with an offer of $6.25M. Mark hired a property manager, met with a commercial mortgage broker, and then created an LLC with help from an attorney. He had investors lined up and a property inspection that also went well.

Two weeks before the contingencies in the contract were to be removed, his investors had backed out. He then needed to urgently raise $1M for the down payment. He found a man willing to sell him a $1.25M commercial building and reinvest the profits into the self-storage facility for an 80% ownership stake. Mark convinced the self-storage sellers to give him more time to arrange everything in exchange for the good-faith deposit becoming non-refundable.

By then, it was the end of 2007, which is when the recession started. The mortgage broker called and told Mark he "lost" some of the funding. This is because the Wall Street money for it had dried up. The $1M became non-refundable. Mark and his new investor were crunched for time and had to get new financing, which they were able to do. On the day of the closing, the bank decided to change the amortization schedule from 20 years down to six, which then increased the monthly payments by $10K. They had to still close, and the bank knew it.

On February 28, 2008, Mark became a self-storage owner again. Those first few years were terrible due to losing 5-6% of occupancy and then having to spend a lot of time on collections. Needless to say, the property did not have the projected growth that Mark had originally expected. It took six years of frustrations, but he finally got the property into good financial shape.

We learn more from our mistakes than we do from our successes. Mark has learned a lot through this. He now never goes over a 70% loan-to-value (LTV). He always makes sure his investors get paid to maintain their confidence and while maintaining his reputation. Your reputation is vital to your success with real estate. Mark says that comes down to being transparent, being honest, and conducting business the way you would want others to do it. Real estate is not a get rich quick scheme. However, it does allow you to get rich slowly over time.

Conclusion

Self-storage has become an increasingly popular real estate investment in the past few years. It's unique in that you are buying both the property and the business within the same deal. Mark's book teaches you the basics about how to outsmart the competition and set up your self-storage business for success. If you are serious about investing in self-storage, you should most definitely buy and read his book!

Additional Reading

Sales & Service: The Cutting Edge of Self-Storage by Christel Land

Crush Your Competition: 101 Self Storage Marketing Tips For The Fastest Way To Huge Profits by Marc Goodin

Chapter 20: Apartment Syndication

Best Ever Apartment Syndication Book by Joe Fairless and Theo Hicks

Introduction

Joe went from owning four single-family homes to more than 4000 units worth $400M. If you are going to learn about real estate syndications from anyone, he is awesome at it! This book has the perfect mix of humor and expertise. You should check out Joe's and Theo's daily podcast Best Real Estate Investing Advice Ever Show.

This book provides a step-by-step process on how to be a real estate syndicator. It will teach you all the terminology, the necessary goal setting, how to build your brand, determine the market that works best for you, how to build your real estate team, expand your network, determine your business plan, find awesome off-market deals, make good offers on deals, present the offer to your investors and get funding, and then effectively run the syndication. There is a TON of information in this book. Joe and Theo walk through it in such detail for you. This is because they are dedicated to helping you succeed.

Even if you lack any money, real estate experience, access to deals, or execution of big plans, you can still learn how others have overcome the same challenges as you and have succeeded. Any challenge you're facing, others have already overcome it. Learn from them!

The first thing to know is what the heck is a real estate apartment syndication anyway?! Essentially, it's where people pool their money and resources together and execute a business plan for an apartment building. The sponsor, also known as the general partner, is the person/people in charge of setting up the deal and finding the investors for it. The limited partners are the people who invest passively in the deal. Use syndication when investing in a larger apartment building or complex of buildings.

To be a passive investor in a syndication, you have to be either accredited or sophisticated. An accredited investor is someone who either has $1M+ in net worth OR makes $200K or more per year OR they and their spouse together make $300K or more per year. Instead of meeting these income or net worth requirements, a sophisticated investor is just someone experienced and knowledgeable in business matters and financing.

Joe and Theo are value-add investors and wrote this book to teach others to do the same. They buy apartments and increases the profits by decreasing expenses and/or increasing the income that the apartments produce. Maybe, the rents are under market rate and can be increased. Maybe, they can update the property for it to make sense to raise the rents. Maybe they can improve the efficiency of how the property runs.

Joe and Theo talk about how he bought a property for $14.1M, put $2M into it, then it appraised for $21.6M a mere 16 months later.

The $2M in updates/improvements allowed for the rent to increase. Being able to increase the rents will, in turn, increase the returns and the value of the property. For example, if you have a 250-unit apartment building and you raise the rents by $100 per month each, this then increases the value of the property by about $4M!

How to Get Started

Joe and Theo examine several questions, including: Do you have any hesitations about investing with partnerships? If you were partnered with your friends, would your relationships with them be changed forever? Are you afraid of using other people's money? I recommend both options: using both other people's money, as well as other people's mistakes (both OPM). You don't have to figure everything out on your own as it's a lot quicker and easier to learn from others.

There are two requirements to become a syndicator:

1. To set yourself up for success, you need to start by educating yourself. In the back of *Best Ever Apartment Syndication Book*, there is a glossary of 86 terms and definitions you need to know. These will come up all the time in conversations you have with other investors, brokers, and lenders, etc. Knowing them can help give you credibility in the business.

2. You need some experience in things like real estate, being an entrepreneur, business management, or even earning promotions and awards in your day job can qualify as well.

If you lack experience, there's no time like the present to start getting some!

You should get educated, so you at least have an idea of what's what. Second, you should build a team, which might consist of real estate brokers/realtors, other investors, lenders, a coach, an accountant, a lawyer, and property managers. You should focus on the cash-on-cash return (CoC) and the internal rate of return (IRR). They will let you know if a deal is good or not.

How to Make Money Leading a Syndication

There are six main types of fees you can make as the general partner (GP). DO NOT take a fee unless the interests of yourself and the investor are in line. If your efforts increase the profitability of the property, then you deserve a portion of that additional money. This is done in quite a few different ways.

1. Profit Split – the GP gets a portion of the profit of cash flow and sales proceeds. A passive investor or limited partner (LP) normally gets a preferred rate of return before the profit split with the GP takes effect.
2. Acquisition Fee – Usually, around 1-5% upfront fee that goes to the GP when the deal closes.
3. Asset Management Fee – Ongoing annual fee for overseeing the property management. This is usually around 2% of rents or a per-unit flat fee, such as $250 per unit each year.
4. Property Management Fee – This is an ongoing fee for managing the day-to-day operations. This is normally 2-8%

of the collected rents. It is worth it to have a good property management company. If you are new to syndications or are busy, you should hire out a third-party company to manage the property.

5. Refinancing Fee – If the mortgage is refinanced, the GP may get a fee of 0.5-2% of the loan amount. This usually happens when the syndication cashes out the original investments to the LPs, but they will then continue to get cash flow.

6. Guarantee Fee – This is around 0.5-5% of the principal balance when the loan is closed. It goes to whoever had guaranteed the loan. The variance on this fee amount depends on how risky the loan was.

Setting Your Goals

Do you just want to replace your current income, have enough to live in luxury, or control a billion-dollar empire? Your 12-month goal needs to be both specific and quantifiable. For now, you should keep things simple and conservative. Joe and Theo recommend that you set your income goal for the next year. You should then see that amount as equaling the 2% acquisition fee you will get from raising capital. If you want to make $100K, you will need to create $100K ÷ 0.02 = $5M worth of deals. This will vary depending upon the terms of your deals(s). The other fees you get on top of that will just be a bonus. Also, 35% of $5M equals $1.75M, which is how much you will need to raise for you to make that $100K. Based on this calculation, you should write down a goal like "On DATE, I have raised $X in equity from other investors that I then used to do $X worth of real estate syndication, which earned me $X in acquisition fees."

You should create your vision of the future. What is it that excites you about real estate? How will you benefit once you achieve your 12-month goal? If you don't achieve that goal, how will you be negatively impacted? Since you haven't yet achieved this goal, what negative consequences have you already faced? These questions then help frame your "Why." You are better set up to achieve your goals when you focus on *why* they are important to you. The more specific and quantifiable this is, the better. It helps when your goals are 50/50. This means that they are 50% based on achieving the outcome and 50% based on learning a lesson or skill along the way that you can apply to your business long term.

Tony Robbins has what he calls The Ultimate Success Formula:

1. Know your outcome.
2. Know your reasons why.
3. Take massive and intelligent action.
4. Know what you are getting.
5. Adjust your approach as needed.

Building a Brand in This Business

Building your brand means that you are building your credibility. When starting, this is a piece that you are probably missing. What are you currently known for in your sphere of influence? That's your "brand" as it stands today. What do you want to be known for in the coming years? You should start right now to shift your brand to that. In 1997, when Apple was in major disarray, they made the slogan "Think Different." That is exactly what you need to do now. Skipping this step of building your brand would be a major misstep due to how it would limit both your growth and expansion.

What and who do you want your brand to attract? If your brand gives you "general fame," then you will be recognized wherever you go. If you have "selective fame," then you have two or three thousand high caliber people who then respect you. Selective fame is what you want. Choose specific criteria of who you want your brand to attract. Determine their age, gender, location, occupation, and any other criteria that you like.

To get selective fame, you should build a thought leadership program (TLP). This is a collaborative interview-based online network that provides free content, which is valuable – for example, a podcast, YouTube channel, blog, Facebook group, or a newsletter. This gets you noticed and perceived to be an expert. You need to be entertaining while you educate people through your TLP. To develop your TLP, you should consider what your goal is from it, who the target audience will be, what you will name your platform, why your audience will be interested, and what the flow of each episode/video/blog/post will be.

In addition to your TLP, you should start an in-person Meetup group. It's easy to start and is a great way to expand your network and knowledge. You might be wondering why all of this extra work keeps getting piled onto you. Well, how badly do you want to take your finances to the next level? You have to be willing to do what it takes to get there. Your Meetup could be as simple as chatting with other investors over some beers at a taproom for a few hours. Joe structured his Meetup in five parts. He begins with a short presentation by an active investor, people share their opportunities, people give a short update about their real estate business, there's time for networking, and then people share their goals for the coming month.

Your brand has three main components.

1. *Your company name, logo, and business cards*: Does your company name include your name? If so, it will be dependent on you. Select a name that's easy to pronounce and remember. Create a compelling logo, which can be done at www.LogoGarden.com and www.Fivrr.com. You should put your logo on your business cards, which are inexpensive on LogoGarden and www.VistaPrint.com.

2. *Website*: This is the most important step because it is the first thing people see when they search for your company online. It gives you credibility and generates leads of potential investors. It's a good idea to include a blog on your website.

3. *Company presentation*: Create a company presentation that identifies challenges and PROVIDES SOLUTIONS. This introduces your business, says why people should invest in apartments, provides an overview of your investment strategy, explains the roles between you as the general

partner and them as the limited partners, and finally lays out what your process is for buying a property. Your investment strategy should include a description of your target market, how you source your deals, how you analyze your deals, and also how you structure your deals.

You should explain to your potential investors that you source your deals by following the 100:30:10:1 rule. Out of about 100 properties, you look at, look closely at 30, put offers in on the top 10, and then of those, you will acquire one. For analyzing deals, choose your submarket location, review the history of the property, consider the condition of the property, look at the surrounding competition, and then make a business plan that maximizes the return.

For the structure of the deal, Joe and Theo look for properties with 100+ units, purchases them with 70-75% long-term debt, aims for an 8% preferred rate of return to the LPs, and plans to keep each property for 5-10 years. The LP's role is to provide money for the investment. You should focus on finding deals that match the criteria that your investors want to see. The GP's roles include finding and researching properties, negotiating offers, coordinating inspections, getting the best financing, having attorneys create partnership agreements, performing due diligence, hiring and supervising property management companies, and then overseeing and following the business plan.

You should wrap up your company presentation with an example of a deal from your past. If you haven't done a deal yet, you could go through an example from your mentor's past or your business partner's past. This gives LPs a much better idea of what they can expect.

Three Immutable Laws of Real Estate Investing

1. Buy for cash flow and not for appreciation.
2. Use long-term debt to your advantage.
3. Have sufficient cash reserves to handle things that come up now and then.

Deciding on Your Investment Market

There are 19,000+ cities in the USA, so don't try screening deals from all of them. However, if your market research area is too small, it will then be more difficult to find deals. You should select seven potential target markets that you have some knowledge about and/or interest in them. Joe and Theo use reports that look at different aspects of the real estate economy, including Marcus & Millichap's Annual US Multifamily investment Forecast, the Zillow Annual Consumer House Trends Report, as well as the RCLCO Quarterly State of the Real Estate Market.

Joe and Theo use the following six steps to evaluate a market:

1. Record the demographic and economic data, such as unemployment, population, age, job diversity, top local

employers, the supply and demand, and miscellaneous things such as local property taxes and friendliness towards landlords.

2. Interpret that data.
3. Rank your seven markets in each of the above-mentioned criteria.
4. Select one or two of those markets to take a closer look.
5. Analyze 200 properties in *those* "one to two" markets.
6. Finally, create a market summary report.

www.Census.gov and www.City-Data.com have great reports that you can use to analyze those criteria in those markets. Analyze the trends for the past five years. You want a market that matches your target group of renters. Also, it's best to choose a market with good job prospects so that tenants can afford to pay you the rent. You should make a ranking chart of how your seven markets compare in the different criteria. You can even use a simple 1-7 rank score for each criterion, 1 being best. In the example below, Markets E and A have the lowest scores, and would then be your top 1-2 markets. Then, to analyze deeper, add weight to certain criteria. Job diversity and supply/demand are the most important of the criteria.

	Market A	Market B	Market C	Market D	Market E	Market F	Market G
Unemployment	3	4	7	5	1	6	2
Population	4	6	2	7	3	5	1
Population Age	1	3	2	6	4	7	5
Job Diversity	4	5	6	7	1	3	2
Top Employers	3	4	5	2	7	1	6

Supply/Demand	5	6	1	7	3	2	4
Miscellaneous	2	5	4	7	1	6	3
Total	**22**	**33**	**27**	**41**	**20**	**30**	**23**

When you analyze 200 properties in your top 1-2 markets, you should take note of the market name, property name, address, neighborhood, total number of units, rentable square footage, rent for each sized unit, year it was built, whether the owner or tenants pay the utilities, whether it is a value-add opportunity, the source of your info, owner's name and address, appraised value, and year the owner purchased. This info can usually be found online or by calling the property if need be.

After you narrow down your 200 properties, you should look at the best ones in person. You can have a local person do that for you if you do not live near the market that you are analyzing. From there, you can then start reaching out to the owners and local brokers to move toward purchasing. A market summary from a broker can list the top ten reasons to invest in a particular market, or you can also do a more detailed market overview to impress your investors. Joe and Theo give examples of both of these approaches in his book.

Building Your Real Estate Team

Through doing a Meetup or mastermind group, you will meet and attract various real estate professionals. This is also a great opportunity to meet people for your real estate team. Your core team should include a real estate agent or broker, mortgage broker, real estate accountant, real estate attorney, syndication/securities attorney, property management company, and a mentor or a consultant. However, meeting them through referrals is even better.

While you might be able to figure everything out on your own, it is much easier to have someone who is experienced and can also guide you through the process to avoid the major mistakes. Even experienced investors have mentors to keep up-to-date with things. A good mentor provides expertise, a step-by-step system, opportunities to work through problems, and connections to network with others within the field. The most effective way to find a mentor is through a word-of-mouth referral. Joe and Theo also offer their excellent mentorship program through www.BestEverAptProgram.com.

Not all investors agree on the need for a mentor. If you do choose to get a mentor, find someone who already has the knowledge and skills that you want to learn. Have they already been an apartment syndicator? They should be willing and able to explain the steps that you need to take to get to where you want to be. They should also help you network with others to help you with your success. Do not expect your mentor to do all the work for you or solve all of your problems. They are more of a guide to help you while you do the work.

You cannot be successful by doing everything on your own. This is especially true in apartment syndications. When you interview people to potentially join your team, they are also interviewing you at the same time. Ask them questions such as these: How many transactions have you done? How long have you been a broker? How long have you been focusing on apartments? How many listings do you have right now? How do you find your deals? Do you have off-market deals in addition to on-market deals? What is the state of the local apartment market? What do you specialize in? How do your fees work? What sets you apart from the other brokers in the market? Can you provide me with your references? Is there anything else I should know?

Real estate brokers want investors who can close deals, the quicker, the better. Show them that you can do this or that you have team members who have a proven track record. The ideal broker will send you lots of off-market deals that match your criteria. You will probably have to put in the effort to build trust with them first before that happens. Your real estate broker should also be local to the market in which you are investing. Communicate with them regularly, so they know you are serious.

Brokers will also have questions for you, such as: What property management company are you using? How many units do they have? Have you or one of your team members previously bought an apartment building? What criteria are you looking for in deals? What is your funding like? Are you willing to sign an exclusion agreement? (Joe and Theo do not recommend signing an exclusion agreement because it limits the flow of leads.)

You will definitely need a good property management company. Start looking for one at the same time you look for a broker. Ask a potential property management company questions such as: How long have you been in property management? What is your range of geographic area that you cover? How many apartments do you currently manage? How many units does your company itself own? Do you have any specialty in a specific property class? Do you work with value-add properties? What sort of due diligence do you do on potential properties? What is your process for managing a renovation? What are some other local properties that you manage? Who would my main contact person here be? What do you consider to be the duties of the site manager? May I have final approval of who the site manager will be? What sort of updates/communication can I expect to receive from the site manager? What do you charge for your various fees, and what is included with them? What is your use of technology – property management software, online payments, marketing? Can you give me references from some of your current clients?

Also, you want to work with a property management company. They will want to work with you as well. Show them that you are interested in them and that you won't be a total pain in the butt. They will also want to know what kinds of properties you are looking for, how you underwrite your deals, what your expectations are, and what you and your partners will be like.

Paying for a good accountant and possibly a bookkeeper who both understand syndications will save you from paying unnecessary taxes. Ask them things such as how their fees are structured, how conservative their tax positions are, whether they have a secure portal for file transfers, how proactive they are with tax planning, whether they can file tax returns in every state/local government, what they expect in their clients, and if they can provide you some references for you to call.

Finding Passive Investors

Good returns aren't the only thing investors want to see when deciding whether to invest with you. The more important factor is being able to trust you. You can then gain their trust through time, expertise, and personal connections. Trust can build over time. However, the more expertise you have in syndications, the less time an investor needs to know you to trust you. More expertise means more credibility. The expertise could belong to your team members if you are newer to the game. If you can build a genuine human connection with an investor, they are more likely to trust you as well.

Here are five good methods of finding passive investors for your investor list. Regardless of where you meet them, you can find ways to add value to them.

1. Create a thought leadership platform, such as www.InvestWithJoe.com.
2. Join BiggerPockets, use your profile for advertising what you do, and participate in the forums.
3. Network at real estate Meetup groups and/or start one of your own.
4. Volunteer at a nonprofit organization and connect with the board members, who are usually affluent people.
5. Connect with your personal connections – friends, family, coworkers, etc.

Once you have your investor list, it's time to start talking to them on the phone. Take lots of notes about the conversation you have to help prepare for future calls with them. See it as more of a conversation and not a sales pitch. Your aim here is to understand their background and investment goals. Paint a picture for them to show how investing with you aligns with their investment goals.

Inevitably, you will encounter questions and objections from potential investors. Joe and Theo cover the 49 of them, but here are some of the top questions and how to answer them.

1. What is your experience? Talk about the experience and skills you have in real estate and/or business. If you don't have much of your own, you can talk about your team's track record and any syndications you or they have succeeded with before.

2. Why should I invest with you instead of another syndicator? Focus on describing how you and the investor have an alignment of interests, show them that you will have good transparency throughout the deal, and build trust with them.

3. How will investors get paid? Have a well-defined and easily understood plan for returns lined up already. This includes how often distributions are made preferred rates, profit splits, the projected IRR, and the exit plan.

4. How will taxes work for investors? Explain that you provide Schedule K-1 tax forms each year, which describe investors' distributions and tax write-offs from depreciation.

5. What are the risks involved? Show how you have done conservative underwriting if things don't go as planned. Be honest that the absolute worst-case scenario is that you lose everyone's money, but that it is not likely because of your good planning. Your Private Placement Memorandum (PPM) covers the plan in depth.

6. What if there is another recession? By planning for cash flow, which increases by adding value to the property and by having reserves, you insulate yourself from a downturn economy. The property will probably make less money during a recession, but you will wait to sell it until you can do so for a profit.

7. What are the responsibilities of the general partners? Finding deals, getting properties under contract, performing due diligence and underwriting, lining up the financing, raising capital, managing the property manager, manage the asset, and communicate with investors.

8. What is the minimum investment? This is up to you. Higher minimums mean that you have fewer investors involved. Lower minimums mean you can include more people in the deal, but you may have more work involved as a result.

9. Do you have any references? Have a list already of other investors who are willing to be a good reference with you for new investors.

Real estate investors invest in either equity or debt. With equity, you own a share of a deal and then might receive a preferred return between 2-12% and/or a profit split. The profit split between the investors/limited partners (LPs) and the GP can be anywhere from 50/50 up to 90/10. It's most common to have an 8% preferred rate with a 70/30 profit split where the LPs get 70%. Debt investors, on the other hand, loan money to the GP like a bank would and then receive a specific interest rate back on an interest-only loan. The debt investors could, for example, get a 12% annual return on their money and then get 100% of their money back when the property is either sold or refinanced. Equity investors can get a larger payday in the end. Also, debt investors get a more stable income.

Finding Great Deals

Decide on the specific investment criteria you are looking for a deal, and only look at deals that match those criteria. This will save you from wasting time on deals that won't work with your plan. Are you looking for value-add, distressed, or turnkey investments? Distressed are riskier and require more work, but can have potentially larger returns. Turnkey has both lower returns and lower risks. Joe and Theo prefer value-add as it falls in the middle of those two extremes. Next, you should decide on one or two markets where you will be searching, the age of the property, and the range of units you want. You will generally need to raise 35% of the cost of a property to cover the down payment, repairs, fees, and reserve. If you can only raise $1M, then you are limited to just looking at properties that cost $2.86M or less. If the units where you are looking average $50K each, then you are limited to properties with 57 or fewer units.

For around every 100 deals you look at, 30 might match your criteria. You might put an offer on 10 of those. Also, if you close on one of those, you are then in good shape. Your search could take anywhere from a few months to a few years.

Deals could either be on-market where they are listed by a broker. Or they could be off-market where the owner wants to sell but does not have a broker. On-market deals are easier to find, whereas off-market deals can have more profitability and are worth putting in the effort to find. You have less competition with off-market deals and then don't have to pay a broker fee. Brokers can find you good deals for sure, but you should just be ready to move faster on those due to the competition.

Here are ten tactics for finding good off-market deals:

1. Direct mail campaigns are when you send batches of letters to owners of properties that match your criteria. You can get a list of these owners from a title company, "driving for dollars" to find distressed properties, as well as looking through www.Apartments.com. You can also look in public records to see which owners are evicting tenants, facing foreclosure, are late in taxes, have taxes that went way up in the past year, live out-of-state, have probably paid off the mortgage, or have building code or health code violations.

Joe and Theo include some templates and scripts that you can use with this approach.

2. Use your direct mail list to do cold calls and cold text messages to introduce yourself and say that you are interested in purchasing their property. ListSource and CoStar can help you get the phone numbers.

3. Your team members can be a good resource for finding off-market deals within their network.

4. Your thought leadership platform brought you team members and private money, and it can also get you some promising leads as well.

5. Look at "for rent" ads online or around time. If they have vacant units, they have a problem that you could potentially fix by buying the property.

6. Title companies close on deals daily and can also give you some referrals.

7. Join the local apartment association group to meet and talk with other investors.

8. Vendors like electricians, plumbers, and property managers might be willing to share info with you about off-market deals.

9. BiggerPockets is a huge real estate resource, including hearing about deals.

10. Connect with local people who have a large network, such as insurance salespeople, restaurant owners, fitness trainers, etc.

Track the results of the method(s) you use to know what is effective. Keep tweaking your approach to find what works best. An Excel spreadsheet works well for this. Joe and Theo have one that you can get a copy of by emailing info@joefairless.com.

Once you find the owner of a property you want, you should find out what motivates them to sell. The highest price isn't always the deciding factor. Sellers may also be interested in having specific terms of sale or knowing that the buyer will also take good care of the property.

How to Underwrite a Deal

If you like math, then you're going to love underwriting! Underwriting is the process of confirming whether a deal that looks good is actually good. Regardless of how much the owner wants for the property, your analysis will determine how much you can pay for it. Until you have it under contract, you will have to make some assumptions about your underwriting numbers. This process could take a few weeks or a few months, depending on the deal.

Obtain the current rent roll, the trailing 12-month profit and loss statement (T-12), and the offering memorandum (OM). The rent roll should detail how much rent was collected from each unit, unit square footage, info about the leases, and the unit types. The T-12 provides a description of the income and expenses of the property in the past 12 months. The more details you get in the rent roll and T-12, the better. However, they vary widely in their details and quality of info. The OM is a sales package about the property prepared by the broker if it is an on-market deal. The OM usually includes highlights about and description of the deal, an analysis of the location, an analysis of comparable local properties (rent comps), and a financial analysis.

Since the broker's OM always looks at the property with the angle of the best-case scenario, you will need to use a separate underwriting financial model. It's their goal to sell the property for the highest possible price, which is not in your best interest. Ask lots of questions, especially when you see discrepancies.

After reading through the OM, input the rent roll and T-12 info into your financial model and then set assumptions for how you plan to operate the property, calculate how much you can offer, conduct your own rent comps, and tour the property for further due diligence. You can either buy a financial model or create your own from scratch. (If you have a mentor/coach, they may have one you can use as well.)

Plan out how much you will need to have for the closing costs, down payment, renovations budget, and saved in the general operating fund. With your calculations, you should take that into consideration whether any of the units have already been renovated, what other things need to be updated such as the roof or landscaping, what sort of rent increase you would be able to get after renovations, and how long the renovations would take to be completed.

You will need to include various assumptions in your calculations. Aim for the renovations to take 12-24 months. If the market rent growth is 5%, you should calculate your numbers conservatively and assume it may only be 3%. Your expenses will increase over time, perhaps 2% annually. You might have vacancies at around 8% during your renovations, and then at 5-6% after the renovations. There will be some income loss if you have any model units or employee/administration units. Annually for each unit, expect to spend around $1100 for payroll, $300 for maintenance, $300 for contract services, $250 to turn each unit, $150 for advertising, $200 for admin costs, $800 for utilities, $225 for insurance, and $250 for lender reserves. You can get the projected tax numbers from the county assessor. The property management company will also charge perhaps 3-5% of rents to manage the property.

To calculate the price you can offer, you should enter in all of your assumptions, operating costs, fees, profit return goals, and holding period into your financial model. Both your mentor and property manager should review your underwriting for accuracy.

Analyze your own rent comps both when you do the underwriting and later during your due diligence. You can do this partially online and also in person by touring other properties as if you were interested in renting there. Look at properties that have similar age, proximity, number of units, types of units, sizes of units, quality of units, and amenities. The more similar the other properties are to your property, the more accurate the rent comps will be.

It's important to visit your potential property during your due diligence, especially if you are living out of state. It's the best way to get a feel for the property, neighborhood, and competition. Tour other properties to do your rent comps during this visit.

Submitting Your Offer

Deciding whether a property is a good deal or not is entirely up to your own criteria and investment goals. If a property passes all of your criteria through your underwriting process, it's then time to submit a letter of intent (LOI) to the seller. The LOI includes the purchase price, structure of the financing, earnest money and deposit plan, length you need for due diligence, schedule for closing, as well as the schedule for the sale agreement. You are not legally bound to the terms of your LOI. This is because it just shows the seller your terms and intent to buy the property.

The seller may then reject, counter, or accept your LOI. If it's an on-market deal, you might be invited to the best and final offer round. If your LOI is rejected, you can then decide whether to submit a better offer. If your LOI is countered, run your model with the countered numbers to see if it still works for you. You can then accept or counter their counter offer. If your LOI is accepted, then you submit your purchase and sale agreement, which is legally binding. If you are in the best and final offer round, convince the seller that you can close the deal and have an awesome business plan for it. Of the potential buyers, the seller will then decide who will win the contract.

Conducting Due Diligence

Once a property is under contract, you can begin your due diligence to confirm whether your underwriting assumptions were accurate and that the property doesn't have too many skeletons in the closet, figurative or literal. You usually have 60-90 days to do the due diligence before the closing date. During this time, you'll also be finalizing the financing from a lender and also the capital from your investors.

There are 10 due diligence reports you will need. Using the information from these reports, update your financial model to see if you can proceed as planned, need to ask the seller to adjust the price or terms, or have to walk away from the deal entirely.

1. The financial document audit compares the property's historical operations against your budgeted income and expenses. This is done by a commercial real estate consulting firm. See whether this confirms your assumptions with the income and expenses.

2. The internal property condition assessment (PCA) is made when a licensed contractor inspects the entire property and gives you a sort of a to-do list of the needed repairs.

3. The market survey report is when your property manager does a more in-depth version of your market comps. This lets you know what the market rate is currently for rents.

4. The lease audit report is when your property manager inspects the leases for all the units to take note of their

rents and security deposits, etc. If there are any discrepancies, see how they would impact your financial model.

5. The unit walk report is when your property manager walks through every unit to document their condition. This helps you make a solid renovation plan.
6. The site survey is a map of the boundaries and lot size of the apartment community done by a third-party vendor. You should pay attention to any potential zoning issues.
7. The property condition report is the same thing as the PCA but is done by a contractor that your lender has chosen.
8. The environment site assessment is done by a third-party vendor to see if there are any possible environmental contaminations.
9. The appraisal is done by an appraiser who determines what the property is currently worth. Hope that this shows the property is worth at least as much as you offered for it.
10. The green report is an assessment that determines if there are opportunities to make the property more energy-efficient. Making the property greener can really decrease your operating expenses.

Finalizing the Capital

The capital comes in two main parts: mortgage from a lender and cash from investors. When you meet with a lender for the first time, you should bring a short biography about your company, one to three years of the property's financial statements, your business plan and the budget you will require, and personal financial statements for anyone who is a loan guarantor. You will need to compensate the loan guarantor(s) with either an upfront fee or equity in the deal.

The lender financing can either be a permanent agency loan or a bridge loan. A permanent agency loan typically has a loan length of between 5-12 years and an amortization of between 20-30 years. A bridge loan typically has a loan length of 6-36 months and usually has interest-only payments. When the loan length is done, you will either need to pay off the loan, refinance, or sell the property. There may be an extra fee if you pay off the loan early.

Before you have even found your deal, you should have already had passive investors lined up ready and willing to invest in a deal like yours. Once the property is under contract, you need to immediately begin getting investment commitments from those investors. To do this, you will make an investment summary and email your list of investors to tell them about the investment opportunity. You should also let them know that you will have an informational conference call. Then you should do this conference call and send a recording of it to your investors who weren't on the call, follow up with each investor, and then send commitment paperwork for them to sign. Raise 50% more money than you need so that some investors are on your waiting list in case other investors drop out for whatever reason.

Your investment summary includes an executive summary explaining the deal, highlights of the investment with your business plan, an overview of the property, an analysis of the financials, a market overview, examples of other deals you or the other GPs have done, and an appendix that also includes your biography.

When emailing your investors, you can use an email service such as Mail Chimp because you will be sending out A TON of emails about your investment opportunities. Your emails should include general information about your deal and how they can participate in your conference call. Ask your investors to reply to your email if they are interested in hearing more.

There are free websites such as www.FreeConferenceCall.com or www.Zoom.com, where you can make and record your conference call. To make a successful conference call, start by having the mentality that you are there to serve the investors by sharing an opportunity to help them make money. During the call, you should welcome the investors to it and describe the outline of what the call will include, your experience, the deal, the market where the deal is located, your team, and your business plan. After this, you can conduct a Q&A session. Joe and Theo list out the 30 most commonly asked questions, such as what is covered by insurance, what the minimum investment that is required, how often you will communicate updates, and when the investors will start to see a return on their investment. You should end the call with a conclusion and the next steps.

There are five forms you need to have your investors sign to participate in the deal. The private placement memorandum (PPM) describes the property, risks involved, required investment, and info about the sponsor. The operating agreement (OA) describes the responsibilities and ownership of both the general partners as well as limited partners. The subscription agreement describes how much shares of the investment cost, such as $1 per share. The ACH application is needed if an investor wants their distributions direct deposited into their bank account. The accredited investor qualifies form is required if you set up your syndication as a 506(c) offering to confirm that the investors are accredited.

The two main types of syndications fall under Rule 506(b) or 506(c). With 506(b), you can have as many as 35 sophisticated non-accredited investors; however, you cannot publicly advertise your offering. This means you are limited to only having your friends and family as investors. With 506(c), you can only have accredited investors but can publicly advertise. To be accredited, an investor must either have a net worth of at least $1M not including their personal residence, an annual income of at least $200K, or a combined income with their spouse of at least $300K. (To be sophisticated, an investor must have good net worth and depth of real estate experience/knowledge.) Consult a securities attorney to make sure you use the right approach for what you need and are following the related laws.

Closing the Deal

Three days before the closing date, you will sign the loan and title documents. The day before the closing, you will sign the closing documents and transfer the closing funds into escrow. The day of the closing, the title company will issue you the deed, your property manager will take care of the property, and you and your investors can celebrate that you crossed the first finish line. Send your investors an investor guide that explains how often you will communicate with them, what will be included in your updates, how the tax documentation will work, and what to expect with distributions.

Following the Business Plan

You have ten main responsibilities as the asset manager:

1. Implement the business plan as written and follow the budget.
2. Conduct performance reviews with your property manager every week to keep things on track.
3. Pay your passive investors their correct distributions on time.
4. Send out monthly emails to your investors to keep them updated on everything.
5. Manage the updates and renovations to the property.
6. Keep the property rented out to maximize the revenue. This can be done through things such as a marketing campaign, a tenant referral program, and awesome customer service.

7. Plan monthly in-person trips to the property to observe the day-to-day operations.

8. Analyze the competition to keep up-to-date with what market-rate rents are.

9. Analyze the market to know when the best time to sell will be.

10. Fix any problems as and when they come up.

As much as your investors will enjoy the distributions from owning the property, they will love the huge payday when you do sell it. You should be flexible on the timing of when you sell it based on market conditions. A broker can help you with the sale and to create a bidding war where you can choose the best offer from someone who can close the deal. You should use an attorney to create the purchase and sale agreement. Provide any needed documentation to the buyer during their due diligence. Then, you can distribute the sales proceeds to your investors after the closing. There's a good chance many will want to invest with you in future deals.

Conclusion

The way to set yourself up for success with syndications is to take consistent action and also get connected with people who can help you in the process. Best Ever Apartment Syndication Book is very thorough and makes the syndication process easy to understand. If you are serious about becoming an apartment syndicator, you need to buy this book! It is 428 pages long and goes in much greater detail than I could have included here. There is another type of syndication that involves using a fund which is called Regulation A (Reg A). However, there is not yet a good book about Reg A offerings. Another type of syndication is crowdfunding, which is covered in the next chapter.

Additional Reading

The Complete Guide to Buying and Selling Apartment Buildings by Steve Berges

Apartment Syndication Made Easy: A Step by Step Guide by Vinney Chopra

Chapter 21: Crowdfunding

Real Estate Crowdfunding Explained by Salvador Briggman and

Krystine Therriault

Introduction

You should think of this book as a starting point for crowdfunding. You will need to do additional research to fully understand it. Essentially, it is a style of real estate syndication that allows syndication sponsors and investors to easily connect with each other on investments. It uses modern technology and regulations to make this happen.

Crowdfunding is Booming

The real estate industry is based on old practices and is about to be completely transformed. Essentially, real estate crowdfunding is just a way for you to invest in properties through a secure third-party vendor. These vendors are called platforms or portals and allow an investment company to quickly obtain funding from the public. This is a more efficient and faster way to raise money than what is used by the traditional real estate model.

A crowdfunding sponsor is a person or company who is raising the money for deals. Some crowdfunding sponsors focus on single-family homes, but most invest in commercial real estate like apartment buildings, offices, and retail space. The crowdfunded deals are generally not developments from the ground up.

To list your deal on a crowdfunding platform, you need to be able to answer questions about your company and the deal to confirm that everything is a hundred percent legit. Platforms prefer established real estate companies and solid cash flowing investments. Platforms normally will raise between $500K-$5M but are not permitted to hold onto the money themselves. The minimum amount needed to invest will vary from a few hundred dollars to thousands of dollars. The opportunities through these platforms mainly give investors cash flow as well as tax benefits.

Crowdfunding is not a type of real estate investment trust (REIT), even though they both allow you to invest in real estate passively. Crowdfunding allows you to be in control by investing in a specific property that can have a great return. REITs are more like a fund for multiple properties that are chosen by the fund manager, and their returns are averaged together. Unlike REITs, you cannot sell your shares whenever you feel like it.

When you invest in a crowdfunded deal, it can be either on the debt or equity. Debt deals work in such a way that you are part of the bank controlling the mortgage that an investment company has to pay to you. Senior debt is prioritized over other debt and is then usually invested in through a fund. Mezzanine debt is any loan that is junior to the senior debt. Equity deals are when you have part ownership in the property itself. Equity, also called joint venture equity, is when multiple investors put their money together separately to acquire a deal. Preferred equity is when the investors have the highest priority to receive cash flow from a deal.

Deals can also be direct or indirect. Direct investing is when investors interact with the sponsor of the deal. The sponsor then has the contact info of the investors and can reach out to them for future deals. Indirect is when investors interact only with the crowdfunding platform instead of the sponsor. Special purpose vehicle (SPV) funding structures involve separate legal entities for each deal to help limit legal as well as financial risks. With SPV, sponsors don't have individual investors because the SPV is the investor. Sponsors don't even know who invested in the SPV.

There are various big platforms out there. Fundrise allows investors to buy into the equity of individual properties. RealtyMogul charges you fees to invest in both their equity and debt real estate deals. RealtyShares provides investment opportunities in a wide variety of asset classes and charges the fees to the borrowers as opposed to you. CrowdStreet connects you with properties that are professionally managed in both equity and debt offerings without any fees. Groundbreaker is an online tool that allows sponsors to raise money directly from investors. Similarly, Patch of Land focuses on residential debt investments and commercial equity deals. Salvador and Krystine especially love CrowdStreet's platform due to their comprehensive approach.

Regulations

Crowdfunding is governed by not only the usual real estate laws but also the laws around selling securities. The Securities and Exchange Commission (SEC) regulates crowdfunding and is also allowing it to continue to grow. Crowdfunding started as only being allowed for accredited investors who met specific criteria with their income or assets. To be accredited, an investor needs to prove that they have at least $1M in assets, not including their personal residence, make at least $200K per year, or together with their spouse make at least $300K per year.

The purpose of the JOBS Act of 2012 was to reduce SEC regulations on general solicitation by small businesses to create more jobs. It is what has allowed crowdfunding to begin as a new way to sell and manage securities. Crowdfunding was not possible before the JOBS Act. The JOBS Act is split into sections called Titles. (All of the regulatory compliance aspects can get complicated. Therefore, you should consult with a securities attorney if you plan to sponsor a crowdfunded deal.) It will cost between $5K-$150K in fees to start a crowdfunding campaign.

Title II offerings are primarily for accredited investors and do not have a limit on the amount that you can raise in capital. Title III began allowing non-accredited investors to invest through crowdfunding, starting in 2016. It came with additional regulations to protect non-accredited investors. For example, they can only invest 5-10% of their annual income depending on their income level. To make offerings under Title III, you have to be a broker-dealer or just a portal intermediary. Platforms under Title III have to complete additional disclosures and audits, provide educational materials about the risks involved with crowdfunding, and then make an effort to prevent fraud.

The SEC allows crowdfunding to be done through 506(b) and 506(c) offerings with differing rules. These rules are set up to protect investors who do not fully understand their investments and/or do not have enough net worth to handle a big loss. If a sponsor breaks these rules, they can either be fined or shut down.

With 506(b), sponsors cannot advertise any deals on Facebook or elsewhere, but they can advertise their platform. Investors in 506(b) must have an existing relationship with the sponsor. There is a limit of 35 non-accredited investors with no limit to accredited investors. On the other hand, sponsors can advertise specific deals anywhere with 506(c), but can only accept accredited investors. These investors must verify their accreditation with documents such as bank statements.

Regulation A+ (Reg A) offerings provide opportunities for more non-accredited investors to participate in deals than 506(b). Non-accredited investors are only allowed to invest 10% of their income or net worth through Reg A. Reg A offerings can raise up to $50M and may also have to follow state regulations. They must be listed in the federal registrar of the SEC for 60 days before people can invest in them. Sponsors can advertise their REG A offerings anywhere. Reg A is the most expensive offering to create. It is like doing a mini version of an initial public offering.

Advice for Investors

Crowdfunding portals make real estate investing safer and easier for ordinary investors who are both accredited and non-accredited.

Instead of trying to buy a property yourself, you get to pool your money together with other investors to purchase bigger properties. That way, you can earn passive income from a property without having to spend the time or energy managing it. If you prefer having total control and all of the income from a property, then crowdfunding might not be right for you.

You should be aware that there will still be a risk that you might lose some or all of your investment money. The return on your money will average between 12-14% annually. You have to keep your emotions out of it when you analyze each deal to make sure they follow your investment criteria. Only you can decide what your investment criteria will be and the level of risk that you are comfortable taking. Do not invest more than you can safely lose.

To feel confident in an investment, you need to know how to analyze the risks regarding the three following factors.

1. The quality of the sponsor is the first thing to examine regarding their leadership, track record, and how well their deals match with their experience/expertise.

2. The deal's structure is also key to consider. The higher the position your money has in a capital stack, you will have higher risk alongside the potential to make greater profits. For example, equity investments have better returns than senior debt since senior debt has a better chance of making money. Equity deals also offer added tax benefits.

3. Location is more than just the old real estate adage. With crowdfunding, you are not tied to just investing locally

where you live. You should ask yourself if a specific property will remain a good investment at its location during the entire holding period. Think about job trends and population growth in that property's market.

Salvador and Krystine recommend having a diversified mix in your portfolio of low, medium, and high-risk investments. That way, you can still make profits if one investment unexpectedly goes bad. This may vary depending on where you are in the growth stage of your portfolio.

Explore the different platforms to find one that suits your needs. Curated platforms analyze and underwrite deals for you. Uncurated platforms make you do all of the due diligence to verify what the sponsors say about their deals. Most of the investments are the ones that provide cash flow. Only some of the deals are developments since it can be difficult to gauge whether they will or will not be successful.

Multifamily investments tend to be stable since there are so many tenants. Office and retail can provide great returns but involve higher risk since one vacancy can greatly reduce profits. Peer-to-peer investments are more akin to owning the mortgage on other properties.

You should do your own research to prevent being scammed by fraud in the world of crowdfunding. Consult with an attorney when necessary and only work with sponsors who have a proven track record of successful investing. New sponsors may not have the skills or experience necessary to limit risks. Good sponsors and platforms will be very transparent with you regarding the risks.

Three influences may trick you into making a bad investment. Social proof is the idea that if other people are investing in a deal, then you may convince yourself that you should too. Urgency is when there is an impending investment deadline that might rush you into a decision. Expert authority is where you may inaccurately think a platform is an expert because they work with real estate all the time.

Advice for Sponsors

Crowdfunding gives sponsors opportunities to raise more capital for more deals faster with fewer fees than they could have otherwise. Platforms make it easy for sponsors to become more well-known and also help them connect with investors by handling many of the investor relations tasks. A sponsor's first crowdfunded deal is the hardest, but it then becomes easier due to having a proven track record. Different parts of the securities laws provide different rules and exemptions. Study them to know which path you want to take for a deal.

Sponsors will need to consider which platform is right for them due to the varying rules and policies. Some platforms will fund a sponsor's deal with the platform's money if they believe in that sponsor and their deal. Some platforms pool investor capital together under one LLC to make a single investment while others provide a funnel of investors to the sponsor's website. Some platforms accept both new and old sponsors, and others only accept experienced sponsors. Experience managing real estate is the key thing that platforms look for in a sponsor.

Most platforms will require sponsors to do background checks, have good credit, prove that there is a good business plan, and show that the deal is solid. Platforms do not like sponsors who have bankruptcies, foreclosures, or a criminal history. When a sponsor first connects with a platform, they will need to create a profile about themselves and the deal. Properties that cash flow soon after closing tend to work well with crowdfunding. The platform will then ask questions about the deal. You should know that not every deal will be accepted by a platform. Accepted deals are posted publicly to potential investors.

As a sponsor, you should make sure you adequately underwrite a deal and have a good understanding of its market. The cash flow and investor capital need to be enough to buy a property, manage it, and cover all expenses. Open and honest communication will help build your credibility and ability to raise capital for deals.

Advice for Platforms

Having competing platforms is good because it helps with both innovation and progress. The trick, like any business, is to stand out above the crowd. You must add value to others to build solid and positive relationships so that people know, like, and trust you. Tell your story in a way that really connects with people's hearts and minds. Also, it always helps to stand out if you provide the best deals.

Starting your own platform from scratch takes a lot of time and effort. Your business will need to be staffed with engineers, operations managers, accountants, marketers, real estate experts, attorneys, etc. You will also need to line up sponsors in advance who will list their deals on your platform when you launch. Attracting good investors takes even more effort than attracting good sponsors.

Luckily, there are easier ways to get started. If you already have a good investor base, there are white label front-to-back services that will help you build crowdfunding capabilities on your own website. Groundbreaker, CrowdStreet, CrowdEngine, Katipult, CrowdfundHQ, and CrowdFund Connect are companies that provide white label service while supporting you with things like compliance and IT.

Platforms need to spend their time providing education to the public, marketing, research and development, networking, developing partnerships, and supporting sponsors with things like campaign advice and social media. The education can be through things like podcasts, blogs, as well as videos. The goal of the education is to teach investors how to become savvier and to understand the crowdfunding process. Social media is a great way to connect with potential investors cheaply.

The customers of platforms include both the investors and the sponsors. A platform's reputation with them will be everything. You can provide user-friendly portals and ongoing education and support to them. The main costs include the development and maintenance of the platform, staffing, marketing, and providing education. The revenue is usually a 4-6% commission fee when a project is successful. Some platforms also charge investor fees.

Crowdfunding in the Future

Real estate in the USA is worth around $40 trillion as of 2016. Crowdfunding itself was worth $2.5B back in 2015. (The World Bank is predicting it will be worth $93B by 2025.) This is amazing growth that will likely continue as more people see crowdfunding as a safe investment strategy for real estate. This growth also benefits other businesses that support sponsors, such as those that provide tools for investor support and regulatory compliance.

There will continue to be new platforms in the USA and internationally as crowdfunding increases in popularity. Previous generations, in comparison, tended to be hands-off with their investments. The new demographic of investors will be more hands-on and knowledgeable of investing and the changing technology. The transparency involved in crowdfunding is also quite appealing to millennials.

Conclusion

This is the shortest book I have included in my Book About Real Estate. It is both packed with great information to learn the basics while also being an easy read. Whether you are looking to be an investor, sponsor, or create a platform, this book is a good jumping-off point with your crowdfunding education. Salvador invites you to check out his website www.CrowdCrux.com/RealEstateCourse to get additional crowdfunding training at no cost.

Additional Reading

Equity Crowdfunding for Investors: A Guide to Risks, Returns, Regulations, Funding Portals, Due Diligence, and Deal Terms by David Freedman and Matthew Nutting

Step by Step Crowdfunding: Everything You Need to Raise Money From the Crowd by Joseph Hogue

Chapter 22: Real Estate Development

Making It in Real Estate: Starting Out as a Developer by John McNellis

Introduction

When John started out investing in real estate, there wasn't a good book written about real estate development. He had to learn it the hard way, by doing one deal at a time. He wrote his book to help save you from having to learn some of the hard lessons on your own. However, much of your understanding of real estate development will still have to come from real-world experience.

The best thing you can learn from his book is knowing to maintain control over every risk that you can. While you can't control interest rates, market shifts, or even the weather, you can control your plan for preventing and handling various issues. The second edition of this book is much longer than the first one. It has various stories from John and his advice about things related to business, real estate, and even life in general. This chapter focuses more on the material related specifically to real estate development.

Starting Out

Businesses tend to only pay their employees just enough to keep them from quitting their jobs. Most people think they should be paid more. If you are more dissatisfied with your job itself than your income, then it may be the right time to quit once you have enough cash flow to survive. If you have the heart of an entrepreneur, then you need to be able to focus on creating opportunities instead of managing the daily grind.

If the only reason you start a business is to get rich, you will probably fail. You need a deeper driving force that keeps you going strong. This could be that you love what you do in your business, you want to be your own boss, you have a passion for helping people, or another great reason.

A career doing business in real estate is not going to be all sunshine and rainbows. Nothing ever comes easy, and hard work is a major ingredient to get where you need to go and achieve your goals. As of 2020, nothing related to real estate even made the U.S. News & World Report's Top 100 Jobs list. This list does not reveal that you can create great wealth by just investing in real estate on the side. You could not do that with any hourly side gig. If you don't have the cash flow to quit your job and want to quit, you can start buying real estate one property at a time until you can do so.

Cash Flow

Don't expect to make money in every deal you do. Depending on your numbers, you will need to make money on more than 80% of your real estate properties so you can avoid bankruptcy. Many people in real estate think breaking even is the same as making money. It's best to thoughtfully consider each property before you purchase it so that you will be ahead of the crowd. You make money when you buy real estate and not when you sell.

In 2014, John made the cover of the *Wall Street Journal*, but not for the reason he had hoped to be. His shopping center in California was right in the path of the flooded Russian River. Luckily, he had flood insurance. Unluckily, he had a five-figure deductible. If you own enough properties over your real estate career, you too will face some sort of disaster.

Any properties you bought during the 2004-2007 bubble would have lost big time, but only if you had to sell them. You can make money in real estate regardless of the market, as long as you can hold onto your properties for long enough. There's a fine line of where to balance your real estate debt. On one hand, using other people's money is leverage that propels you towards wealth. However, too much debt at the wrong time can destroy you.

Suppose you use $1M cash and a $4M loan to buy a $5M property. It appreciates up to $6M in a year, which then gives you a 100% return on your money. If you had bought that property with $5M cash, then you would only have gotten a 20% return during that time. However, if market conditions forced the property down to be worth only $4M, it really doesn't matter as long as there is enough cash flow to wait out the market for it to increase again. Net worth doesn't mean anything because cash flow is king.

Believe it or not, a $15M deal isn't much more work on your part as compared to a $150K deal. If you want to scale your business, it may be easier to focus on a few big deals as opposed to many smaller ones. However, that is not always the case. John started out buying a duplex for $24K and was doing a $15.5M deal as his sixth deal just seven years later. He had some success with his first five deals. However, that last one proved to be a lemon from which he needed years to recover. You should not be afraid to do bigger and bigger deals as long as you manage the risk involved.

Specializing

Which real estate investment type should you choose? There are many options available. To be honest, it doesn't matter as long as you pick one and focus all of your energy on it. Specialization is a key to success in real estate. Find a niche and do it better than anyone else. And most of success comes down to simply putting in the work for it. John cautions you to stick with what you know well about making money. For example, he was lured from development to invest in startups during the dot-com bubble and lost much of that investment capital.

John bought some warehouses in an area where someone else owned a lot of land, andhe loved building new warehouses on it. After ten years, John was lucky to sell his warehouses for what he paid for them. He then developed a shopping center that was so successful that he modeled his future developments off of it.

John's niche is developing shopping centers in an area that fights tooth and nail against new developments. There is less competition that way because big development companies can't compete with his local knowledge and decisive action based upon it. If you choose a specialty that becomes unprofitable at some point, then it's a good idea to move on and find a new niche.

Retail space has been struggling, even before the COVID-19 pandemic. There is still money to be made in it, though. However, John recommends using an abundance of caution with retail. The internet is unlikely to kill off retail space, but will likely continue to shrink it. The USA has twenty times as much retail space per capita as compared to Europe. It's simply overbuilt in the USA. (At the time of this book's writing, we have yet to see if working from home due to COVID-19 will also show us whether office space is also overbuilt.)

Why even go through the long process of building projects from the ground up when you can just buy properties that are already finished? This is because there is significantly more competition for turnkey properties. A ton of people are buying properties, whereas few are developing from scratch. However, it's a good idea to adjust your strategy based upon the market conditions. Buy premade properties when prices are cheap. Do developments when the market is hot.

Brokers

You may be tempted to be a licensed real estate broker who acts as the broker for your deals, thus saving money on broker fees. However, this is a terrible mistake as it will prevent you from seeing many great deals. A listing broker simply would not care to share their commission with you on a good deal, especially when the market is red hot. They neither need nor want your help if it means cutting their commission in half.

If you can close deals while paying brokers their full commission, they will bring you more good deals in the future. Real estate is a relationship business. If you only use people, you will burn all your bridges and find yourself alone on an island. Giving value to others, whether it be commissions or otherwise, is the right way to go. You need to be friendly and treat brokers well to ensure you have great deal flow. At the same time, you should be cautious with brokers. Since a great deal of money is involved, some brokers convince themselves that it's okay to have unethical practices.

Buying Right

Too many new real estate developers chase after off-market deals and then overpay for them. In truth, a current owner who is content with their property is not likely to sell it for a song. If a broker is involved in an off-market property, then it's not truly off-market.

You're better off finding a seller who is motivated by one of the four D's – death, divorce, dissolution, or disaster. However, even motivated sellers may not have an urgency to sell ASAP. This means you will either be good at negotiating or just waiting them out.

Often, there will be multiple investors bidding to win the purchase of a deal. If you end up overpaying for a property, then it could end in your financial demise. It's better to walk away from a deal than to overpay for it.

When no one else is buying, that's going to be a great time for you to find motivates sellers. If you could go back in time to 2009, how much real estate would you buy? It is almost impossible to time the market, though. Instead, you should focus on things you can control, especially the price, contingencies, and a closing date that is right for you. You should befriend the seller if you can to help things go your way.

You need to be wary of how listing brokers describe their listed properties. They may describe a less than stellar property as a no-risk sure win. Don't fall into the delusion of looking at properties with the same rose-colored glasses as those of listing brokers. If a property is described as "core," you need to know the definition of that varies quite a bit throughout the real estate world. A core property could be top-notch in a large city, or it could just mean it is a similar type of property to someone's other properties.

You may remember around 2012 when North Dakota had a boom with its production of shale oil. Real estate around the oil rigs also became quite hot. And when the price of oil dropped, so did the real estate there. As you can see, real estate is strongly tied to the local economy. If you can figure out how to time the market, then you can make your way to Wall Street.

It's more realistic to create enough value in a deal that it can weather the storm of a market correction. John believes that if a property only has 50-60% of its value tied up with debt, then that is the best range to balance building wealth while also ensuring safety. This can be done by buying deals at deep discounts, putting enough of your own money into them, or changing the property in some way that increases its value. Changing the property could be something like fixing it up, renting out the vacant units, or just demolishing it and rebuilding it better.

Partners vs. Employees

If you think you can do real estate development on your own, you are gravely mistaken. It is possible to pull off a deal on your own if you wear all the hats. That includes real estate broker, mortgage broker, contractor, property manager, custodian, lawyer, accountant, etc. However, if you try to do everything, you will do it all poorly. Plus, your time is too valuable to do all the things like maintenance or bookkeeping, as that will keep you from building and sustaining your business.

The thing to ask yourself is whether you should seek help from partners, employees, or both. The beautiful in-between step is to hire consultants. You can rent professionals for any job without hiring them as full-on employees. You should consider the cost analysis of hiring consultants vs. employees.

Consultants can easily be fired and replaced. You should have backup consultants ready to go just in case. If you do hire consultants, find the most experienced ones you can afford and show them sincere appreciation for their work. It's better to hire individual consultants than a large firm that might assign an inexperienced person to you.

Employees and consultants are cheaper than partners if you are successful. Giving partial ownership to a partner doesn't mean that you will get the best support from them. Employees will often be just as dedicated to your business as will actual partners. The right partners can help you towards incredible success. You need to decide for yourself what the right path for you will be.

Getting the Capital

Unless your pockets are filled with cash, you will need to raise money for your development deals. Most people start by raising money from their family and friends (F&F). It's normal to give them a 5% preferred return on their income with a 50/50 split on the profits above that. Simpler deals might just have an 80/20 split where you get the 20%. F&F tend to be more willing to give you control over the deals and the most understanding when there are problems. Only take money from people who can afford to lose it.

Eventually, you will have to expand to raising capital from outside your immediate circle. The vast majority of developers need financial partners, especially when first starting. These partners could be individuals, institutional investment firms, or banks. An individual partner normally puts in 90% of the equity into a deal while you pay for the rest. This means that for a $10M property where the bank loans you $6M, your partner would put in 90% of the remaining $4M balance.

Money from institutional investment firms and banks is limitless, as long as you don't actually need it. This capital comes from professionals who understand business and expect you to produce results as well as the projected returns. You can do well with intuitional money as long as you can stick to the budget and the timeline to build.

If you are borrowing money from the banks for your projects, then you will need to prepare your annual financial statement for them to review. This is to prove that you're able to produce results for them. The banks will scrutinize your financial statements and property appraisals. John tends to value his properties based upon a cap rate between 100-15 basis points lower than market rate to be conservative. This makes it so you don't know just what your net worth is. John's billionaire friend says, "If you know how rich you are, you're not that rich."

John's financial statement shows that 99.4% of his net worth is in the equity of his holdings. However, equity doesn't mean much until it's cashed out. Equity without cash flow is nothing. When it comes to getting money from banks, they want to see that you can pay back the loans they give you. Your cash flow and cash reserves will get you more money from the bank with much better terms. Bank money is the cheapest money you can get for doing real estate. You need to build great relationships with the lender, and they will keep lending you more money. John recommends doing this with three bankers at three separate banks so that you will always have available options.

There are two main types of loans for real estate. You can either get a lower-risk permanent loan if the property is stabilized or a higher-risk loan to do construction. The first type tends to be nonrecourse, where you aren't personally held financially responsible if the loan defaults, unless you were purposely committing fraud so you could take the cash to Las Vegas. Construction loans are almost always full recourse, where you guarantee the money will be paid back.

As long as you finish the construction, you can always use the building itself to pay back the bank if needed. It is possible to prevent a construction loan from being full recourse if you put in a higher down payment or agree to a relatively higher interest rate. You will need to choose your path with this since there is an inherent risk in development no matter which way you slice it. By accepting risk, you also open yourself up to some nice rewards.

Having financial partners allows you to do more deals than you could on your own. If neither you nor your financial partner has any personal liability, then you can make good money with limited risk. However, if you fund your deals yourself, then you have no one to whom you have to answer or be held accountable. John decided at one point to stop having financial partners and do smaller deals on his own. Only you can decide the best course of action for yourself.

Handling the Politics

There are usually a ton of zoning regulations and permit hurdles to overcome to complete a development deal. They are well-intended but can be quite inhibitive at times. Some places, like Houston, allow developers a sort of free-for-all such that they can build what they want, where they want, and when they want. This makes it easy to do developments, but also brings on a ton of competition. In such places, you often have to buy at high prices, which eats into your profits. Places like California have more stringent environmental regulations. This means that you have a ton of hurdles to jump through if a nearby dry cleaner spilled any chemicals years ago.

You have to decide if you prefer bothersome regulations that limit competition or fewer regulations with deal-killing overbuilding. If you choose a place where the zoning and approval process feels like torture, then you are more likely to make money on the developments that go through. There are huge profits to be made by rezoning in first-class places that make that difficult.

To get things rezoned, you will need to convince the local politicians to do it, and that may not be so easy. They see themselves as defenders of the people. And they see you as controlled by self-interests. The public might show up to a rezoning meeting feeling angry because they see your development as blocking views and traffic.

Your play here is to give the politicians an easy excuse to vote in your favor. Start by meeting the people who oppose your rezoning application and understanding their point of view. You can compromise by adjusting your project or adding more benefits for the public.

Next, find out who leads the different levels of approval, which may include an architectural review committee, a planning commission, as well as the city council. Tell the decision-makers of those groups that you will meet with the people in the neighborhood to learn about their suggestions and objections to the project. Meet with each member of the different committees individually to plead your case with them before the public hearings. You can also write letters about approving your application to any of them who refuse to meet with you.

Conduct outreach meetings with the neighborhood before each public hearing to gain genuine support from the public. You should give sincere thanks to the neighbors who speak well of your development during those outreach meetings. It is best to not bring a Rolex or a lawyer to these meetings. This is because you want people to see you as down to earth. You must be the bigger person by politely listening to the naysayers and keep any promises that you make during the outreach meetings.

Selling vs. Holding

One of the hardest things to decide in real estate development is whether to sell or hold onto a completed project. How do you know when to cash out on the profits as opposed to keeping an asset that can be passed down to your children? The answer to that depends on your investment goals. The first option helps launch you to doing flashier development projects as a merchant developer. The second gives you cash flow that lasts as an investment developer. You can certainly have a hybrid between these two options if you so wish.

You have to decide on your investment goals before you begin doing developments.

Merchant developers sell their projects right after completion so that they can pull out the profits to finance more projects. (This is somewhat like flipping houses, only on a much larger scale.) They make money from charging fees from the investors and getting proceeds from the sale. They normally plan to get a return on the cost of around 1-2% above the going capitalization (cap) rate. Each project typically takes three to five years from start to finish. Investment developers don't charge high fees, so they can benefit more from cash flow later.

A merchant developer's approach may force them to sell upon the project's completion regardless of what the market conditions are at the time. John prefers having options for each property to minimize risk. His strategy is to sell about 2/3 of his developments and keep the few properties that have the highest quality and lowest debt. He looks at each property individually to carefully determine the best course of action with it.

Internal Rate of Return

Real estate brokers usually provide you accurate information about a property they are selling. This is because that information can be verified; otherwise, they could be sued if it is not. However, you should be wary of any information they present of how they believe the property will perform in the future through their calculated internal rate of return (IRR).

The IRR is calculated by first adding the projected cash flow from a property during a certain period. Secondly, you add that to the projected worth of the property at the end of that time. For example, if you get a 5% cash flow from a property for ten years and then it sells for double what you paid for it, you would have an IRR of just under 11%. There are various assumptions you would need to make to calculate a future IRR. Unless you have a crystal ball, you don't know what rents, cap rates, interest rates, vacancy rates, population changes, income shifts, and the market will be like years from now.

Predicting just when the next real estate crash or boom will be is like predicting the Super Bowl winner ten years into the future. You should take projected IRRs with a grain of salt regardless of how fancy they are presented by listing brokers. It's better to examine a property's return on investment (ROI) by seeing what the net operating income (NOI) will be once a development project has been completed in its entirety.

Architects and Contractors

You need designers who bring beauty to your projects so that your properties are more than just egalitarian gray boxes. Architects want to make you happy by designing exactly what you request. However, they won't save you from your terrible vision if you have no idea what you are doing at all with real estate development. If you decide to build condos next to a fire station, your architect may not warn you that the condos won't sell very well there.

It's not unusual for contractors to hire subcontractors to complete much of the construction. The contractors then charge a little extra to make some profit in the overhead. However, there are a ton of ways to go broke as a contractor. You may be tempted to go into the construction business to save some cash. Unless you have the skills and experience for construction, it will likely be cheaper for you to hire that out as opposed to doing it yourself. It's a good idea to require bids from multiple contractors. The cheapest bid isn't necessarily the best one for you to accept.

Analyzing Deals

The best deals are rare and hard to find. You will have to sift through many bad deals to find the ones you actually want to purchase. Many times, good deals don't appear to be good at first. You will need to figure out how to turn mediocre deals into better ones. The deals you look at might be overpriced, but could work if the price can come down. Either the seller of an overpriced property will be willing to negotiate after a while or someone will pay way too much for it. You need to remain patient and focused during your search for good deals.

The numbers will tell you the truth about deals, as long as they aren't eclipsed by inaccurate assumptions. If a deal doesn't make sense by analyzing the numbers on a napkin, then it's best to move on to looking at the next deal. A calculator and middle school math are all that is needed to do the initial analysis of a deal.

The Net to Me

John's best advice he can give you is the "net to me" (NTM). It is a question that you ask before investing in a deal, accept a job, or join a partnership. It will save you from some headaches and regret. Make sure your NTM will be worth the effort, as well as the sacrifice required.

Suppose you are offered a job with a base salary of $150K plus 10% of the profits from your projects. Those projects normally net $15M. Before accepting, you should determine what your NTM will be. Perhaps you discover that the company has investors who get 70% of the net profits and a project financer who gets half of the remaining money. This dwindles your $1.5M bonus down to $225K.

NTM looks at how you will be impacted over time. You have to look at a few things in that regard. How long will it take to obtain your desired profit? How many hours will you have to work to obtain it? Perhaps the above scenario is still appealing to you. If you become an entrepreneur as a developer, then you will have to make sacrifices with many risks. However, there are great rewards to be obtained on the back end.

Legal Considerations

It is very important to protect yourself from litigation whenever possible. Even if you win a lawsuit, you can still come out scorched from it. Lawsuits will cost you time, energy, and money no matter the outcome and regardless of which side you are on in the lawsuit. If a CEO privately tells you that their company is going downhill and you then sell your stocks in it, you may end up in jail. However, if you own the building for that company's headquarters and sell after that disclosure, you legally save yourself a ton of money and headaches.

Conclusion

John's book includes a lot of humor that you don't always find in real estate books. The second edition is much longer than the first one and includes many more of his various stories about the market, real estate investments, as well as operating properties. He includes some practical advice on handling things during hard times, such as the COVID-19 crisis. The book ends with a glossary of development terms that will help demystify the language you will need to know.

Real estate is the business of relationships, and you will need to communicate effectively to be successful. It is imperative to choose good partners and treat them with respect. Your reputation in the real estate development world will take years to be built. Real estate development is a long-term investment strategy. There are a ton of challenges involved in it. There is also a ton of money to be made. This is because not everyone can overcome those challenges. If you choose the path of real estate development for yourself, you must have the vision and the fortitude to see your projects through to completion.

Additional Reading

The Complete Guide to Developing Commercial Real Estate, The Who, What, Where, Why and How Principles of Developing Commercial Real Estate by Robert Wehrmeyer

Introduction to Real Estate Development and Finance by Richard Levy

BONUS

Real Estate Loopholes
Loopholes of Real Estate by Garrett Sutton, Esq.

Much of the real estate law originated in medieval Europe. *Loupe* in Middle English meant window. A *loupehole* was a window in your castle where you could shoot arrows to defend your property. A landlord was a lord who had absolute control over a parcel of land and answered only to the queen or king. *Tenere* in Latin means "to hold." A tenant was someone who would hold and take care of the land for the landlord. This book starts with a quick crash course about the book *Rich Dad Poor Dad*, which I have covered in another chapter in this book. If you want to learn ways to pay less in taxes and protect yourself from potential lawsuits, then go to www.HawkwingCapital.com/free and download this bonus chapter for free today!

Conclusion

There are many other ways to invest in real estate. I've covered most of the main ways for you. Now it's up to you to decide which path to take. I recommend that you choose the one that matches your interest, abilities, and personality to the very best. If you allow yourself to be controlled by the Shiny Object Syndrome, then you might never take action. This is where many different avenues of real estate investment are appealing to you such that you want to do them all, and then you can't decide on just one.

Real estate investing is undoubtedly an incredible vehicle for wealth creation. Countless people have found success with it, and you can too. It all comes down to NET. Network with other people and add value to them. Educate yourself about what you need to know to be successful. Finally, take intelligent actions towards your goals. Information is nothing without the follow-through action. I wholly believe that you can do it. What are you waiting for? Get started on real estate investing today!

About The Author

Matt Jones is a real estate investor based out of Minneapolis who specializes in investing in both small and large multifamily properties. He is the CEO of Hawkwing Capital, which syndicates large apartment buildings. He has a master of science in mental health counseling which comes in handy with building positive relationships in real estate. Matt co-hosts the Pillars of Wealth Creation podcast with Todd Dexheimer. As an avid reader, he loves talking with others about the powerful books he has read. When not doing real estate, you will find him cooking amazing meals, traveling the world, and going hiking with his amazing wife. He has a passion for helping others to become the best versions of themselves. You can find out more about Matt and his real estate investing at www.HawkwingCapital.com.

www.ingramcontent.com/pod-product-compliance
Lightning Source LLC
Chambersburg PA
CBHW060113200326

41518CB00008B/816